Data Analysis in Qualitative Research

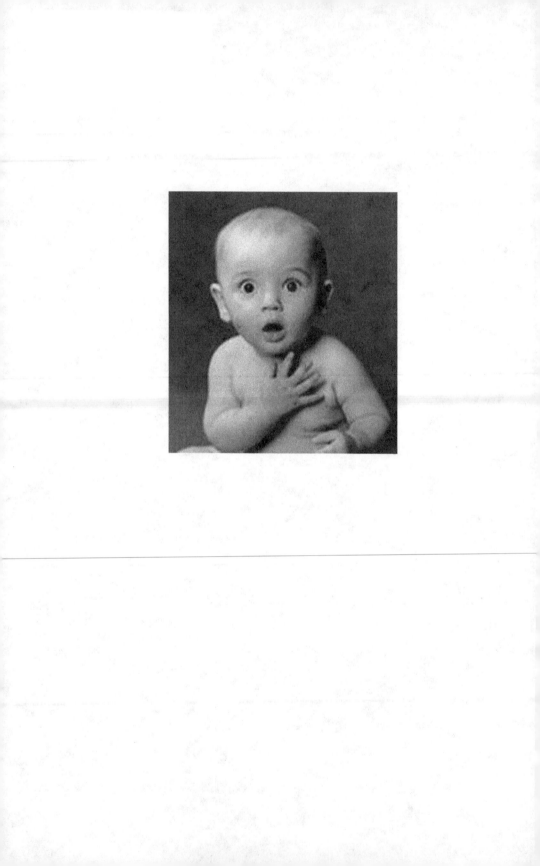

Stefan Timmermans and Iddo Tavory

DATA ANALYSIS IN QUALITATIVE RESEARCH

Theorizing with Abductive Analysis

The University of Chicago Press · Chicago and London

The University of Chicago Press, Chicago 60637
The University of Chicago Press, Ltd., London
© 2022 by The University of Chicago
Published 2022
Printed in the United States of America

31 30 29 28 27 26 25 24 23 22   1 2 3 4 5

ISBN-13: 978-0-226-81771-2 (cloth)
ISBN-13: 978-0-226-81773-6 (paper)
ISBN-13: 978-0-226-81772-9 (e-book)
DOI: https://doi.org/10.7208/chicago/9780226817729
.001.0001

Library of Congress Cataloging-in-Publication Data

Names: Timmermans, Stefan, 1968– author. | Tavory,
    Iddo, 1977– author.
Title: Data analysis in qualitative research : theorizing
    with abductive analysis / Stefan Timmermans and
    Iddo Tavory.
Description: Chicago : University of Chicago Press,
    2022. | Includes bibliographical references and
    index.
Identifiers: LCCN 2021036688 | ISBN 9780226817712
    (cloth) | ISBN 9780226817736 (paperback) |
    ISBN 9780226817729 (ebook)
Subjects: LCSH: Qualitative research—Methodology. |
    Abduction (Logic)
Classification: LCC H62 .T534 2022 |
    DDC 001.4/2—dc23
LC record available at https://lccn.loc.gov/
    2021036688

CONTENTS

1: SURPRISE

Surprises[1] are the fuel that powers research engines. Drawing upon data of millions of research papers, patents, and scientific careers, sociologists and computer scientists Feng Shi and James Evans concluded that "science and technology advance through surprise."[2] Decades earlier, sociologist of science Robert Merton already noted "the serendipity pattern" in empirical research whenever an "unanticipated, anomalous, and strategic" observation becomes the basis for developing a new theory. Merton's formulation was, as usual, insightful. While we may think about surprises as anomalous, we typically don't think of them as "strategic." But the observer needs to be able to recognize the theoretical implications of a serendipitous finding strategically. Merton added that this "requires *a theoretically sensitized observer* to detect the universal in the particular."[3] How can we systematically cultivate surprising findings? How do you sensitize yourself to detect emerging surprises? This book helps you do just that.

Our first book, *Abductive Analysis: Theorizing Qualitative Research*,[4] staked out a claim in an increasingly unrealistic field of qualitative data analysis. Our major concern was that the conventional approaches to data analysis impoverish the potential of qualitative research. At best, most qualitative researchers pay lip service to an epistemic model that they don't follow in practice. The methods sections of research articles—both inductive and deductive—are most often formulaic fantasies divorced from the real-life drama of analyzing qualitative research data.

Joining other scholars who had mined the work of the early pragmatist Charles S. Peirce,[5] we argued that abduction—the mode of inference drawing from surprise—is an underappreciated aspect of the research act, especially in the context of theory discovery. Focusing on abductive reasoning is a productive and logically sound way to rethink qualitative research and data analysis. Abductive analysis requires in-depth familiarity with a broad array of social theories and an intensive engagement with observations in order to develop theoretical contributions. Most methods books in qualitative research are either about coming up with something from scratch, or about testing, verifying, and generalizing theory. Instead, abduction in abductive analysis refers to the process of crafting theory—figuring out both what surprising observations are a theoretical case of, and where the theoretical case and the findings diverge in interesting ways.

While not quite philosophically precise, a cooking metaphor is useful to explain the difference. If you open Yotam Ottolenghi's bestselling cookbook *Plenty*, you will find his famous recipe for poached baby vegetables with caper mayonnaise. The recipe begins: "To make the mayonnaise, place the garlic, egg yolk, vinegar, mustard, salt, and lemon juice in the bowls of a food processer. Start blending and then very slowly dribble in the oil until you get a thick mayonnaise. Fold in the capers and lemon zest and set aside."[6] If you follow the instructions, using the given ingredients, you should be getting the meal Ottolenghi describes. That's a deductive logic. You have a good idea of what you're going to eat; it's pretty delicious, but is often estranged from the local foodstuffs. Even though Ottolenghi is an Israeli-English chef with several delis and restaurants in London, his recipes remain the same whether you live near the Park Slope food co-op in Brooklyn or have access to the farmer's markets from Los Angeles. By contrast, a purely inductive logic would probably have us grab something from the fridge; fry, roast, or boil it; and hope for the best. Perhaps, in the grounded theory tradition, we would compare the flavors of different food combinations for patterns.[7] If the resulting dish grows on us, we may decide to include it in the family rotation of meals, following the recipe that we "discovered." While deduction starts with a theory and makes empirical predictions, induction generalizes from observations.

An abductive logic is different. You are craving those poached vegetables with caper mayonnaise. You have memorized Ottolenghi's book pretty much by heart, with grease spots on the pages of your favorite recipes. His book is tucked in among other cookbooks on your kitchen shelf. You open the fridge and scan the food in front of you, push the cauliflower aside to see what's behind it, notice that you are out of garlic and that the baby carrots are way beyond their prime. But look, there is a basket of kumquats you purchased impulsively during last Saturday's shopping trip. What a pleasant surprise and interesting cooking challenge! You don't have the ingredients for Ottolenghi's dish but maybe you can make something novel that incorporates the sweetness and tartness of the kumquats. What would be the best way of using these grape-size fruits? You'll skip the caper mayonnaise and maybe try a citrus syrup instead. The flavor palate of the dish is going to be completely different from Ottolenghi's poached baby vegetables. You invent your own dish. Abduction, then, is a creative moment where you take what you know and go beyond it to try out something different. It occurs when you have a surprising observation and formulate the most promising hypothesis. Of course, the original recipe inspired the new dish, as did the different cookbooks on your shelf, but the moment of realization of the local possibilities is exhilarating.

Abduction in scientific research is a logic that organizes the process of coming up with a new hypothesis based on surprising research findings. Abduction intervenes in the tension between knowing what you are interested in by chasing usual suspects and remaining open to new unexpected findings for which a usual-suspects explanation is inadequate. It requires in-depth familiarity with a broad range of theories that help you navigate familiar landscapes and point the way when you run into alien terrain. The logic works best when you gather data in an innovative way—a new site, a new set of questions, an overlooked group of stakeholders. You also need to have enough data to examine variation across analytical dimensions. In short, theoretical surprises do not grow spontaneously but are seeded by how you read your theoretical peers and how you conduct your research.

The purpose of *Abductive Analysis* was to carve out a new epistemological position. We developed the pragmatist semiotics of meaning-making, explained why the defamiliarization generated by coding procedures is helpful, and emphasized the critical importance of writing with an eye on a community of inquiry. We included some examples, but it was more a rethink than a how-to book. Observers pointed out that some researchers were already doing something that resembled abductive analysis. In that sense, the book met its promise: it found an audience across disciplines and most references to abductive analysis are from researchers relieved that they can report what they did as a legitimate methodology. However, we were and are more ambitious than repackaging current practice. Our purpose was to stimulate theorizing that plays to the strengths of qualitative research. But, we admit, you would not know how exactly to do this from the first book.

The challenge is that we don't—and indeed can't—have a simple foolproof protocol for surprise. Think back to the cooking example. While a deductive approach gives you a recipe to follow, and an inductive approach might tell you what a meal could look like if you combine the stuff in your fridge, the flash of abductive insight that we depicted requires careful attention to what's in the fridge, a deep knowledge of different cookbooks, and insight into how to coordinate cooking time for various ingredients in order to come up with a new dish. How can something like this be ever taught in a book format? This is the kind of knowledge that comes from years of apprenticing in different kitchens. You do not become a chef by memorizing recipes. Yet while there are no abductive culinary shortcuts, we can still tell you something about how to go about organizing your shopping trips, what to look for in your fridge and pantry, and how to read cookbooks.

The current book aims to translate our ideas about abduction into concrete research practices. We contend that abductive analysis means doing qualitative research *differently*, not just relabeling what you were already doing. Abductive analysis means designing research explicitly to maximize the chance of data surprises; engaging the literature in a different way; approaching data coding with a mindset aimed at defamiliarizing the familiar; and writing research up deliberately and reflexively to evoke abductive insights. We show in the next chapters how working abductively permeates a research project from the moment you muse about doing research, through collecting the first observations, through the final write-up. It demands an analytical sensibility that immerses you in the literature, guides the collection of empirical materials, and requires working with these observations as they come in. Surprising findings do not fall out of thin air: you will need to cultivate them. This book shows you how to discover surprises by thinking differently about your research.

What this book is, and what it isn't

Our kind of qualitative research intertwines empirical and theoretical narratives. We agree with Loïc Wacquant when he wrote that "far from being antithetical, vivid ethnography and powerful theory are complementary and that the best strategy to strengthen the former is to bolster the latter."[8] We presume that you share our goal of theorizing based on qualitative research; why else would you be reading this book? But maybe we shouldn't assume a shared purpose; maybe we should make the case first that theorizing is a worthwhile endeavor. There are, after all, other compelling ways of working with empirical materials where theory isn't really at the center of the work.

In many of the hotspots of qualitative inquiry, researchers don't primarily theorize but engage in applied research. Plenty of qualitative health researchers, for instance, work towards better outcomes within a public health, medical, or health services framework. They examine why patients are noncompliant with medication regimes, or how direct-to-consumer advertising sells pharmaceuticals.[9] Other qualitative researchers apply their skills for technology companies to make products that will find a market. For more than twenty years, Xerox had a research division that included ethnographers to study human-computer interaction in order to design copiers that would be intuitive to use. While some of this work, especially by the principal investigator Lucy Suchman,[10] engaged in theorizing, the purpose of the unit was to help engineers design user-friendly machines. Globally, many, probably most, qualitative researchers conduct contract research, write bids for government projects, apply to foundations, and submit proposals to granting agencies. Since such agencies are rarely interested in advancing a theoretical agenda, this renders a qualitative researcher much more of a consultant or expert working towards an institutional portfolio. Grant agencies often pay for data gathering but provide few funds for analysis, and the resulting publications provide mainly descriptive insights.

Some superb research also doesn't aim for novel theorizations but convincingly proves what many people already suspected. The research of Devah Pager on the racial profiling of job seekers using experimental methods is such an example. She found that employers were more likely to hire a White man with a felony conviction than a Black man without a criminal record.[11] This research is not theoretically innovative, but it is critically important to uncover institutional racial biases in the labor market, and Pager's work meaningfully intervenes in an important political struggle. At Pager's memorial service, the writer Ta-Nehisi Coates talked about how her research validated the experiences of people of color—giving them a decisive argument against people who said discrimination was "all in their heads."[12]

Still other researchers are attracted by the humanistic side of qualitative inquiry rather than by the goal of abstracting and theorizing. Whatever else we do, qualitative researchers closely chronicle the human condition. In that capacity, we are not alone but part of a crowded field of journalists and documentary makers, as well as fiction writers. Chronicling is done by people from the outside looking in, but also by people from the inside looking out. They tell their own and each other's stories on social media, in interviews, blogs, documentaries, news articles, op-ed pieces, reflections, diaries, internet groups, videos, and memoirs.

While humanistic, exemplifying, and applied qualitative projects constitute alternative goals for conducting qualitative research, they also benefit from theoretical engagement, even if the goal is not developing novel theories. Maybe they should be more theoretically adventurous. In fact, some of the strongest exemplars of these research traditions engage implicit theoretical agendas.

It is no accident that Suchman's work for Xerox was so influential; it was due, in large part, to her deep engagement in sociological interactionism and ethnomethodology. Applied studies that sidestep theories risk shortening their reach. Similarly, some of the best studies that seem to only "exemplify" theory actually do more than that. Thus, for example, Annette Lareau's excellent *Unequal Childhoods*[13] can be read as an exemplification of Pierre Bourdieu's theory of habitus formation and cultural capital. Lareau's book is notable for its innovative methodology: she inserted herself into the homes of working- and middle-class parents to observe class-based socialization in action. While methodology is surely part of what makes this book such compelling reading, *Unequal Childhoods* specifies, empirically and theoretically, the mechanisms through which classed socialization occurs in the home and at schools.

As for humanistic research, a common warrant for qualitative research is that the work itself reveals and bridges a discrepancy between what an audience thinks about a community and how the members of a community behave.[14] The researcher shows through the richness of observations that those ostracized as deviant are human after all, and those in power or exalted in the media are actually more flawed than we imagined. This kind of interview study or ethnography folds the extremes of behavior into a universal humanism, while still mapping cultural idiosyncrasies. It is difficult to pull this off without engaging theories and concepts, even if they are banished to the endnotes. Some of the most popular works of qualitative research—Mitch Duneier's *Sidewalk*, Matt Desmond's *Evicted*, or Tressie McMillan Cottom's *Thick*[15]—draw extensively from social theory but you need to know this literature to recognize who they are in conversation with in the text. Again, not just inserting but also developing a theoretical dimension in such a humanistic project may expand its reach beyond those already interested in a substantive research area, as well as help distinguish it from the journalistic human interest stories.

While there are many warrants for qualitative research and all of them benefit from a strong theoretical backbone, the path we advocate fully embraces the theoretical craft of academics as scholars. The theoretical contribution of qualitative research is the endeavor's protection against irrelevance. Theory is how research travels beyond a small substantive niche. The warrant for our kind of research is that we find something counterintuitive, unexpected, or surprising and develop theory from it. We aim to foster a particular craftsmanship of working with qualitative data in light of existing bodies of scholarship in order to make a theoretical and conceptual contribution. These concepts and theorizations not only abstract relevant experiences but, if successful, can open new perspectives and produce new research foci. If theory shows how a pattern found in one place illuminates what happens in another, then there is something deeply humanistic about it.

To take one example we both admire and that we return to later on in this book, Leigh Star and James Griesemer coined the notion of "boundary object" when they studied the acquisition of bird specimens for a natural history museum. They conceptualized the boundary object as a negotiation strategy for situations where parties with different interests do not need or want to confront each other. A boundary object is unified enough that it has a common meaning but also sufficiently plastic that it may have vastly different meanings in different communities.[16] The concept of boundary object exemplifies its own power *as* a boundary object. The notion traveled and was used to mediate very different situations. This concept caught on in dozens of studies. Researchers incorporated boundary objects to examine how the same issue is able to mean different things for different groups without splintering or settling as one dominant trope. At the same time, the concept illuminates a deeply existential aspect of social interaction: the productive role of ambiguity in facilitating action and bridging perspectives. Well-crafted theories and concepts are useful and transcend their origins. They become intellectual passage points, ways of seeing and framing the world, extensions of traditions and inspirations for future scholarship.

Buckling down as scholars does not mean that we greenlight a jargon-heavy, impenetrable academese or favor rigid theoretical frameworks. Despite our attachment to Peirce, who had an unfortunate penchant for abstruse terms, we aren't in love with his terminology. As will become clear, we much prefer nimble concepts that abstract observations by lifting salient dimensions and middle-range theories that prove their mettle through repeated usage. But it does mean that thinking explicitly about theory—and starting from a bedrock of alternative theoretical framings—characterizes our approach.

We search for surprises in observations. They don't just pop up; we cultivate serendipity by analytically interrogating and comparing observations in light of existing theories. When we encounter an anomalous or puzzling set of findings, we need to adjust our theoretical framework to do justice to these findings. We examine alternative explanations while gathering more observations. Abductive analyzing is then as much a research orientation and a sampling strategy as an analytical approach. Following pragmatist thinking and more than a century of social science history, we view theorizations as work in progress.[17] They are introduced in a community of inquiry and their value depends on whether they capture your sociological imagination and inspire more research or end up forgotten in dusty library stacks.

But again we return to the same questions: How, exactly, do we get to theorize surprising findings? If we do not follow the routine stages of grounded theory work, what *do* we do? One set of answers, which we have found useful for our own work, focuses on tricks of the trade.[18] Several methodology books are crammed with heuristics—which we recommend as a source of inspiration—and focus on different ways to jog your observations and limber them up so you can look at them anew and figure out how to go about your work. If you return to our cooking metaphor, it's something akin to the writer telling you to see what happens if you organize your ingredients by texture, then by basic flavor, then by cooking time, and see how that would allow you to think about your cooking opportunities anew. In many situations, this is exactly the inspirational muse you need to get your culinary imagination going.

This book goes beyond heuristics. We aim to give advice on the core practices through which you organize the fridge, how you can structure your shopping in ways that would allow you to experiment with interesting recipes, and how you learn to think about the possibilities that different cookbooks provide. Leaving the cooking metaphor aside, our aim is to organize the research arc to sensitize you to appreciating surprises with theoretical potential. While tricks are useful, they often are only part of a researcher's repertoire and they often come too late in the research process. Prepping for theorizing occurs at every act of the research journey—from the moment you decide that one field site is worthier than another to your decision to ask this and not that question in an interview.

As a qualitative researcher, you mediate a relationship between your research and readers. Your contribution will likely contain insights that violate how some people assume their world worked. You make connections where others see clear divisions. You show that consequences people presumed were common are actually only exceptionally achieved. And at the same time, your research violates not primarily the folk representations of the world, but those of your fellow researchers. Qualitative research is therefore often intellectually subversive on theoretical grounds. As we show, the potential for subversion resides in the questions you ask, the perspectives you take in your research, and the materials you gather.

Coordinates

This book walks you through different moments of the research process. After outlining some of the basic tenets of abductive analysis in the next chapter, we dive right into how to set up research for surprises. We begin with the question of theory: what you should read, how to engage readings, and when to stop reading. Using the metaphors of *map* and *compass*, we show that literature provides you with "landmarks of expectation" against which new theoretical paths may be tracked. We advise you to familiarize yourself with the layout of your subfield. Besides substantive theories, sociology also contains more abstract navigational tools. Theories like Bourdieu's habitus-capital and field, interactionism's definition of the situation, or actor-network theory's view of assemblages don't really tell you what any particular field would be like. They do tell you, however, how to traverse diverse terrains and what *kinds* of phenomena you can expect.

Social scientists are not the only people in the business of constructing theoretical maps to make sense of social life. We all devise theories in the course of everyday life, to help us learn how to act based on what has already happened. We urge you to pay careful attention to the ideas of the people you study, and to their ongoing concerns. We term this the *principle of engagement* and return to it throughout the book as one of the most important methodological precepts of qualitative research. While you shouldn't define a particular social world as your interlocutors inside it see it, we argue that you will benefit from seriously engaging their concerns and ideas. This is not just a good ethical position but a practical analytical standpoint too. Listening to how people order their world is as generative for surprises as reading in your research area. Moments of abduction emerge in relation to all these sources of theoretical inspiration. We encourage you to read literature strategically—as a staging ground of expectations for your own research.

Our next chapter addresses questions of research design. Taking ethnography and interview research as our two primary methodological anchors, we argue that the crux of qualitative research design is an interplay between focusing and defocusing research, between zooming in on specific questions and zooming out at the interconnectedness of social life. All research needs to gather data rich enough to provide possibilities of surprise, but different qualitative methods face different challenges. In participant observation, a method that is almost infinitely flexible, we need to *focus* our evolving research. We might achieve this by adding a site as a comparative case or by shadowing our participants across the places where they live their lives. In interview design, which due to question format and time constraints is much more rigid than ethnography, we build breadth into our interview questionnaires, strategically *defocusing* our questions, especially early on, to maximize possibilities of surprise. The interplay of focusing and defocusing leads to organizing our research differently than how these methods are commonly practiced across the social sciences. We advocate a constant agile adjustment of bringing the phenomena into sharp detail and a move back to explore aspects others have ignored to note surprises.

Moving beyond research design, we enter the analytical labor of coding in chapters 5 and 6. We begin our coding with a more systematic version of grounded theory's open coding. In the initial rounds of coding, we attempt to get a deeper, defamiliarized sense of the data. We do so primarily by mapping and detailing the dramatic structure of our data. Thinking through a modified version of Kenneth Burke's *grammar of motives*,[19] as well as rhetoric passed along since at least Aristotle, we focus on who does what, when, where, how, and to what practical effects. This rhythmic questioning of our observations raises aspects of our data that we either took for granted or ignored in the interview or the field. Such open coding produces two more benefits—first, it allows us to ask about how action and interaction move forward in our data, priming us to look for processes and privileging mechanism-based explanations of our field. Secondly, it helps us to see what we still don't know—both in terms of what our interlocutors refer to, but also in terms of the silences and gaps in our data. Coding then gives us marching orders of where to go next in our data collection efforts. That's why it needs to happen early and steadily throughout the fieldwork, not at the end.

Complementing the discussion of open coding, chapter 6 centers on *focused coding* and the *index case*. Where open coding tries to decipher a promising theme in the noise of your observations, focused coding elaborates on a theme you surmise—from experience and your familiarity with the existing literature—as promising. While such themes capture patterns in your data, they do not "emerge" from the data, but already stand in relation to the theoretical traditions you engage. An *index case*, a kind of "patient zero" in our data, serves as an anchoring device for the empirical and analytic narrative that your work ends up telling. Choosing and assessing the power of your index case, and then examining variation in light of the index case, constitute the thrust of focused coding.

In chapter 7, we show you the single most promising path to take when you are still not sure what is worth pursuing in your research project. We return to the principle of engagement—your responsibility to take your research subjects seriously. Based both on a rich tradition of theoretical writing and on our practical experience as researchers, we focus on *tensions* within the social world we study as a way to deepen our familiarity with the social world. Relying on cultural anthropologist Mary Douglas's work on humor and ritual, we outline the value of looking for "jokes in the structure" of the worlds we study—not as a way to expose what is *really* going on but because understanding the pattern underlying these tensions clues us to theoretical questions tailored to our research project.

In chapter 8, we show that the process of writing is rife with analytical decisions on what to include, how to narrate, how to respond to the dreaded reviewer 2, and how to engage your audience. These decisions are not mere window dressing; they quite literally constitute your theoretical contributions. Writing up your research becomes a trial of strength: Is what you considered surprising actually that novel and unanticipated? It may require extensive revisions to what you thought your surprising findings were and what your theoretical intervention is. Abduction lends itself to an organizational format of setting up a surprise followed by a theoretical denouement in the text. We encourage you to work with this format, and to adopt a writing style that reinforces rather than obscures your theorizing. We argue for a reflexive writing engagement with words-data-ideas to persuade your audience of what you want them to walk away with.

Chapter 9 wraps the book up with reflections on qualitative research, and we add an appendix about the place of abduction in the emerging world of computational social sciences, where abductive "big data" approaches have been developed over the past few years.

Finally, our own approach needs to pass though the sieve of the pragmatist maxim: what difference does it make to the research process if we highlight the moment of surprise? This book will be judged by its ability to make you work differently, both in designing the big picture of the research and in a myriad of small ways—in the folders you will open on your computer screen; in the questions you add to your interview questionnaire; in how you structure the writing of your data in the articles and books you write. It's our hope that these small and bigger differences contribute to innovative and creative theorizing.

2: BEGINNINGS

One of the core elements of abductive analysis is theorizing while engaging a community of inquiry—the fellow travelers who read your work, who write the books that inspire you, and whom you interact with. You do not start from a blank map as the first social explorer, but enter a terrain already charted by multiple researchers. Creativity, as pragmatists saw so well, stands out against habits.

Abductive analysis similarly builds on the work of others. We have been inspired by other approaches to qualitative data analysis—from Glaser and Strauss's grounded theory through the current elaborations and extensions of grounded theory by Kathy Charmaz and Adele Clarke; from Jaap van Velsen's and Michael Burawoy's renditions of the extended case method in ethnography through Jack Katz's and Howard Becker's takes on analytic induction. While we are inspired by these traditions, we also look at them critically. Major approaches to qualitative data analysis carry the epistemological baggage of their origins. The point is not that they are old—there is quite a lot of "old" work that should be reread, not ignored. The problem is rather that given the lay of the land when those works were written—given *their* communities of inquiry—their arguments have been warped over time and distort some valuable aspects of logical inference. Both inductive and deductive legacies in qualitative research have shown their limitations to the point that researchers ritualistically mention them in their methods sections but almost invariably do very different things in practice.[1]

This isn't just a matter of closing the gap between what researchers report and what they do. As researchers, and especially students, follow the recommendations of such approaches to qualitative research, they may find themselves in a tight spot. Perhaps nowhere is this problem more apparent than in grounded theory's admonishment to let the theoretical narrative arise from observations inductively. The problem is that all too often, the analysis does not contain a theoretical kernel—and when nothing is surprising, all we can do is endlessly collect and classify observations. As we were writing this chapter, we found the following cry for help on a bulletin board aimed at qualitative researchers:

> *I have been utilising in vivo codes on various established definitions in two fields of study in order to determine if theories derived from the code analysis can be grouped into the two fields of studies. What has emerged is 141 codes that have been grouped into 11 logical categories.*
>
> *These categories can be linked to some prominent theories such as [. . .] but others cannot.*
>
> *I need assistance with:*
>
> 1. *Are there any principles in linking coding outputs to established theories?*
> 2. *Are there any principles in handling code categories that do not logically link to established theories?*

"In vivo codes" is grounded theory jargon for codes that your respondents articulate, an abstract insight grown out of self-reflection.[2] As the responses to this slightly lost soul noted, description is not enough. But the danger of turning data analysis into a kind of butterfly collection of themes and subthemes is a risk inherent to methods that eschew theorization. The problem wasn't that this scholar didn't read grounded theory carefully enough. It was, rather, that they read it too literally.

In this landscape, abductive analysis is a way to bring what many good qualitative researchers already did closer to what they said they were doing when they pored over interview transcripts and field notes. Abductive analysis gives qualitative researchers a language to describe their analytical practice, not just to please funders or reviewers but also to think differently about how they were conducting their research. While varieties of grounded theory may help you say something about what is going on in your observations, abductive analysis shows in detail what it would mean to tie this question to another: "what are these observations a theoretical case of?"[3]

We do research to be surprised, not to confirm what we already know, theoretically or empirically. This is absolutely fundamental for anything that follows in this book: research is about asking questions to which you don't know the answer. You may have a hunch, but if you are unwilling to ask questions that may give you answers you didn't expect or, worse, want, you are not doing research.

The concern that the established data analysis approaches tried to solve—unsupported theorization—is real. There are still scholars whose main purpose for doing research is to illustrate some grand theorist's musings or to implement a preset theoretical agenda. These scholars know before they even gather any observations that W. E. B. Du Bois, Pierre Bourdieu, Karl Marx, or Judith Butler was right and will explain their findings. They are convinced of what they will find and selectively ignore all signs that may suggest otherwise.

Our ambition, however, is different: we aim to conduct research that breaks new ground while building on those who came before us in order to inspire others. You may think of this position on professional and career grounds (value of originality, impact of research, etc.), but for us, this is fundamentally an existential issue: life is finite, research takes a lot of time. Are you going to spend the good years of your life saying something most people already know, or are you aiming for things that inspire others—not to mention yourself—to look at the world differently? The moments of surprise, and our ability to account for them, are thrilling. Puzzling out research surprises is what keeps us going.

As a scientific logic of inquiry, abduction complements inductive and deductive scientific reasoning. Inductive reasoning, and this is often misunderstood by grounded theorists, looks for more facts based on resemblance and strengthens the empirical base of a research project. It's a bottom-up logic that helps us reject or gain confidence in a theory. It is, as Charles S. Peirce put it, *ampliative*. The accumulation of facts makes a theoretical premise probable, suggesting that individual observations inform more general conclusions. Deduction, in contrast, interprets facts in light of predictions drawn from theory. It's *explicative*. Deductive reasoning sets an expectation of what we should be able to find based on prevailing theories, which can then be falsified if our observations violate hypotheses, or accepted until further notice. It's a top-down logic to test theories.

Abductive reasoning, like induction, starts with an observation and seeks a likely explanation. The observation is unlike others we have. It is a surprising finding in light of our expectations. Abduction is contextual: something is surprising in light of what should have happened. As Burawoy points out: "A *good* theory makes predictions and fosters surprises."[4] A surprise by definition is a foiling of expectations. Our current theories cannot fully account for this finding. The analytical task is to puzzle out what these findings could mean, how they could fit, and what consequences they produce. If these observations are robust, then something else—a theoretical conjecture—is required to make sense of them. Abduction refers to the interpretive leap we make when we have a surprising finding and come up with a provisionary theoretical claim that may make sense of this anomaly. It takes us away from the known and into the realm of inference.

Peirce explained that the leap from facts to a provisionary hypothesis rests on a logical relationship that can be postulated. He put it in a syllogism where C is the surprising finding and A is the abductive inference: "If A were true, C would be a matter of course."

> The surprising fact C is observed.
> But if A were true, C would be a matter of course.
> Hence, there is a reason to suspect that A is true.[5]

The abductive inference is an educated guess that renders the surprising finding understandable as a matter of course: "Abduction," Peirce says, "is, after all, nothing but good guessing."[6]

An abductive inference thus cannot be where we come to rest. At best, it's a plausible hypothesis focusing on the surprising aspects of the findings to be pursued with additional research. Abductive reasoning by itself is only provisionary: a hypothesis on probation. To strengthen an abductive inference, researchers need to change or refine their theoretical apparatus to incorporate the new claim and then deduce what could be expected based on the invigorated theory. Abduction thus leads to deduction: an abductive inference specifies what you should expect to find in your research. Then gathering more observations can strengthen the theory inductively, although it is more likely to be falsified with more findings through a process of continuous refinement that requires new abductive inferences. This is why abduction complements deduction and induction. In every research project, even quantitative projects that are written up as hard-core deductive hypothesis testing, you will find some deductive, inductive, and abductive moments.[7]

The point of abductive analysis is that we should practically and analytically center the process of creativity, the moments of discovery of new theoretical insights. But how do we produce those novel insights? Should you close your eyes and wait for a muse to inspire you? There isn't some mysterious "context of discovery" that is the realm of mystics or psychologists. Abduction is also not an intuitive flash of insight. In fact, this is one point where we part ways with Peirce. For all his attention to the context of discovery, he was too enamored with instinct, thus inserting a magical black box into the heart of his philosophy of science. Influenced by Darwin's evolutionary theory, Peirce argued that people have evolved to pretty much instinctively come up with a likely fitting hypothesis. But this mystifies the process exactly where we need clarification. Instead, we argue, abductive analysis follows from reasoning and depends on how plausible a preliminary explanation is. It is something that we can hone in our work.

There are countless abductive inferences possible, so how do we know which one to pursue? Despite being smitten with instincts, Peirce provided some elementary guidance of what constitutes a good abductive inference. Since abductive hypotheses are tentative, their consequences will need to be deductively traced out and inductively compared with the results of new observations. An abductive moment thus suggests what we should observe and, once collected, how these new observations can be theorized.[8] This sounds good in principle. But how do we go about abducting? Ultimately, we need to go with what seems the most promising abductive inference, but there are ways to make the process more effective during the research journey. Before we get to how you can stack the deck in your favor in the next chapters, we outline some of the central tenets of abductive analysis we developed over the past decade. You'll need to understand these in order to grasp what comes next.

Cultivating abductive reasoning

Rather than waiting for muses to whisper abductive inferences in your ear, abductive reasoning can be stimulated by organizing favorable research conditions. While spontaneous surprises are possible, many surprises such as marriage proposals or birthday parties are meticulously planned. Surprise takes coordination and quite some work behind the scenes.

To favor abductive reasoning, we play to the strengths of qualitative methods. Compared to the strengths of other social science methods, qualitative research has distinct disadvantages. It is virtually impossible to generate a random sample in the way survey researchers value. Consequently, qualitative research is vulnerable to the criticism of sampling on the dependent variable, selection bias, and having limited generalizability.[9] You similarly set yourself up for a losing battle if you make causal claims with the same conviction as experimentalists. Researchers manipulating one variable in a controlled setting using double-blind procedures are going to have the upper hand over your convenient "natural" observations of unfolding events.

Yet qualitative research offers an opportunity to observe social life in its full complexity, as you and others experience it, and as it ricochets off in different areas and directions. Playing to the strength of the method means taking advantage of the close contact and probing while you go along, examining alternative explanations, and working closely with your observations as they unfold over time. It also means being aware of when an extrapolation crosses into a figment of a theorist's imagination, when a theory is no longer grounded in your materials, or when you just don't have the evidence. In *Abductive Analysis*, we emphasized four key elements that take advantage of the strengths of qualitative research and tip the scales in your favor for abductive insights:

1. Familiarity with multiple theories

If you want to contribute to a literature, you must participate in a community of inquiry; you need to familiarize yourself with the prevailing ideas and theoretical notions. There is no way around it. A surprise is surprising only in light of a set of expectations and, by default, those expectations will likely be commonsense notions of how people should behave. In order to make theoretical sense of a research finding, we also need to have theoretical groundings of what we hope to find in a site. Each research project is embedded in a theoretical library of relevant readings.

Here, we want to distinguish between situating a project in an empirical and a theoretical literature—between reading "theory" and "the literature." All researchers need to query databases for studies on similar or related subject matters. For instance, a researcher studying the stigma of having a bipolar diagnosis may do a keyword search in a medical database and find five similar studies. The researcher then summarizes what these other researchers found: whether or not a bipolar diagnosis was associated with stigma. Exactly because this literature review extracts exclusively empirical findings, it is not what we have in mind.

As an aside, often the researcher justifies a study by stating that there is a gap in the literature; no one else has looked at the specific variation of stigma and bipolar disorder. Filling such a narrow gap is often presented as a warrant for a study. Generally, trust us here, this is a terrible warrant. The fact that nobody looked at a particular phenomenon does not mean that you should. We are not in the business of faithfully copying the world, looking for nooks and crannies that went unnoticed by past cartographers. What makes a study worthwhile is that you have something interesting to say, not that you point to its existence.[10] Who knows, maybe no one looked at your topic precisely because it is so similar to other cases that it makes your proposal pointless.

Another, more practical, reason why the "no one has looked at it" warrant for a study is a weak one is that it depends on your ability to review the entire literature. Chances are, in a world full of social researchers, someone, in fact, *did* look at your topic, or one that is quite similar to it. Imagine, then, a reader or reviewer of your work who thinks that she has done a study very similar to yours. Now you are at double disadvantage: you have shown your ignorance of the literature, and you have likely annoyed a reviewer by implying that her research does not count. A much stronger justification of a research project is a positive reason. A study is interesting because it solves a consequential puzzle and thus adds something new to a preexisting conversation. Your job is to convince your readers that your study creates a new road, not that it fills a pothole.

To return to our example, in a study of the stigmatization of having a bipolar diagnosis, we would of course want to know what others have found in order to avoid restating what is already known. The more relevant literature we are interested in, however, explores underlying theory. What are the stigmatizing associations of mental health conditions? Where do they come from? How are they anticipated? What are their consequences? This is an enormous literature where some of the best sociologists of mental health have left their mark.[11] This abundance of literature is both a challenge and an opportunity. On the bright side, you have a lot of interlocutors to engage and potentially a large audience of readers who already care about your research topic. But this presents a challenge: you also have the responsibility of mastering an extensive literature and finding your place within it. To be surprised in a populated field, you need to be able to see how your observations relate not just to one theory, but to a complex landscape of writing and thinking.

We cannot emphasize this strongly enough. The only scenario worse than claiming to go into the field without a theory is entering it with only one of them—your "favorite" theory. A single theory or theoretical tradition means a limited range of observations that can surprise you. This, in turn, leads many good researchers to rediscover social capital, hide a lack of originality behind flowery prose and a string of citations, or make contributions that are so painfully obvious from the get-go that the reader just prays that the empirical data will be strong enough to keep their attention.

Moreover, as theories and concepts travel across substantive research projects, simply reading the literature immediately related to your topic is not going to be sufficient because of selection bias. You will insert yourself into a network of like-minded individuals who have already agreed on what the topic or site is about and on what a surprise looks like. But thinking more widely opens up possibilities of surprise—and as importantly—expands your ability to think of how you would explain what you have found. As we will outline in detail in the next chapter, we are advocating for far-out reading, outside the comfort zone of subdisciplines, outside the confines of your field, into the domain of other researchers.

Here is an example we like: Anna Mueller and Seth Abrutyn conducted a study of suicide. Coming from a background in social networks research (Mueller) and social psychology (Abrutyn), they initially envisioned their work as a social psychological elaboration of Durkheim's pioneering writings on suicide. They proposed a study of the role of emotions and dyadic ties in suicide clusters—communities in which a number of suicides take place in close proximity in time and place. They settled on "Poplar Grove," an affluent neighborhood in northern California that had an ongoing cluster of teenage suicides.[12] As Abrutyn told us, when they conducted focus groups with Poplar Grove residents, they realized that the stories they kept hearing didn't fit a focus on the emotional dynamics of "dyadic ties": "Anna and I had both independently become aware of (a) a massive awareness of a suicide problem within the community, and not just some dyadic dynamics, (b) the level of solidarity was quite high and, like a small rural town, everyone was in everyone's business." This was an unanticipated puzzle.[13]

Faced with a community with strong cultural and social cohesion, Durkheim's categories of "altruistic" and "fatalistic" types of suicide should have been most relevant, but these categories did not fit the kinds of narratives of intense shame, tremendous pressure to succeed, and desperate attempts to fit in that Mueller and Abrutyn found in their observations. They also noted little assistance in the epidemiological literature, as it tended to be too descriptive and talked of correlations rather than processes. They were fascinated by this puzzle, and the themes of their analysis emerged as salient precisely because of its uneasy and puzzling relation to prevailing theory.

At the beginning of the research project, we consider these concepts and theories mostly as heuristic tools to orient us, help us think, focus our observations, develop questions, and form research puzzles. One way of being innovative is to bring something from a different field or discipline to bear on your own site.

2. Methodological kneading of observations

The complementary key to stimulate abductive inferences is to work intensively with the empirical materials the first day you start your research. Such work was emphasized and developed usefully in the coding paradigms of the grounded theory program. For abduction to work, however, we need to rethink some of the ways grounded theory suggested we consider the analytical categories and sets we "discover." Whereas in grounded theory, coding often seems to be the destination of data analysis, in abductive analysis the point is to open up moments of surprise and help determine what kind of case you have. By slowing yourself down and becoming mindful of your observations, you can grow more deliberate about what it is that you see, find puzzles you glanced over, and allow yourself time to focus on what makes them puzzling. Coding is the analytical labor of data analysis.

By abstracting your findings in light of existing theories, you oblige yourself to determine what kind of theoretical claims you can support and to become more precise about how and where your findings deviate from what others have claimed. Coding then forces really close reading of your own observations. It is a process of figuring out what you have: defamilarization by isolating observations, and refamiliarization by putting observations in dialogue with each other and your ongoing reading.

Field notes and interview transcripts do some of that work. Researchers sometimes feel that perhaps they should really just transcribe the "important bits" of an interview, or that they can skip a lot of the "boring" details in their fieldwork. Now, while you may feel that the twentieth time you saw the same observation you might not need to write it up in as much detail, writing and transcribing the specificities can't be replaced. Beyond theoretical preparation, in order to be surprised you often have to strip away some of the ways you take the world for granted. And as researchers in literary theory have shown, defamiliarization techniques are ways in which we can nudge ourselves to appreciate anew aspects of the world that we thought we already knew.

Beyond defamiliarization, in this book we advocate two different kinds of coding: a more rudimentary form where you interrogate your data with a pragmatist variation of the basic rhetorical questions since antiquity of "who does what, when, where, how, with what kind of consequences." Going systematically through your observations alerts you to the range of parties, actions, and consequences present in your field site. It helps the process of defamiliarization by bringing into relief what is taken for granted and left implicit by participants because you force yourself to spell out how different parts of social action have an impact on people's lives. But more than that, it shows you what kind of claims your data can support by showing you patterns and exceptions. Are you capturing the actions you think you are? Are there other places you should be? This is why coding occurs during the process of data gathering. If you wait until you have wrapped up your observations, you can no longer go back and ask new questions. Open coding thus also gives you marching orders on where to go next. Open coding prompts you to read other people's research and theories when you start feeling that a theme is emerging in your observations. This, in turn, will further stimulate new ideas of what to look for in your materials.

The second form of coding starts with a specific theme that you feel is particularly promising in your observations based on an *index case* that captures that theme particularly well. In focused coding,[14] you examine your materials for similar scenes, interactions, and situations and then code them as a group. Reading pertinent literature also becomes more focused.

Again, the goal is to figure out systematically what kind of theoretical claims your materials can support.

Coding aims to discover the pattern and variation in your observations and explain both the dominant forms and their deviations. We are particularly keen to encourage qualitative researchers to explore variation in their data because qualitative research with its repeated observations is particularly good at finding variation across seemingly similar situations. To get a handle on variation, you build a dataset of cases based on similarities and dissimilarities. Qualitative researchers also are able to follow phenomena over time and therefore can also map processes across temporal variation. The third kind of variation is most unique to qualitative research: we can switch settings and see how the same people act at home, on the street corner, at work, in the park hanging out with buddies. Or we can follow a grocery item from its origins through its journey in stores to its final consumption. We call this intersituational variation.[15] Coding across temporal or situational dimensions for variation will give your research project analytical heft. However, mapping variation is insufficient as an abductive research strategy because it gives you a typology of what you have in your observations but does not lead to a theoretical argument.

3. Finding puzzles

You read other people's work and you code, but to what end? What are you reading or coding *for*? As social scientists, qualitative researchers want to both show something and explain something, implicitly or explicitly.[16] Our explanatory work rests on identifying a puzzle in the form of a poignant moment or pattern and then examine how this puzzle could possibly get resolved. The puzzle is about the particular pattern we find in the social world, and the explanation is an argument about why social life works the way it does.

We refer to this as the Jeopardy principle of qualitative research. Analyzing observations is a quest to find out what your research is an answer to. You have the answer; your job is to ask the right question. In the Jeopardy quiz, participants answer a clue with a question. Thus, the quiz master may state: "Unlike the tech version, there's no 'A' in the name of this apple named for the finder of the first seedling in 1911." The contestants phrase their answer in a question format. In this case, the correct answer in the form of a question was "What is McIntosh?"[17] Similarly, in qualitative research you acquire some ideas of an answer to a research question over the course of the project. Your observations are your clues. Now you need to come up with a question that fits those clues. Analyzing your observations is then a process of casing, finding an answer to the question "what is this a theoretical case of?" that leads you to theorizations. Unlike the quiz, analyzing observations is not just a hit-or-miss clue. You don't really passively receive the clue: as we will show, you create your own clues by collecting observations and cultivating abductive insights through coding and engaging existing theories. The key issue is that each project is good for answering some questions rather than others (though, inevitably, more than one question). What argument do your observations support? What is the strength of your data?

You need to answer this challenge as honestly as you can because often researchers realize at the end of their project that they wish they had probed their data more in a particular area and they really, really want their research question to address that area. Your best shot is to go with where your data is strongest, not where you wish it would have been stronger. And gathering more data in an adjoining area may risk setting you on a pursuit of that ever-elusive greener grass because when you add more data, you may find that if you just keep adding data in yet another area, you *really* can answer the most interesting research question. But when you get there, you find that if you just got some more data.... The problem is that you have much too narrow a vision of what makes for a good garden. Stop looking for greener grass, and start watering and fertilizing the pasture in front of you.

And, of course, it is not just observations that can set up a research puzzle. Some research puzzles originate from a theoretical riddle. The dominant story in the immigration literature is one of assimilation with its challenges, moments of racism, achievements, and discontents. New immigrants orient to the norms of the dominant White culture.[18] Research overwhelmingly treats White Americans in the U.S. as the standard bearers, defining the norms and parameters of academic achievement against which to compare minority achievement. Blackness and Latinxness are measured against White achievement (and often fall short). Asians are considered a model minority, but still Whites set the norms of success and remain gatekeepers to belonging. Researchers have marshaled these theories to explain the academic achievement gap between minorities and White Americans.

Studying East and South Asian immigrants going to high school with third-plus-generation White students in the heart of Silicon Valley, however, Jiménez and Horowitz's results did not follow this pattern. Rather, in light of the earlier literature, the findings were not merely surprising but truly astonishing. The schools were academically hypercompetitive with the Asian immigrants setting the norms of achievement of which their

White fellow students fell short. An Asian "fail" in high school was receiving a B or B+ on a school assignment while a White "fail" was receiving an F. "Being White" meant opting out of AP (Advanced Placement) courses. Students referred to White students who were studious as "Asian at heart," while Asian students who partied or emphasized extracurricular activities "acted White" and were "Americanized" or "Whitewashed." Teachers would be more lenient with White students, making sure they passed the class. Cupertino's students, parents, and teachers had embraced an inversion of White and Asian norms of achievement: Whiteness stood for lower achievement, laziness, and academic mediocrity while Asianness was tied to high achievement, hard work, and academic success.[19]

These findings are staggering in light of the received theoretical consensus in the migration literature that treat White Americans as the gatekeepers to belonging, determining the ethnoracial and class segments of U.S. society into which immigrant populations will assimilate.[20] They also run counter to what would be expected from the influential racialization theories that view a historically rooted racial social system of White hegemony as relegating minorities to a subordinate status.[21] Jiménez and Horowitz explain this dramatic inversion of achievement norms with the large, concentrated immigrant population (Cupertino was 29 percent White and 63 percent Asian at the time of their study). However, relative size is not sufficient: in other settings, White students have been able to define norms of achievement when they are in the numerical minority. The class structure also mattered: the immigrants' socioeconomic status equaled or exceeded that of the dominant group. There was no third competing ethnic group, although the researchers' predicted that even if Cupertino had large Latino or Black populations, Whites still were unlikely to set the achievement norms. Jiménez and Horowitz's work supports the immigration literature that emphasizes a more dynamic exchange. Some assimilation theories, building further on the original theorizing of Park and Burgess, relax the notion of assimilation as a process of group absorption into the dominant culture for a process of group convergence.[22]

Again, the detail of your observations will facilitate such explanations and theoretical developments. Jack Katz reviewed how ethnographers develop explanations through the rich and vivid particularities of their observations.[23] An observed scene may prompt curiosity about why it occurred, but the answer to the *why* resides in the *how*, the process by which things come to be. You ask a student why she opted for law school, and most likely you will receive an answer, often reiterated in a personal statement in the application file, that reflects a cultural repertoire of motives related to why people pursue higher education: making money, helping clients, pursuing justice. If instead you turn the question into a *how* question—how did you end up in this law school program, what was happening in your life, what other choices did you have, and how did you end up here?—you are more likely going to receive an answer that combines planning with serendipity, covers loose ends, failed attempts, and other potential careers. You will uncover a process where confidence is mixed with doubts, and other much more interesting aspects that open rather than foreclose an analysis. Juxtaposing how the people answer the two kinds of questions often produces yet more puzzles.

The idea is to examine observations for luminous events that may take the form of unexpected interactional turns, paradoxes, conflicts, contradictions, enigmas, dilemmas, absurdities, uncertainties and then to work backwards or, "retrodict." The researcher examines what is needed to make this observation a matter of course within the situational specificity in which it occurred. Turning the saying "necessity is the mother of invention" on its head, the researcher's task is to search "for circumstances of necessity" in order to explain moments of inventiveness.[24] What could otherwise be crude explanations based on social forces becomes instead flexible, playful, and unexpected explanations. Sounds familiar? Indeed, this is the abductive logic applied to processual explanations.

One implication is that abductive analysis does not start with a single research question but ends with one as the result of a process of chipping away at what you are studying. You start with hunches, supported by literature and your own stamina. Maybe you lived, worked, or volunteered among the people you are interested in studying. Your own position, never completely reduceable to the categories sociologists often look at, shape your expectations and where you could be surprised.[25] Your hunches may be quite specific. But figuring out what exactly it is that you are studying, what your site is good for, is an outcome of the research process. Throughout the analytical journey you are refining the question.

4. Peirceian semiotics and research

This is a book about abduction, and about how to make abductive analysis actionable. But our work also draws from other aspects of pragmatism. And so while you don't need to subscribe to any of *that* in order to read the book, it might make our examples and our thinking throughout more legible.

Besides abduction, we also build upon a semiotic foundation from Peirce. This elucidates the most fundamental unit of analysis for qualitative research. For conversation analysts, the most basic analytical element is the turn construction unit (TCU): a turn in a conversation that completes an utterance. In the small exchange between two people, "How are you?" "Fine. But my back still hurts," there are three TCU's, the question, the initial response, and the elaboration, as long as there's a new intonation contour at "but," and the utterance does not run straight through. Conversation analysts studying disparate topics from presidential press conferences to police-citizen interactions will slice their data into these basic units.

The equivalent basic "bottoming out" unit for ethnographers and interviewers is the processes of meaning-making: the semiotic act where a sign signifies an object and produces some kind of effect in the world. Peirce conceptualized this basic act of meaning as a threefold semiotic partition:

> I define a sign as anything which is so determined by something else, called its object, and so determines an effect upon a person, which effect I call its interpretant, that the latter is thereby mediately determined by the former.[26]

Meaning-making thus consists of three interlinked parts. The first of these elements is the *sign*—whether an arbitrary convention or a characteristic that is more intimately tied to the object. The sign, in turn, does not exist on its own but is always in relationship to an object: a sign signifies or provides meaning about an object. A sign reveals something, and due to the limits of human perception this revelation is inevitably partial: the sign focuses only some aspects of the object. The second element, then, is the *object*, any entity about which a sign signifies—including both actual things out there in the world as well as ideas in our head and in public culture.

Peirce's most original insight in this tripartite division, however, was that meaning-making is a practical achievement. To capture this point, Peirce argued that every act of meaning-making includes an *interpretant*— the effect of the sign-object through which any act of meaning-making is completed. We cannot talk of meaning-*making* unless it has some kind of effect upon actors—an emerging understanding, emotion, or action. With the interpretant, Peirce argues that future semiotic chains indicate whether a particular signification had an effect. To understand meaning, we need to follow the sequence of signification. The three elements of his semiotic theory form an irreducible triad. A sign thus *stands for*, *denotes*, or *represents* an object and *shapes* an interpretant. An object, in turn, constrains the range of signs that are possible in the situation at hand.

To return to the short exchange about the hurting back, there are two basic semiotic units: the question leading to a response, and the elaboration of the response, which qualifies and signifies the word "fine." Semiotic acts of meaning-making go beyond utterances. They include behaviors such as a person running away from a barking dog (as well as the dog barking), turning on the stove to boil water, noticing smoke on the hills while listening to music. They include shifts in thinking and emotional re-actions such as the feeling of desire when a lover touches your inner thigh. They can be mechanical, intentional, or accidental; human or nonhuman. Anything that gives meaning to something else or adds an interpretative dimension to a previous thought, action, or feeling spurring some kind of effect is a basic semiotic act of meaning-making. Compared to the TCU, the basic semiotic unit is less cleanly delineated and more comprehensive.

Exploring the semiotic underpinnings of meaning-making as a start-ing point constitutes a theoretical heuristic to help qualitative researchers make sense of the minutiae of observations. Taking on the key insights of this semiotic legacy—that we can approach action and interaction as itera-tions of meaning-making in action—provides a flexible set of sensibilities that fits the strengths of qualitative research particularly well. Regardless of whether you are interested in the patterns of conflict between workers and management on the factory floor, or in how African American Mus-lims navigate the challenges of a rapidly gentrifying neighborhood, your observations will consist of acts of meaning-making in the moment, antici-pating future use, and building on past experiences. Pragmatist semiotics gives you a way to tease out, isolate, and relate these basic units. They pro-vide a granular way to see how action unfolds.[27]

Where do you start?

Jorge David Mancillas, then a doctoral student who had just finished his first quarter in graduate school, sat down at the table in Stefan's office, pulled out a copy of *Abductive Analysis*, then made some space to put down two transcripts of interviews. The interviews were with two men who were affiliated with a gang, one a thirty-eight-year-old OG, or original gang-ster, and another with a younger friend. Jorge had asked them questions about how they lived with the possibility of dying. He opened his bag again and took out some more books. All about death and dying. He had Ernest Becker's Pulitzer Prize–winning book, *The Denial of Death*,[28] a general soci-ology textbook on death and dying, and a couple of other books. Pointing to the orange cover of our first book, Jorge began delicately, saying how much he liked reading the methods book over the break but it was clear he had a burning question. "How," he wanted to know, "do I generate these abductive insights? Where do I start?"

This question about beginnings is a good one. Jorge was eager to get a head start. So where does he start with abductive reasoning? One way to think about this question is to look at the things Jorge spread out on the table and pick one up as the place to begin. Should he start with the interview transcripts or with *The Denial of Death*? It depends on what drives your research: are you fascinated by how a psychoanalytical theory about death withstands time and Illuminates the contemporary moment during Black Lives Matter and the COVID pandemic, or are you more committed to the people you interviewed? There is no wrong answer, but the next steps will differ based on how you can tie the two together.

Jorge's foremost commitment was to his interviewees. He wanted to study his childhood friends in the gang—and how they dealt with the closeness and omnipresence of death at such a young age seemed a promising theme. One good start is indeed to begin with the transcripts. In most research projects, the transcript is the object requiring signification. As such, it will constrain the theoretical signs that are possible. If the data motivates the project, it does not make much sense to spend months in the early stages of a research project trying to master a theoretical literature because it may turn out to be irrelevant to the project. You definitely will need a to get a working acquaintance with this literature and then delve deeper into it once you see resonances with specific literatures in your observations. But the data will show whether this literature is a relevant orientation point for the project.

Jorge and Stefan looked over the transcripts together. Jorge's first question was about associations with death but the response of the younger man immediately veered off into poverty:

> *Death? I mean. . . . It kind of scares me—I mean it doesn't scare me but like, I fear death because I'mma leave my family alone. I don't want to leave my family without being able to support them or being able to leave anything that makes them happy. Like let's say money, money-wise. I know my family's fuckin' poor, so I'm afraid of dying because they're poor and I'm not leaving them with millions, you feel me? I want to accomplish something in my life in order for me to not have to worry about money so my family could stay straight.*

The OG also touched on feeling poor:

> *And like I told you, dog, I didn't know I was fuckin' poor until I came over here [the United States] cuz over there [Oaxaca, Mexico] my childhood was never about "aw shit I got some fucked-up shoes." Sometimes I wouldn't even wear shoes, I'd run on the street with no shoes! You know, second-hand clothes. . . . Nobody was over there trippin' like I got fucked-up second-handed clothes from a thrift shop, or fuckin' shoes, or huaraches [Mexican sandals]. Sometimes*

I don't even have shoes. You ate, you go to sleep, and you're fuckin' happy. It wasn't until here [USA] till we're like "Fuck. What the fuck? We're poor!" Like, I got a scar on my hand, dog. Cuz my mom couldn't afford to buy me a shirt on my twelfth birthday and I punched a fuckin' glass on a door—not cuz I hated my mom but because I was frustrated at that age and I was thinking like, "Why the fuck are we so poor?"

When he talked with Stefan about the poverty theme, Jorge explained that this particular gang used to call one of the wealthy Westside Los Angeles neighborhoods its home but the members had been priced out of this neighborhood and were spread out in East Los Angeles, even though they would regularly return to their home turf. The family he was closest with was living in a small motel room with eight people in Southeast Los Angeles. The transcript teemed with references to being poor, needing money, and wanting money. Maybe Jorge needed different books. Instead of reading an anthropologist's integration of Freudian theory about death in the mid-seventies, it made more sense to think about poverty and death, about absolute and relative poverty. This brought up different literatures on the economics of gang life[29] and the reproduction of social class,[30] and even Merton's on reference groups.[31] *The Denial of Death* needed to stay on the table for now, but there were other books and articles that went to the top of the pile.

The second way to answer Jorge's question was to retrace his research project and think when it began. Jorge didn't actually start with these transcripts. As an undergraduate student, he had written an article as part of the McNair mentoring project on how gang members anticipated and considered the possibility of an early death.[32] The current project built on these provisionary research feelers. Jorge also had been hanging out the entire first academic quarter with a family of gang-affiliated young men. However, the observations were all over the place. Some of the gang members tried to break into the formal economy by setting up a marijuana dispensary. Jorge also had observations of the conflicts between the family and landlords, and between the brothers in the family. Since he had a driver's license, almost every set of notes included a run to liquor stores and the troubles of finding a parking spot in Los Angeles.

The point is that the analysis did not start that day in Stefan's office. Some projects truly begin when we officially enter the field, but many more don't. Researchers shape their interest over time. It is usually not a dramatic moment of choice. They serendipitously read something here, take a class there that exposes them to some other literatures, and more or less wander into their project, rather than making a momentous decision. Jorge had already had made countless choices of what he was going to study, and the range of possible tracks to take had already been narrowed. He hoped the study would be related to living with death, dying, or addiction. If the goal of abductive analysis is to figure out what kind of case one has, the parameters of this project had already been quite well-defined.

To answer Jorge's question most directly, abductive insights are not going to pop up right away in a research project, after you have transcribed the first two interviews or read some books on death and dying. Neither are they going to develop on a daily basis. The reality is that you spend a lot of time laying the groundwork for abductive reasoning with a combination of coding observations and reading various literatures. Most observations are going to fit with what others have observed and theorized. Most reading will be off-target. You may get excited for a while about a possible connection to the literature but then you drop it again. The bar for making creative inferences in increasingly maturing fields such as urban ethnography is growing higher and higher as much of the low-hanging fruit has been picked and the literature accumulates. The answer is to sit with your materials, go to the field, read widely, and discuss your thoughts and findings with your community of inquiry. There are ways to discipline these processes, as we outline throughout the book, but there are no shortcuts to the abductive process.

Abductive insights are going to be few and far between, but, and this makes it worth pursuing them, they are likely disproportionally influential. The corollary is that even if your ambition is not to move the theoretical goalposts but to make sense of your data on an elementary level, you will still find much useful advice for conducting qualitative data analysis in this book because most of the groundwork of working with data and integrating it into a literature is helpful regardless of theoretical aspirations.

In medical school, physicians warn each other not to go for out-of-place diagnoses when a more common diagnosis is more likely. They say: "If you hear hoof beats, think horses, not zebras." Abduction looks for zebras but most of what you will find is horses, and that is how it should be. Zebras, though, may pop up in unexpected places, as many people driving Highway 1 from San Francisco to Santa Barbara experience when they pass Hearst Castle. This book is a field guide for finding the lone zebra in the herd of horses.

Reflecting on this advice, a colleague and friend of ours, Pamela Prickett, added, "Zebras, yes. But not unicorns." Indeed, we are not interested in chasing fantastical beasts but in empirically observable life.

3: THEORIES

A paper that does not have references is like a child without an escort walking at night in a big city it does not know: isolated, lost, anything may happen to it.

BRUNO LATOUR, *Science in Action*[1]

Too much of what researchers do when they think they are theorizing is illustrating observations with more or less impressive abstractions. Such work "uses theory" to make findings more compelling and legitimate. Even this chapter's epigraph, in Bruno Latour's signature evocative prose, assumes that citations to other scholars are first and foremost a matter of strength rather than of intellectual discovery. While it is true that, as Latour would put it, each reference is recruited as an ally to bolster your claim, such a view overlooks a more compelling point. "Using a theory" is not only about strengthening your argument, but about your ability to see surprises in your data and join an intellectual conversation. Theorizing should not repeat what you have found in other words. Neither should it primarily solidify your work through a string of citations, though it will do that too. Rather, theorizing should allow you to join an ongoing disciplinary exchange about the world, *and to say something interesting*.

The best theoretical engagement achieves two goals: (a) it gives you a better understanding of your own empirical field, opening up new questions, new surprises, and axes of variation; and (b) it allows other scholars, both within and beyond your subfield, to recognize and anticipate new patterns in their own work. In other words, theorizing needs to do some "internal" work, pushing your own work forward, and some "external" work that has to do with how well your arguments travel.

Yet if theories need to travel in order to be thought-provoking, do they always travel in the same way? To the same destinations? To be thought-provoking, after all, is not an intrinsic property but a relational one: thought-provoking *to someone*.[2] Who, exactly, is that special someone? And beyond everything else, if abductive analysis is partly about entering the field with theories, what theories should we carry with us?

Have theory, will travel

Scholars have divided theories, or even what the word theory may mean, in different ways. When Gabriel Abend realized how many versions of theory he found as he was scouring the qualitative research literature, he just numbered them all the way to seven.[3] We find it more useful to think about two ideal types of theories: those that are directly aimed at others working on similar topics within a subfield, and those that cover a broader area of social life at a more abstract level. These constitute different types of theoretical engagement that move in different ways, to different audiences, and thus require a different kind of preparation. Here, Latour's quote is inspirational because a theory allows us to navigate difficult terrain. But how? Pushing the metaphor further, we would like to suggest that one way of highlighting the two kinds of theories is to think about the difference between two orientation tools: a map and a compass.

Let's decide you're going somewhere in a woodsy park for the first time. You might look up the park on a mapping app, to orient yourself to the location and what's where. The map will give you sets of possible directions, both to get to the park and for trails inside the park. Like a child lost at night in the city, losing your way in the woods could be dangerous. And if you're visiting a park in a land far from home, where you don't speak the local language, a map is essential. A compass, on the other hand, is a very different kind of instrument. It will give you less guidance in finding an exact desired destination (unless you are going to the north or south pole), but it will help you get where you are going across diverse landscapes. What it lacks in specificity, it gains in flexibility. While a map links a description to a landscape, a compass provides direction but requires continuous adjustment to make it work in the moment.

Map theories produce a picture of the social world as the general coordinates of what is out there. In other words, these are *substantive* theories about what a particular slice of the world looks like. Examples of map theories are most middle-range theories that form the backbone of any discipline and constitute subfields. Organizational sociology will have theories such as "institutional logics," "resource dependence," or "institutional isomorphism." The sociology of religion will have its own set of theories, people arguing about varieties of the "secularization theory," about the "subcultural theory of religion," and so on. In whatever subfield we find ourselves, we have to locate ourselves in relationship to one or more such theories. Without doing so, we would be coming into the field, meticulously mapping things that everybody who has looked at a map would have been able to tell us. One can imagine such a modern-day cartographer victoriously presenting us with a map of the eastern shoreline of the USA: nicely done, but a little pointless.[4]

But there's a hitch. While a map theory describes a set of studies and the relationship between them, our site is always unique and different from places others have mapped. It may be tempting to think that by mapping it, we are necessarily doing something different and theoretically interesting, but this is only true as a descriptive attempt. "Yes, there may be a forest," you are effectively saying, "but won't you take a look at this beautiful tree!" This is fine if you see your contribution in a variety of nontheoretical ways, which, as we noted in the first chapter, also presents viable warrants for qualitative work. But if it is a wider-ranging theoretical contribution that you're after, then you shouldn't be taken aback when others are not impressed.

Compass theories are different. They are what we think of as *grammatical theories*, in the sense that they provide the social grammar of life.[5] They tell us how social life is organized beyond a specific field. They lay out the general way in which you should approach the terrain—how you should walk, rather than exactly where you should walk to. The mark of such a theory is the set of keywords that it evokes. Rather than belonging to a subfield, a compass theory highlights general concepts: think of "exchange," "interaction," "boundaries," "class conflict," or "structure." These are also the kinds of theories that graduate students often think of first when they think about what "theory" is—Foucault's general approach rather than his specific genealogies; Bourdieu's general sociological insights beyond his contributions to education or class; Latour's actor-network theory instead of his sociology of science. In this sense, theory does not circumscribe the boundaries of the case, but rather provides the grammar for a broad range of possible stories that transcend a unique case.

One example of such a theory, which we are both partial to, is the pragmatist-inspired theory of interactionism. The symbolic interactionist teachings are, as Anselm Strauss writes, "open ended, partially unpredictable . . . interaction is regarded as guided by rules, norms, mandates; but its outcomes are assumed to be not always, or entirely, determinable in advance."[6] Symbolic interaction is thus a theory of the ways in which the social becomes both partially embedded in structures and negotiated in everyday life, always open-ended and subject to rearticulation by the agents in the field. In this sense, symbolic interaction answers questions of process. Remaining agnostic to the actual structure of the field and interests of the agents within it, symbolic interaction provides a theory of the social grammar of everyday life.[7]

Substantive and grammatical theories differ as to what counts as a theoretical contribution, and to whom. In the case of substantive theories, the contribution is aimed at a relatively well defined subdisciplinary audience. It needs to convince a set of researchers who work in a similar field of two goals: one easier, the other harder. First, you need to convince them that you really did encounter something surprising in the field. But then, what makes it into a *theoretical* contribution is that you ask these researchers to change or at least closely examine the maps they have been using. That is, you need to show researchers in your subfield what makes the feature you have found transposable to the substantive field as a whole. And while there are different ways to do so, the explanation for the feature found in your site needs to be on a level that is more generalizable than the substantive specifics of your data.

Grammatical compass contributions are harder to pull off. While not all compass theorizations are as all-encompassing as interactionism, they still need to transcend the particular map of the field. A compass should work just as well in California as in New York. This means that there are two tasks involved in their production. First, much as in substantive theories, you have to show that there was an interesting and unexpected feature in your field. But then, in the second moment, you need to make the case that across different subfields there are a family of problems that researchers should now approach differently; that there is something about how you navigate the social terrain that requires rethinking. This is more difficult for a simple reason—the audience is less well defined. It will be composed of people within the subfield who would read the work because of its substantive resonances, of theorists who will read it for its coherence as a general contribution and its resonances with other such theories, but also by a diffuse audience of people in different subfields whom you are trying to convince should adjust the grammar of the social, even though they are dealing with different substantive concerns.

The differences between these theories are relatively clear. They do different things, operate at different levels of generality in relation to specific research sites, and ideally reach different audiences. Articles developing map or compass theories end up being published in different journals. Moreover, as we outline in more detail below, they also afford researchers different kinds of surprises and lend themselves to different forms of abduction. The metaphors of map and compass are useful for one more reason: if we are serious travelers, we do not go into the field with *either* a map *or* a compass. It is not really an either/or kind of decision. Instead, a traveler to the wilderness should obviously both study her maps and have a good compass to work with. In other words, we never go to the field with only substantive or grammatical theories. We go in carrying both.

Choosing maps and compasses: choices and surprises

As with actual travel, you need a different map for every new place that you visit. The idea that you stay with one map is like saying that you will only take your vacations in one little town in Connecticut. Possible. Even if you are partial to the Northeast, you would probably want to go to different areas. And even if you stay in one little town, you will have to update your maps every so often. New places keep popping up even in narrowly demarcated spaces. Subfields are constantly evolving.

But how do you know which map to choose? Every social world is complex, full of overlapping phenomena that are all going on at once. Imagine a neighborhood map that only contains the sewage system, another map that locates each form of vegetation, a third map that shows the foot traffic, a fourth map that lists the toxic substances, and so forth. That's what substantive theories do: they each draw out some aspects of social life. Take a morgue, or an ad agency, two places we spent some time in. A morgue is about death and dying. But it's also a workplace, not that different from other workplaces. It's also, broadly speaking, a medical facility. Since there are people in the morgue (the living ones, we mean) who are categorizing other people (the dead) following scientific protocols, it may also be useful if you brush up on your sociology of knowledge. An advertising agency is also a workplace, but it is a workplace in which public culture is produced, as is knowledge about what "culture" even is. After two minutes in the field, or reading any book on advertising professionals, you realize that there are interesting questions of professional jurisdiction among different positions in the organization. And then, there are definitely also critical gender dynamics and racial politics that deserve attention (there are very few women in "creative" jobs and almost no people of color in the advertising industry). You quickly realize that there are *many* maps to consult.

Taken to the extreme, this is an Alice in Wonderland rabbit hole of epic proportions. There is simply no way that you could read everything that is relevant to every possible framing of your field. You can't look at everything that is going on. It's endless, and a little dispiriting. So what do you pack? What maps should you definitely carry with you?

In our experience, there are two complementary ways to find out what maps are most relevant to the work you do. First, *go for what is obviously relevant*. If you are planning to start an interview project about people's experiences at work, you simply need to get some handle on the sociology of work and occupations. Whatever else is going on in your data, given that your choice of site is determined by occupational activity, this is a literature you need to know. The same goes for ethnography. If you study a church group, you better immerse yourself in the sociology of religion; if you study poverty in an inner city neighborhood, you better have a sense of urban sociology and the rich sociology of race and ethnicity.

This may seem self-evident, but you would be surprised how often researchers enter a field without reading the obvious. This is not necessarily because they are beholden to grounded theory, lazy, or clueless. It is because sometimes people think that they can ignore the obvious because of the special angle with which they enter the project. For example, they want to study fictive kinship and thus focus solely on the sociology of the family in an ethnography of a street gang, ignoring the large literature on urban gangs. Or they want to study the organizational structure of churches, and thus read exclusively in organizational theory without familiarizing themselves with the religion literature. Or, and this drives one of us crazy, researchers study social health networks without consulting the sociology and public health literature on health and illness. They limit their reading to social network ideas under the assumption that the substantive issues of illness and mortality don't matter.

Instead, it's your responsibility to acquaint yourself with what others have written about your topic and related topics. There are really no shortcuts to doing this: when we contemplate a new research topic or settle upon an analytical theme, one of the first steps we take is to check an academic database of articles to see what others have written. We plug in some keywords and start scanning titles and abstracts, pick out a couple of articles that may be useful, branching off their references to slowly reveal the terrain. We check some syllabi in a field we don't know; we look at award-winning books and articles to get a sense of what people in that world think of as representing some of their best work; if we are lucky, we ask a colleague who knows the field more intimately and try to get an initial footing. When we wrote an article that uses Peirce's semiotic categories to trace and parse out videos of racist encounters in the United States,[8] we spent months reading in the sociology of race and badgering colleagues who knew much more than we did for recommendations, even though the primary reason for writing the article was to outline the contours of a semiotic interactionist approach.

The second, and no less important, way to figure out what map theories you will need is what we call the *principle of engagement*.[9] This is one of the key marks of serious analytic work in qualitative research. Our work as qualitative researchers takes as it starting point what our interviewees or research subjects find central. Yes, we see the social world through theoretically tainted lenses; we ask certain questions and not others. But still, the people we talk to will go about their life, and share what they care about.

The principle of engagement is simple: qualitative researchers have to take these emic preoccupations as seriously as they take the obvious theorizations of the field.

Here is a counterintuitive example: people struggling with drug addiction lie. They lie about taking drugs, about where they were, who they were with, what they did, where their money went, and they lie about lying. What do you do with these lies as a qualitative researcher? Should you give deference to lies? How should you engage them? In a project evaluating the effectiveness of a substitute drug for people addicted to opioids and other drugs, anthropologist Todd Meyers examined how lies operate in the context of addiction treatment: not just their destructive potential within personal and clinical relationships but also how the drug treatment system aims to "trick" the body into accepting a treatment drug as the real drug. These drugs are double agents: embodying both healing and poison, creating a deep ambivalence about the purpose of treatment. By listening carefully to the work lies do and accepting lies as lies rather than as distortions of a truth to which the researcher has access, Meyers showed that deception is closely tied to hope and is embedded multiply in the therapeutic context.[10]

These field explanations, however, have a different value than existing theorizations within your community of inquiry. We do not look to our interviewees for theory. They will theorize their lives, inevitably and often perceptively. People in a morgue will have an idea of why they autopsy some people more than others; people in an advertising agency theorize why some clients are considered "good clients." However, if all we have done is to repeat such first-order theorizations, then we have failed as researchers. Indeed, this is one of the most common hallmarks of mediocre qualitative research: a repetition of the categories and folk theories of our interlocutors.[11] Instead of treating these concerns as social theories, you need to treat them as pointing towards social science literatures to consult. For example, when Sonia Prelat, one of Iddo's students and coauthors, found out that the Argentinian businessmen that she was interviewing kept talking about past economic crises to make sense of their current precarity, she had to take a break from reading the literature about work and occupations and dive into the literature on collective memory. When another student, Eliza Brown, found that her ethnographic field notes of doctor-patient consultations of IVF treatments constantly returned to the question of money, she had to read up on economic sociology. As qualitative researchers, we need to treat our interviewees and research subjects' concerns as pointing towards other possible mappings of the terrain.

These two modes of finding maps are not the only ones available. There are other areas of literature that you may want to consult as the research twists and turns. As we show throughout the book, the actual work of qualitative research—both finding surprises and making sense of them—is the work of coding, teasing out variation, and constructing theoretical narratives from data excerpts. As we carefully attend to our data for emerging themes and puzzles, we may find themes that our interlocutors don't particularly stress, but that come up again and again in observations. These moments may call for their own maps.

How do we choose a compass-like theory? This is a question of a different order. There is relatively little in the field that forces you to think in Bourdieu's terms rather than as a rational choice theorist; to compel you to read interactionism rather than Marxist theory. This, of course, may make it seem overwhelming. You can't possibly read everything in general theory, especially not if you are a graduate student under time pressure who also needs to get a firm grasp of the maps of the land.

Here are some guiding principles. First, as you will quickly find out, maps and compasses often come as a package deal. Buy two maps, get a compass for free. That is, there are subfields that have an affinity for one compass rather than another. Much as Adele Clarke and Leigh Star once called interactionism and grounded theory a "theory-methods package,"[12] there are "compass-map packages" that propel researchers to certain compass theories based on their substantive area of research. For example, whether or not this is a passing fad or whether there is a deeper affinity between the map and the compass, most contemporary work in science and technology studies today needs to contend with actor-network theory. Beyond such fields, the pressures toward specific compass theories are more diffuse, though they often still exist. While not all urban ethnographers are interactionists, any cursory review of the subfield will show that this compass theory shaped the field. Some understanding of such theory will be important. Similarly, while education scholars don't absolutely have to read Bourdieu's œuvre deeply, it allows them to better understand the map of their terrain.

So much for the choice of theories. Such navigation tools differ not only in their specificity, but also in how they lead to surprise. One crucial point of abductive analysis, as we laid it out in the last chapter, is that surprise always emerges against a background of theoretical expectations. If theories differ in their fundamental structure, then we must ask ourselves about different classes of surprise that emerge in the research process.

Working through different surprises

What are the kinds of surprises that people encounter when they use a map? What are the modes of abduction in subfields? Generally speaking, maps—especially when you follow the *read the obvious* rule—present two complementary kinds of surprise. The first happens when something that we didn't see on the map is evident in the field. You go somewhere you don't quite know and prepare by studying the map. Then, when you are navigating the terrain, a gorge that wasn't supposed to be there is painfully obvious. You check your map again to make sure that you didn't just miss it. No, there simply wasn't a gorge there. Or else, the opposite might happen. According to the map you follow, at the center of the area you traverse is a raging river, but when you get there, it's more like a shallow stream, which people are crossing without even stopping to gauge the currents. Surprise.

Of course, it is not enough to say "Surprise!" Encountering a surprise is not the end of inquiry. It is the beginning, or perhaps the middle. Once a surprise has set in, the theoretical contribution is in map making, not simply pointing out flaws. From a substantive theory standpoint, making a theoretical contribution is about showing not only *that* the map is flawed, but *how* it is flawed, and something about what changed (or what was wrong to begin with), ultimately offering a revision to substantive theory. Still, the key moment of abduction here is the moment of surprise.

One example of such a substantive surprise can be found in Cecilia Menjívar's book *Fragmented Ties*. The book, an ethnographic and interview study of Salvadoran immigrants in the United States, makes a striking statement. The literature on immigration often thinks about immigrant networks as a source of support and aid (both emotionally and in terms of labor opportunities) under the assumption that immigrants share the same status. Yet the war on undocumented immigrants in the Unites States has created a different picture. Legal status, as Menjívar discovered, percolates into the structure of immigrant networks, creating new and invidious distinctions that the notion of "immigrant networks" misses. In relation to the literature, the differences between the legal status of documented and undocumented immigrants paints a far less rosy picture of how co-ethnic ties work. Against the romantic view that immigrant networks materially, financially, and emotionally support each other, Menjívar finds that the ties between newly arrived Salvadorans and their established friends and family are tenuous, rife with conflict, and quickly exhausted.[13]

The surprise here is precisely in finding patterns that did not appear on the map. The immigrant networks Menjívar studied don't behave as they "should" based on the prevailing literature. Then, of course, the trick is to explain it. Here, Menjívar operates through a double strategy. The first is to say that substantive theory was not careful enough. Immigrant networks are always less simple and tidy than the idea that "immigrants help each other." This is a common trope in qualitative research—things look more complex and varied under the microscope of interviews and ethnographic field notes. But second, and more powerfully, by focusing on legal status, Menjívar also argues that changes in patterns of legality have reconfigured the ways ties work: the US government has differentiated immigrants along legal categories. In a sense, the map doesn't work out because a political earthquake had changed the landscape.

Another example of how researchers encountered and worked through surprise in the field can be seen in Colin Jerolmack and Ed Walker's "Please in My Backyard," an article about the politics of fracking (hydraulic drilling for natural gas) in rural Pennsylvania.[14] The article was based on Jerolmack's ethnography of a community that became a central point for the fracking industry. As he spent time in this community, he found that many of the families were directly hurt by fracking: their drinking water became polluted by methane gas, trucks constantly rumbled through their property, or the pumping noise and the burn-off flares kept them awake at night. And yet, as opposed to the literature he was reading in the subfield of environmental justice, which focused on the powerlessness of the weak in resisting environmental hazards, the people in Jerolmack's field site welcomed fracking and stood by it even when they were personally hurt by the industry. Rather than a "not in my backyard" (NIMBY) story, he found the opposite, a "please in my backyard" (PIMBY) story.

This surprise was a first spark of a surprising finding. It located Jerolmack in a story that was as emotionally compelling as it was theoretically puzzling, at least as far as environmental sociology was concerned. But where Menjívar accounts for her theoretical puzzle by describing the tectonic changes in the political environment, Jerolmack moved in a different direction. Rather than looking at history, he looked at other processes he was seeing in his data. As opposed to the largely individualistic discussions of NIMBY-ism and PIMBY-ism, Jerolmack saw a host of situations in which people came together to talk about fracking and make sense together of their community. These gatherings and conversations were, he realized, a form of mobilization. Along with Ed Walker, a sociologist of political action and social movements, he then related the environmental sociology surprise to literature on mobilization and collective action. They showed the "quiet mobilization" of residents in support of fracking—support that was based on an ethic of libertarian individualism and a suspicion of leftist environmentalists and government intervention, but also on a solidarity with those who made money from leasing their lands. The surprise in light of the environmental justice theory, in other words, is partly explained through the social movement literature—not only explaining why it is different in *this case* but also asking environmental sociologists to consider forms of mobilization that they did not pay attention to before.

Thus, as we crisscross our research field we see that our maps are off. People, organizations, or institutions are not behaving in the ways our predecessors expected. As we spend more time exploring the field, we realize that actors face novel problems that direct us to a different literature. We then read through that literature, trying to get a firmer theoretical grasp. In some cases, such as Jerolmack and Walker's, the second literature helps explain what happens in a domain that was supposed to be secured by the obvious first literature. The point here is not that we "connect two literatures" as graduate students are sometimes told to do. Drawing lines between literatures has no intrinsic value, except for showcasing the writer's ability to perform mental gymnastics. The point is rather that a surprise that emerges with one map is partly answered by connecting it to another map, another body of substantive theory.

A substantive surprise is thus relatively straightforward. Either something appeared that shouldn't have, or something didn't appear that should have. While there are different ways to work through the surprise—the examples above are but two strategies of many—there is something simple about the nature of surprise.

Flaws with grammatical compass theories, in comparison, are less neat. Given the diffuse nature of those theories, the researcher is less likely to know in advance where to look for surprises in light of grammatical theories. There is necessarily something more serendipitous about such surprises. Yet importantly, at least for the theoretical contributions that this book highlights, grammatical surprises, much like substantive theory, emerge from empirical findings.

Let's return to Star and Griesemer's notion of boundary objects. These two researchers did not start with the idea of the boundary object; rather, it was a conceptual innovation to a theoretical puzzle. They wanted to understand the emergence of the research museum in the United States. Early forms of the natural history museum became popularized in the nineteenth century in America through the work of amateur naturalists. But constructing the professionalized museum required a different approach. How was this done?

The Berkeley Museum of Vertebrate Zoology (the MVZ), founded in the early twentieth century, was a fortuitous case to study because its first director, Joseph Grinnell, left detailed accounts of his decisions and their implementation. The archive also contains extensive correspondence with the museum's patron (and avid amateur animal collector) Annie M. Alexander. Through these archival sources, Star and Griesemer began to see how very differently the trappers, director, and amateur collectors went about the work of collecting species. The puzzle here was the divergence between the intent of the director to turn the museum into a scientific enterprise, the rummaging collections of amateur collectors, and the livelihood of trappers, who knew how to capture animals, but often treated them with little care beyond their valuable pelts.

The practical work, as Star and Griesemer describe it, was thus to create a kind of lowest common denominator of collecting that different actors could converge on while still cultivating the ideal of a professional scientific approach. While scientists, collectors, and the general public were all interested in preserving a complete record of California's mammals, birds, and reptiles, for example, collectors were less interested in the scientific rigor of the work. Grinnell thus needed to work hard to standardize techniques in order to ensure the quality of specimen collecting. The trappers who supplied many of the specimens, for their part, were interested more in the money than getting the recording and preserving work done.

Star and Griesemer discovered in the archival records that a set of objects, including standardized procedures, but also wildlife charts—which could be used by trappers, collectors, and scientists alike—acted to smooth over collective action. But what to make of this theoretically?

The starting point of the research, of course, is not theoretically innocent. Two strong grammatical theory influences are immediately apparent. The first is a pragmatist theoretical bent brought in by Star (a student of Anselm Strauss) and Griesemer. Much like Howard Becker in *Art Worlds*,[15] the authors looked at the work of different actors in the museum's history. Rather than assuming that they already knew who those key actors were, they left this question open and created a list based on people's role and influence. From this pragmatist tradition they also took the assumption that the answer they were looking for was an eminently practical one. That is, not what people believed in their heart of hearts, but how they actually went about *setting up* a research museum. Second, throughout the paper, Star and Griesemer are also indebted to the emergence of actor-network theory and its focus on nonhuman "actants" as important elements in any such world.[16]

The theoretical insight Star and Griesemer developed looks simple in retrospect. It wasn't that the different parties negotiated their differences at regular intervals and reached a consensus on the meaning of scientific collecting. Rather, things like wildlife charts, minimal regulations, and even pelts facilitated the coordination of a collective act precisely because they *were* a kind of lowest common denominator of a joint project that didn't need to be negotiated carefully by everyone involved. Boundary objects are crucial for coordinating action across widely diverse perspectives. "Boundary objects," they wrote,

> are objects which are both plastic enough to adapt to local needs and constraints of the several parties employing them, yet robust enough to maintain a common identity across sites. They are weakly structured in common use, and become strongly structured in individual-site use. They may be abstract or concrete. They have different meanings in different social worlds but their structure is common enough to more than one world to make them recognizable, a means of translation. The creation and management of boundary objects is key in developing and maintaining coherence across intersecting social worlds.[17]

Star and Griesemer's theoretical innovation has become a go-to concept for sociologists finding objects and tools that help coordinate multiple social worlds without hashing out all their intergroup differences. In a theoretical context in which the coordination of action between actors was theorized primarily in terms of negotiation and a shared "definition of the situation," Star and Griesemer showed that it is sometimes the *under definition* of the situation—not achieving a consensus—that facilitates people's ability to act in concert. This insight opened a whole new terrain that sociologists could explore, going far beyond the specific map of the sociology of science subfield. Like good compass theories, boundary objects work just as well in different places, such as, for instance, resilience theory.[18] Star and Griesemer's example also shows that making a "compass theory" contribution does not require us to replace the compass we have been using, but to recalibrate it. The notion of boundary objects is still rooted in interactionist theory but it allows for a different orientation. Not all compass theory innovations lead to "grand theories." The point of theorization isn't to throw our old ways of navigating overboard. Much as most contributions to map theories don't require completely new maps, few contributions to more grammatical theories demand completely new compasses.

When to read? When to stop?

This chapter clarifies what we mean by theoretical surprises in the field, and turns a hazy desire to make a theoretical contribution more tangible. A sizable chunk of what stands for a theoretical contribution based on empirical research is captured here. That doesn't mean that there aren't other ways of writing theoretically, e.g., increasing levels of abstraction that culminate in modes of writing where the empirical never seems to dare to show its face. But much of the best theorizing, including some of what people think of as "pure theory"—the work of Pierre Bourdieu, W. E. B. Du Bois, or Erving Goffman, for example—began in data surprises and theorizing that are similar to those we have shown.

Finally, this way of thinking about theorizing also has consequences for *how* we read.[19] In many ways, the problem with abductive analysis is that it requires you to read, and read widely, in a world in which you can read endlessly. If the aspiring grounded theory researcher is in danger of being eternally buried in ever-longer lists of themes and subthemes unencumbered by reading theory, an abductive analysis researcher may feel that they never read enough to be properly surprised. How then should you read? And when? And can you ever stop?

Substantive and grammatical readings follow different rhythms. Substantive theories are usually read in bursts. The first burst of reading will happen before you enter into the field. Dissertation proposals and "comprehensive exams" in graduate school training in the US do some of this work. You have to read widely within the subfield you enter. You'll need a good few months of immersing yourself in the literature. Then it is a matter of following interesting citations and bibliographical references, and—every couple of months—looking to see if something interesting was published in the subfield's outlets. In some disciplines, aspiring researchers are told to look at new abstracts as a way to start their day. While we wouldn't go so far, checking some of the subfield journals every month or so is useful. Then other bursts of reading occur as you spend time in the field, following interesting observations you have found in the notes or transcripts that throw you into another substantive area.

In comparison to this semipredictable reading graph, with its bursts and its relatively quiet periods, the rhythms of grammatical reading are different. Sometimes months can go by without any grammatical reading; sometimes you will find yourself completely taken over by a set of writings or a debate around a concept. Partly, as we outlined above, this is a matter of being attentive to substantive-grammatical theory packages in the field. But this does not cover it. The truth is that grammatical theories are always there, waiting to be read. This, in turn, may feel like a constant, low-grade pressure to read and consider the relevance of different grammatical compass theories. It need not be onerous, though. Treat compass theories— theories of action, of practice, of power, of structure—as an ongoing part of your work. You need not read them fast to "get it all," as there is no defined endpoint to that reading. It's more a constant hum of intellectual life. This curiosity to find out what some deep thinkers wrote is, probably, why a lot of us ended up in graduate school.

If you encounter what seems like a grammatical surprise in the field, however, the pressures for reading change. If you aim to contribute to grammatical theory, you need to read a lot, and read carefully, around the concept or processual approach you aim to contribute to. Indeed, to make sure that you are not reinventing the wheel, you need to treat the grammatical concept or process much like you treat a subfield—you need to know how it has been argued, and why, in real depth. Thus, the peaks of reading grammatical theory emerge through your encounter with the field, but are only possible through the background of ongoing forays into such theorizations.

But then, a harder question. When do you stop reading? This is both a practical and an existential concern. After all, as we outlined above, there are so many possibly important things that you encounter in the field. The factory workers you interview, for example, may have families—something that keeps popping up in the interviews. Should you become a sociologist of the family? But they also talk about themselves as "men." Should you become a sociologist of gender? And then, there is also the matter of education—crucial, actually. So, what now? Should you just go on substantive binges of reading forever?

More existentially, the idea of stopping and writing is, for many people, terrifying. One of Iddo's mentors when he was a master's student in Israel, Avi Cordova—an incredibly brilliant and charismatic teacher who has shaped the thought of generations of students at Tel Aviv University—once told him that he always thought that to write you need a combination of ignorance and arrogance. Cordova had neither. He always felt there was more to know before he wrote; he was never arrogant enough to assume that his way of understanding the phenomenon was the right one. And so, he rerouted his energies and kept teaching, thinking, and reading. But he never wrote.

Fears about reading enough or not enough may waylay the best of research projects. But finding a balance is less troublesome in practice than it might seem in the abstract. One practical answer is about surprise. You stop reading for other substantive topics when you encounter a surprise. This doesn't mean that you will stop for good, but at least for a while you focus on the surprise and the substantive field that formed its necessary background.

The other answer, to both the practical and the existential concerns, requires us to take a step back. The drive to cover all aspects of your respondents' lives, and keep filling the vast swaths of ignorance we all face, implicitly assumes that writing is a solitary thing—that at the end of an article or a book, the author needs to imagine that she has made the decisive and everlasting contribution defining her field. An immutable map, buttressed by an unfailing compass. If that is how we imagine our work, then each failure to cover an aspect of the field is irredeemable, the possibility of ignorance is devastating.

Our writing is part of an ongoing conversation in a community of inquiry. While we hope to have presented a better map at the end of the conversation, we would be poor conversationalists if every time we say something we would expect the conversation to end. That's like hoping that our map is the only map people will every need. If we are in an ongoing conversation, then the answer for when you stop reading and start writing is less existentially fraught. You stop when you feel like you have something interesting to say in relation to the literature you read, and to the colleagues who hear your presentations, and whom you engage in conversations about your half-baked work. Then, you write. And, as importantly, you present what you write for a variety of audiences. It very well may be that someone will then point you towards something you should have read. This is something to be welcomed, not dreaded. And then, if and when that occurs, you will have a first draft to work with rather than only anxiety and heaps of articles and books piling up on your desk.

4: COLLECTING

It is by now a cliché that, as Louis Pasteur put it, "in the fields of observation, chance favors the prepared mind."[1] While surprise also requires preparation, it is not only our minds that need to be prepped for the unexpected. The mind of a social scientist can be thoroughly primed. She may have read all there is to read and developed all the theoretical maps she could ever wish for (well, she couldn't possibly, but let's give her the benefit of the doubt). And yet, for all the texts in the library, if this extraordinary mind does not encounter observations that propel her to see the world in different ways, then her preparation has largely been in vain. She may write interesting tracts, but the kind of theory she will develop will be the theoretical constructions of an armchair sociologist rather than theory developed when you get your hands dirty in research. Acquiring a sense of the theoretical maps of your field is crucial, but it is in the relationship between observations, theory, and your community of inquiry that provocative surprises emerge.

After exploring theory in the previous chapter, cultivating abductive inferences leads us to research design: how to collect data if we want to be surprised. This is harder than it looks. While consulting theoretical maps from the get-go is important, there is no magic spell that ensures that your site or respondents will generate surprises. Indeed, we would caution against knowing too well exactly what is interesting in the site if surprise is what you're after. We cannot tell you how many people to interview or how long to spend at a site. We cannot advise you without knowing more about your project.[2]

We can, however, say something about *how* to collect data in the field if you are looking for surprising findings as well as warn you of some research practices that would make surprise harder to come by. Much like the computer programmer's dictum—garbage in, garbage out—the quality and scope of your observations will help determine how much distance you can cover in your analysis. The basis for an abductive inference is a surprising observation in light of prevailing theories. Therefore, the entire scientific process of discovery will be for naught if you don't know *what* to observe.

In this chapter, we start with some thoughts about sampling that are aimed at in-depth interviews and ethnography. Next, we offer different, actually opposing, guidelines for studies that are primarily interview based or ethnographic in nature. While ethnography and in-depth interviewing have commonalities in analysis, as approaches to gathering data the methods are vastly different,[3] and there is also tremendous variation within these methods as well as in their combinations.[4] The difference is not as simple as doing vs. saying, if only because talking is itself a situated action and ethnography is filled with people conversing. The issue here is that the methods put different demands on the researcher to reach intriguing observations, counterintuitive claims, or surprising findings. Interviews give you limited data, which you can seldom revisit, and your job is to develop an interview guide that will provide the best, and broadest, platform. Ethnography, with its freewheeling observations of groups, is flexible in accommodating multiple foci, even overly flexible, and therefore needs sharpening of an analytical focus.

We argue that taking abduction seriously in an interview study means that researchers need to strategically *defocus* their data gathering after they have sharply focused it. Such defocusing, which means going beyond what others have done in their projects and exploring seemingly less relevant topics, provides space for surprise. Ethnographers need to do the opposite: we encourage them to pay careful attention to the observations they have by *focusing* their materials while they are in the process of collecting data. For both qualitative approaches, we point out ways to build a methodological "confidence interval of surprise" into research design. Thinking about how data collection triggers surprise leads us then to the question of positionality—how our own complex positions shape both surprise and research possibilities. Finally, we warn against some common practices we increasingly see in qualitative research such as reliance on video, qualitative analysis software and large-N interview studies, all of which may set you up for *excerpt analysis*, a fragmentary way of looking at observations that fails to do them justice.

A shared focus: who and where?

Sampling is often ignored in qualitative research (at least in practice; it's often discussed extensively in methods books). In many cases, researchers study a place close to where they are living because it is convenient or they snowball sample interviewees from a few initial contacts that they happen to have.[5] The number of people they talk to is set for both practical and traditional reasons: twenty-five or thirty-nine[6] respondents sounds like a respectable number that would assuage potential reviewer concerns and allows them to examine some variation, and so they try to find twenty-five people who meet some preset inclusion criteria. We cannot cover the full literature on sampling in qualitative research, but here we want to emphasize how important it is to understand the limitations of how you select people or sites, while also thinking of sampling as a methodological pathway to stimulate abductive insights.

One of the most anxiety-provoking scenarios for qualitative researchers is that someone will stand up when you give a talk and ask whether you cherry-picked your data. A telltale that prompts such a concern is that your respondents all sound identical or that you keep quoting the same respondent. Or that other data, say survey research, reveals that what you claim is the most common concern is actually an extreme instance of a pattern. Once exposed in such a way, it is very difficult to recover because the implication is that your research is not empirically supported but driven by a biased (because nonrepresentative) agenda.

Even though in interdisciplinary settings the question of bias is a common challenge, many qualitative researchers find this an unfair critique that applies inappropriate criteria to their research. They are right to some extent: there is no way an ethnography of one or two neighborhoods or an interview study of twenty-five respondents is going to be statistically representative of a large population, and very little will be gained from randomly selecting a small sample. You may as well select one "average" or "typical" neighborhood/American and have them stand in for the entire country.[7]

And yet, even as you should not aspire to statistical representativeness, you should have a sense of how you selected your observations, and there are better and worse ways. As Clifford Geertz reminds us, the fact that there is no completely aseptic environment doesn't mean we should conduct surgery in a sewer.[8] For sampling, this comes down to being deliberate in recruiting people and reflective on how these recruitment processes may not just introduce selection bias into your findings but also hamper abductive inference.

First, concretely, this means that you should plot not only the sites you plan to observe but the other sites that you could have observed but didn't, and examine the differences. A good way to wrap your head around this is by asking yourself, "If I were one of the people in my study, where else could I have gone?" and "Do other people do the same actions in other places or ways?" To keep it simple, let's say you conduct an ethnographic study of a grocery store to understand how everyday markets work: Where else do shoppers go to buy their groceries? What do you gain and lose from studying the store you are observing? Do other people in that area do their shopping elsewhere? How is it different from the places you did not study? How many are there? Where are they? What do they sell?

The same goes for an interview study: if you interview men who have sex with men using an HIV prevention program, the way you gain entrée to this population is going to color who you get to interview and likely misses a large population of potential respondents.[9] You are going to talk to people who are engaged in preventive health or have reasons to think they may be at increased risk for infection. The question then is: who are you missing and how does that affect what your respondents tell you? This is not to say that the HIV program is out of bounds, but it does mean that you need to be aware of how this will frame your findings and what other venues exist for finding these men. Similarly, if you study how people facing eviction take advantage of free legal aid clinics and you focus your research on the interactions in the legal aid clinic, you need to know whether the people that make it to the clinic are typical of people facing eviction.[10] It's perfectly fine if they are disproportionately facing eviction for withholding rent, if they are more educated, live closer to the legal clinic, or are more net-worked than others, but you should have an idea of how the people you see compare to those who are absent. If you don't, any kind of explanation you propose for what the clinic does for a person facing eviction is going to be overshadowed by the concern that it's not the clinic but the kind of person in the clinic that explains the outcome of the eviction proceedings. You can get a sense of this by asking how clients find out about legal aid. Selection bias in qualitative research often mirrors institutional self-selection bias: sites select for certain kinds of people and, in turn, those people are more likely to have the resources and cultural capital to enter particular sites.

There often is some kind of consensus on whom you should talk to in research, but it may pay off to break out of this taken-for-granted frame. Here is an example based on some very old work. Much of the notion that homosexuality was a mental illness in the early twentieth century came from clinicians seeing homosexual patients in their private practice or en-countering them in mental institutions. In the early 1950s, Evelyn Hooker broke this mold by interviewing men who desire and have sex with men in the community. She then found a comparison sample of heterosexual men that she matched by age, education, and IQ with her self-identified homo-sexual respondents. She did not engage in the qualitative research we ad-vocate here. Instead, she asked all the men to take several personality tests that measured their attitudes, emotions, and thoughts. She then asked experts in these tests to determine who of the pair was the homosexual. The clinicians couldn't figure sexual orientation out better than by chance, leading Hooker to tentatively conclude that homosexuals were psychologically as healthy as heterosexuals.[11] It still took until 1973 for the American Psychological Association to remove homosexuality from the DSM as a psychopathic personality disorder, but by going outside the typical clinical population for respondents, Hooker contributed to this change.[12]

So how should you select a site or respondents? To stimulate abductive thinking, you would want to go beyond the obvious ways of studying a group or site. Returning to the example above, rather than focusing on a site catering to men who have sex with men in an HIV prevention program, you may want to ask how men sexually attracted to other men find each other and try to trace all the different ways by which they locate partners. Your sampling strategy mimics how people in their daily lives make decisions and find each other. By following this advice, you make sampling itself an analytical theme: it becomes a process of discovery of how people connect and make choices. You go beyond what others have done to increase the odds of finding something unexpected.

Second, you pick a field site strategically for its presumed theoretical relevance, for extreme or negative cases, or for internal variation. Mario Small advocates for sequential interviewing where a first set of interviews points you to a next set of respondents and questions, and then you follow that trace until you don't find anything new.[13] If you are interested in how African Americans view immigrants, for instance, you may want to look for African American respondents who experienced discrimination from Latino immigrants, move on to those who did not experience such discrimination, then talk to African Americans who felt threatened by an influx of East European immigrants, and so forth. The key here is that what you learn in the interview suggests where you should go next. You build up a theory until you reach saturation, until no new insights appear. Such an approach violates all questions of statistical representativeness but offers a strong defense to the question of how you selected respondents: on emerging theoretical grounds.

Small's notion of working sequentially also pays off if you are thinking of doing a comparative study.[14] Many, probably most, comparative studies start off in the design stage with the explicit goal of comparing two sites or groups. This is often done because of the conviction that if one site is good, two or more sites should be even better—in the sense that a comparison will guarantee stronger lines of analysis because it highlights what is unique and different about a site. However, because the comparison has been decided prior to the observations, you may discover that the sites or groups are either very similar (which renders the comparison moot) or too different to facilitate a meaningful comparison. Hence, many comparisons in qualitative research falter, and too many others present two cases side by side, while weakly depicting the work as comparative.[15]

The key practical difference between sequential comparison and most comparative qualitative research is that the decision to expand to a second research area is not made in the early research planning stage but is decided halfway through the research project based on accumulated analytical and theoretical insights. Sequential comparative qualitative research requires you to first figure out precisely what case you have in your original site and then decide whether it would help to add a second comparative site for analytical purposes, and which kind of site it should be. The benchmark for initiating a comparison should be high. To convince readers that a comparison is necessary, you should show that your study would lose critical analytical insights if the comparison is not pursued.

Third, sampling itself may produce unexpected findings. In Peter Bearman's interview-based study of New York's doormen, sampling should not have been an issue. Doormen are highly visible and they do the kind of things we think doormen should do: hailing cabs, standing outside, and wearing a recognizable uniform. Yet, in the backs of buildings and storage places also work "invisible" doormen. They don't wear a uniform but do jobs similar to those of their uniformed counterparts. Consequently, if you want to understand doormen, a convenience sample of the highly visible doormen would be biased because the invisible doormen would not be part of your study.[16]

Bearman's study shows that sampling itself can produce surprising findings: in his case, the discovery of the coexistence of two kinds of doormen with different levels of public visibility. Bearman found that the nonuniformed doormen were less likely to join a union. This could be an interesting analytical nugget to explore: What is the hierarchy between those two groups? Is there a common identity? How does being a particular kind of doorman affect the relationship with tenants, the reputation of a building, and the kinds of secrets doormen keep?

Being strategic, thoughtful, and reflective about who you talk to and what you observe serves two purposes: it allows you to change the discussion when critics question the representativeness of your sample because you know who else you could have interviewed/observed, and it sets the stage for surprising findings because you go beyond how others design their studies.

The design dilemma and techniques of defocusing

The research design stage is a crucial place to set up analytical surprises. If you think narrowly about design and follow well-trodden paths, chances are that you are going to find similar data to those whose path you have faithfully followed. This isn't necessarily bad, but it circumscribes the parameters by which you could be surprised. The time that passes between research projects may give rise to interesting shifts and transformations, two sites will always differ somewhat, and different respondents elicit varying findings, so you could still get surprised at some junctures. Still, narrow design stacks the deck towards a narrow version of normal science. And so there is an incentive to do things differently. At the same time, in order to intervene in a theoretical and empirical argument in a meaningful way, you will also need a shared point of reference and comparison. Variation is always a variation *of* something held in common. How do you balance these countervailing pressures? How can you both think within the parameters of earlier work and set yourself up methodologically to think outside them?

Becoming an interview

Interviews in qualitative research elicit narratives, accounts told from your respondents' perspective. Each question that you ask is a bet on social life: you ask because you presume there is something socially relevant there. That means that you want to ask respondents about issues they know and have experienced. While there are multiple ways of conducting good interviews, a successful interview is one where the interviewee develops a narrative line in ways that aren't completely defined by your questions.[17]

For interview studies to generate surprising findings, our recommendation is to *strategically defocus* your research design. What we mean is that as you design your interview study, you build additional layers of data gathering that go beyond what others have typically done in this research area. Given that the researchers are constrained by what they asked and didn't ask in an interaction that usually only occurs once, careful planning needs to go into interview design. While interviewers often change their interview protocols in response to surprising findings while they are in the field, and while some respondents can be contacted more than once, interviewers, from survey researchers to in-depth interviewers, need to craft their questions carefully in order to capture surprises.

How, then, can interviewers generate openings for surprise in their design? The challenge is, again, that two contravening pressures operate at the same time. As interviewers know, a completely open-ended interview provides endless opportunities for surprise. If your interviewees have un-limited time to spend with you, then such an approach presents your best chance for surprise. Of course, you don't usually want to know everything about a person's life. There is a reason why you want to talk to that particu-lar person, and this has to do with a certain aspect of their lives. Below, we suggest two complementary strategies for maximizing surprising findings in the research design phase of an interview study.

First, in order to provide interviewers with avenues for surprise, *you need to distinguish between the kind of questions you ask during the initial pilot interview stage and the questions you ask later.* For abductive purposes, the pilot stage needs to be substantively more open-ended than the actual re-search. You can then identify surprising moments and patterns that you have not seen earlier and work them into the shared interview guide.[18] You need to spend time with the pilot interview transcripts—code them in both open and focused coding as we develop in the following chapters. Only af-ter such analysis should you return to the field and restart interviewing. Then, during this second stage, in order to allow for workable variation, semistructured interviews are much more useful—interviews that allow interviewees to develop their narratives, while making sure that they speak about similar experiences or processes, to generate workable variation among interviews.

As an aside, it's OK if a pilot study kills a research project. One of our col-leagues planned to retrospectively interview first-time parents about the stress of having their first child after some of the infants had grown into four- to five-year-old kids. We were skeptical that parents would still re-member what they were stressed about such a long time ago. Together, we designed a pilot study where our colleague would have an open-ended pilot interview with some friends: one parent of a newborn infant and one of a four-year-old child. After the interviews, our colleague realized that the interview with the mom of the four-year-old glossed over the neonatal pe-riod. She received great data on the challenges of parenting a four-year-old but very little on what interested her. Worse, she had talked to her friend four years ago and remembered the confusion and difficulties of the early period, but in the interview all was forgotten, qualified, and overshadowed by the challenges of daycare and keeping a mobile child in check. This expe-rience required a retooling of the research project. It's better to find this out in the early stages than to waste time getting data with limited usability.

If splitting the research design into open-ended initial work and semi-structured subsequent work is one important strategy, *a complementary as-pect of abductive interview design is to strategically widen and deepen the scope of the questions you ask in the interviewing stage.* This may take on different forms depending on the specificities of the project: asking about other actors in the field even if you think that they likely are irrelevant, for example, or extending the temporality of the processes you study by digging deeper into the past. In this sense, after you know what questions you want to ask—after you have focused—you need to slightly defocus your design, allowing "noise" to enter the interview.

Still, before adding noise, you need to make sure that you get a strong signal. Doing abductive research means, as we noted in the last chapter, that we need to take the principle of engagement seriously—while you can write about something that your interlocutors aren't very routinely oriented towards, you are in a much better position to find surprises if you have a rich database and variation to work with. And this, in turn, means that you need to think carefully about what people in the field are actually orienting toward in their daily lives. While studying medical examiners, Stefan noted that when he explained that he was observing autopsies he often received one of two opposite reactions. Some people did not want to hear about such a gruesome topic while others were fascinated with what they presumed was the underbelly of crime. The medical examiner's office is a place where people end up who are fatally shot, stabbed, and hit. But, as Stefan needed to explain again and again, this was not the majority of deaths, and there are many situations that have a different emotional valence: abandoned and abused babies, kids who drowned in pools or in the ocean, unfortunate falls, people who did really stupid things, and just unlucky people who were at the wrong place at the wrong time. For Stefan, this was a research project and not his complete professional life, so even though he got exasperated by the questions, they didn't inundate most of his interactions. Medical examiners, however, have no escape from such inquiries. They have to explain or obfuscate their job. Stefan wondered: if you are a medical examiner, how do you explain on a first date what you do for a living? That became an interview question that caught medical examiners' attention and that they talked about at length. Attending to what people care about not only produces more data, but also often opens up theoretical questions.

So how can we add more noise to such signals? An example of strategic defocusing through a widening of research scope is Iddo's work with Michele Poulin. The research puzzle emerged when Michele and Iddo compared notes about their work in Malawi. Talking about condom use (a research topic Iddo was writing about) and nonmarital relationships (Michele's research interest), they wondered how sex workers navigated the demands of the clients to *forgo* a condom—which a lot of clients preferred, even with the threat of AIDS still hovering. Iddo and Michele hypothesized that since the indigenous *chibwenzi* relationship (roughly translated as sexual partner or girl/boyfriend) assumed exchange of sex and gifts, the sex work and condom use would be negotiated through these relational categories. Negotiating condom use was particularly poignant in the local sex work industry, with "freelancers" who were not institutionally embedded and "bar girls" who worked at bars and also worked as sex workers. How did these positions refract relationships and sex?

Unable to conduct the interviews themselves (neither spoke ChiChewa or ChiYao well enough), Iddo and Michele trained interviewers and sent them to the field with a semistructured interview guide. And, especially in such a situation, some defocusing was crucial. The interviewers were trained to ask the sex workers in as much detail as possible about the economic exchanges that took place between them and their clients and sexual partners, and also about how they negotiated financial issues in their day-to-day lives. Capturing step-by-step details of the exchanges of sex and goods, Iddo and Michele learned that the story about condom use was the least stimulating part of the interviews. While they received some confirmation that bar girls (who also got a small salary from the bar) had more control over their relationships than freelancers, and thus could ask for condom use more forcefully, a much more interesting pattern emerged in the question they added into the interview guide about the specific exchanges. Instead of assuming that people exchanged money for sex, the interviewers asked what exactly was exchanged. They found that in the case of bar girls, where clients often tended to be repeat clients, small shifts in payment dramatically changed the relational definitions of the situation. It was enough for someone to be short on cash and offer to "pay" with a pair of jeans for the relational definitions to shift dramatically from sex work to a *chibwenzi* relationship. The resultant article was about different monies, relational definitions, and gift exchanges—not condom use.[19]

Sometimes it is not just noise but simple silence or questions about absences that end up most revelatory. Asking about the road not taken allows you to get at the social structuring of careers, which are work biographies that take place over time. The point here is that you need both to think about the advantages of a pilot study and to build extensions of the research focus into semistructured interviews. Make sure that you provide enough defocusing to allow space for surprise, while still asking interviewees similar enough questions to allow you to work through variation, and avoid the frustrating situation where you have a wonderful theoretical lead but failed to ask other interviewees about a similar set of issues.

Techniques of focusing

In *Abductive Analysis*, we stressed the danger of ethnographers falling into the assumptions they carry into the field: to only hear what we want to hear and disregard the rest. Some taken-for-grantedness, however, is unavoidable. We always and already carry prototheories into the social worlds we enter. We necessarily filter our perceptions through preexisting categories and expectations. You can put such prototheories to use (as long as you try to be self-aware about the way they structure your data collection). As you collect observations, there are ways to trick ourselves into seeing our observations anew: to interrupt the process of assuming that things just are the way they are because you are familiar with them. Interrupting what you assume because you are a member of a social world constitutes an opening for surprises. As we discussed earlier, we think of these as modes of *defamiliarization*. Such techniques provide an opening through which you can look at apparently familiar objects in a new light.

We want to push our advice further. We highlight ethnography as an instance where focusing is particularly helpful in simulating abductive inferences because writing field notes is quite different from looking at interview data. While interviewers often write notes about the context of the interview, transcripts are by far the most crucial piece of evidence. Seen from that perspective, there is more leeway in writing up observational notes in ethnography, more ways to observe, more things to note. Even the most predictable and sterile research site has an overstimulation of action with too many potential clues you can follow. How you focus your notes sets up the potential for surprising findings.

Being a field note[20]

Let's make one point crystal clear: if you don't write up field notes, the event may as well not have happened. Sure, you remember what you saw yesterday and maybe what you saw last week. But you will only remember the most elementary aspects six months from now. And you probably will not trust your memory to do something with your fading recollections. (If you don't believe us, we challenge you to watch a video and write notes a week from now about what you saw. Then rewatch the video and find out how much you missed.)

The focused notes that best enable abductive analysis are *descriptive* and *analytical*. What does that mean? Descriptive notes capture the events as they are unfolding. These are not mechanical field notes such as "a human subject moved the hand three inches to grasp a steaming container of hot liquid . . ." when we describe someone sipping coffee. To capture this level of granularity, there are better methods than ethnography and the questions you can answer with such observations are also unlikely to resonate with an interpretive project. With rare exceptions, such an "alien's view" is more a curiosity than an actual technique. In most sociological research, we can make *some* assumptions about what's going on.

The other end of the spectrum is much more difficult to avoid, and a far more common pitfall for ethnographers: writing notes rife with imputations. These notes are infused with motivations that reflect the assumptions of the researcher rather than what is apparent in the scene, or that psychologize the interactions. Thus, if you write about an observed instance in a public space by saying, "an exasperated mother shushed her toddler who was looking at ants in the crack of the sidewalk. She was disgusted by the ants, and just wanted to get back home," this observation presumes that you know the exact relationship between the adult and the child and the future sequence of events, in a way a novelist puts a character together.

Imputations creep into the most basic characterizations. For example, sociologists are socialized to see the world through the lenses of particular demographic variables. Whether these aspects of self matter in an observation, however, is something to puzzle out rather than to assume.[21] One could write about race, gender, age, or occupation as omnirelevant characteristics that overshadow everything one does and how a person is perceived, or alternatively as something that is done more or less saliently at particular times than at others. It's the difference between assuming that someone was acting as a "woman" and viewing gender as something that needs to be done by actors, and done to them. Nouns both moralize and freeze social action.[22] Verbs, in contrast, highlight an ongoing process of becoming, being, and doing. So when you take notes about doctor*ing* rather than about doctors, and about *doing* gender rather than about hegemonic masculinity as an identity, you open up rather than foreclose your analysis.

Of course, in some places people aspire to be nouns or others pigeonhole them to certain membership categories in a way that you cannot afford to ignore. Once you start paying attention to this issue, it can become a core challenge of writing up field notes. Typifying people's actions along the same demographic lines risks essentializing these characteristics, but not writing down such things as race impoverishes your notes and may stop you from noticing some important patterns in your observations. Indeed, in many situations, it will become deeply problematic. One cannot be race-blind in a world in which racism is rampant, or gender-blind in a patriarchal world. Twenty-four years after publishing his authoritative ethnography *Forgive and Remember* about residency training in surgery programs, Charles Bosk admitted that he changed the gender of the only woman resident, leaving out how this resident worked in a hostile misogynist environment.[23] This speaks not only to the debate on anonymization in ethnography[24] but also to the ability to document widespread sexism in the workplace.

But then, what do you do? First, we return yet again to the principle of engagement. In most cases, your problem is also a problem for the people you are observing. They also have to take a stance in the ongoing course of their lives to ignore or engage someone's gender, race, age, or profession as salient in the situation. You want to see the world the way people in your site see it. This means that you need to be alert to how people implicitly and explicitly pick up on each other's clues and how this differs over time, across places. It's not just your issue as a researcher; it's everyone's issue.

Second, this is precisely where accumulating observations for variation matters. When you take field notes, you need not decide in advance whether an intersection of membership categories is the right prism through which to understand action, but you need to remain open to the possibility that it does. As field notes accumulate, you likely will become more attuned to the differential treatment of some people over others. Remember, you never work from one particular set of notes but from a collection of observations. Your notes will become more analytically legible the more there are. Here is the litmus test: if questioned about your analytical inference, you should be able to defend the evidence behind your conclusion with multiple observations.[25]

If being careful about motives and membership categories is one way of making your notes more descriptively focused, another way of doing so is by switching your focus. In the first few weeks you are in a field, your notes will be a long jumble of anything and everything. The field will be a buzzing confusion of new and exciting possibilities. But as you settle down, and learn the rhythms of your field site, your notes can have a more sustained focus. As Christina Nippert-Eng outlines, there are different things you notice, and they require a shifting of attention.[26] You can describe the physical layout, or the choreography of movement, the passage of time, or how conversations ebb and flow. In other words, as you stay in the field, train yourself to sustain your focus. While you want to have similar observations as a way to get at variation, after you have depicted the same routine twenty times, you can trust yourself to notice when things happen a bit differently. Then you zoom in on such moments like a hawk. But otherwise, pick out one person, one conversation, one set of actions, one sequence of events and follow it through. You aim for depth, not a scattered bird's eye view.

As the research goes on, you will want to switch the focus of what or whom you observe. Field notes track your movements through the site. Whether your focus can be sustained or whether others will perceive it as a rude intrusion also tells you something about the site. A sustained gaze may then become itself an intervention that reveals something about the community you are studying. When you wonder who can look for how long at what, go and find out, and add these insights to your collection. The gaze may itself be a means of social structuring a site and be part of a moral valuing of people and actions.

Think about some ethnographies you have read and you'll notice that researchers get more mileage out of zooming in rather than panning across people and places. Studying Skid Row in Los Angeles, Forrest Stuart came across a group of homeless Black men lifting weights in the street and egging each other on to build muscle and resist the temptations of drugs, prostitution, and crime around them. Stuart dug into how these men navigate the street, how they read their environment and the omnipresent police, and how they collectively developed an alternative way of inhabiting the area. But there was much more going on at the site. Stuart showed a picture of one of the men lifting weight in a park and in the distance we can see two people sitting on the ground. We observe other people wandering by; from the rest of the book, we know that there are countless people meandering and engaged as part of other worlds. Yet these other characters do not enter the description unless the men comment on aspects of their surroundings.[27]

Being descriptive also means that you show interaction as it is unfolding rather than telling about it. Instead of taking a third-person all-knowing narrator voice, you describe the events as they are occurring sequentially and interactionally. Writing "some people waiting in line looked bored" is a summary sentence that glosses over descriptive specifics of who waited in line and generalizes "bored." This latter term probably reflects a series of body movements such as checking one's phone, sighing, tapping one's feet, each of which has its own sequence. The research skill in ethnography is to become aware of such summarizing shortcuts—since they are the things you and the people you study take for granted—and push yourself to be as descriptive as possible, attentive to sequence, confluence, and rhythms. You could, for instance, pay attention to sequence and place, as graduate student Natasha Bluth did in her field notes of a man waiting to enter a grocery store during the COVID-19 pandemic:

> When I join the line, he is squat-sitting on the small, raised corner of concrete where the ramp to the underground parking garage from the street-level lot

began, hunched over with his feet turned out and hands clasped, elbows resting on his thighs. . . . Despite his fatigued stance, he looks straight ahead, a light-blue medical mask pulled down to his chin. I swerve to the left, cushioning the space between us to maintain a safe distance and claim a taped X behind him, although the way he is flouting COVID social conventions makes it difficult to know where to stand. As the line of shoppers inches forward, he lethargically rises from his squat to sit on the small green bench a few paces ahead. In doing so, he leaves multiple Xs vacant ahead of him, denying me and the other customers who are beginning to congregate behind me the instant gratification of moving closer and closer to our final destination.

His torso is bent over now, looking down at his navy loafers, which are made of velvet or velour-like material with a slight snakeskin embossed look and silver buckles. I guess that he is in his mid to late fifties—his wavy auburn hair stops at the circular bald patch at the crown of his head. He has an olive skin tone and is dressed crisply, in dark pants with a dark-wash plaid blazer-jacket over a navy shirt, all of which complement his loafers. More shoppers are entering the store now, forcing him to rise again. Finding a new position where he can redistribute his weight, he props his right arm upward, using it to lean against a wooden shelf holding succulents and other house plants. His movements are sluggish, but fluid, with a loose-jointed, underwater-like quality. In his right hand, he loosely holds a crumpled tissue; in his left, he grips a clear plastic bag with what looks like a folded piece of tin foil underneath a three-quarters-full bottle of orange-colored juice—I can't make out the exact flavor.

Can you see how the analytical descriptors and verbs convey boredom in ways that quick descriptors would gloss? In ethnographic research, such detailed, focused notes set you up for your analysis, and the richer your descriptions, the more opportunities you create for teasing out analytical traces later on. It may seem trivial to specify the sequence of this mundane situation, but not writing this down forgoes an opportunity to analyze this ethnographic moment interactionally.

Generally, in ethnography, writing descriptively is hard work, but it is work that pays off. You're layering observational granularity into your research. The detail of the description makes the point for you. You can evoke your analytical point rather than having to assert it from other sources.

This leads us to our other important characteristic to help focus ethnography: field notes need to be *analytical*. Field notes are *analytical* in the sense that they tip us off to social processes of people acting together. Peirce (and many others, such as Alfred Schutz)[28] noted that all perception is interpretive. Your job is to open yourself up to these interpretive social processes and channel them in analytical directions.

There is no hard-and-fast boundary between data collecting and analyzing. You're always interrogating your observations analytically while you are at your site and while writing down your notes at the end of the day. When you notice something about your setting, you want to find out more about it. Is this an exception, an extreme on a range of possible behaviors, or is it common in this setting? You wonder, for instance, whether some of the actions you observe are informed by conflicts that have been playing out for years. So the next time, you go on a mission to find out more about what these conflicts could be about, checking whether your hunches hold up. Your notes are not filled with endless descriptions, but you enter your field site to answer a question or puzzle you are pondering. We call this *giving yourself marching orders* while observing: you set yourself a task of figuring something out in your next set of observations.[29] This process of continuously asking questions helps you also to decipher variation.

You will not only observe what is visible but also start asking questions about actors who are not immediately present but whose presence hovers over your site as a concern—about the invisible undercurrents of social life. To take an example from a world Stefan knows well: if you observe forensic autopsies in a medical examiner's office, the staff's routines don't make much sense unless you are aware of the demands of potential legal proceedings. The concern about preserving an unbroken chain of evidence matters greatly when a pathologist has to recount under adversarial courtroom interrogation who had access to a corpse from the moment it entered the morgue until it left the facility. You will not see anyone asking about the chain of evidence during the everyday work of processing bodies. Yet staff members are acutely aware of the importance of documenting exactly who received the body, whether the lock on the body bag was intact, who removed the deceased's personal effects, where they were kept, etc. For people working in the morgue this is unremarkable routine, and a quick ethnographic visit would not give you any sense that the anticipation of being questioned in court infuses this behavior. You get at such insights by standing still by these routines, noting their repetition, their care, and then asking questions about it. Even if the lawyers aren't in the morgue, their concerns permeate the observable.

Why this matters practically has to do with the place of notes within the research process. Inspired by Peirce, we see any description as part of an ongoing process of meaning-making both within a research project and within a community of inquiry. Just as one iteration of one experiment is unlikely to be decisive in laboratory science, research gains credibility if you figure out multiple instances of the same phenomenon. Each set of field notes should be regarded as a set of hypotheses in the making. Your field notes become collections of observed instances and it is while comparing instances against each other, looking for similarities and differences, that you gain insight and confidence in the range of variation and open yourself up to surprising findings. This is why it is so important that you stay on top of writing down notes and ask questions of your data. Just spending time in the field does not make an ethnographer. It is necessary but not sufficient. Asking questions gives ideas and clues to pursue, but collections of observations are going to circumscribe the kinds of claims you can make confidently.

Positionality

Throughout our advice above, we kept going back to the researcher's experiences while interviewing or participating in social life. But such experiences do not originate only from your theoretical preparation and the materials you gather. What you hear, and even the access you are granted, will depend on how other people see you, as well as the things that you are more likely to notice because of who you are. In other words, as so many have written before us, our positions matter. And positions matter in abductive analysis because leveraging your insider- or outsider-ness may alert you to surprising findings exactly because you have insight where others gloss.

At its core, the methodological literature on positionality is simple: everyone occupies certain positions in social life, and these color our vision by allowing only partial access to the field and shaping how our interlocutors interact with us; our position as sociologists arms us with proto-theories of the world in ways that are deeply ingrained in how we perceive social life.[30] While positionality is important in shaping what and how you see your field and what you pay attention to, positionality can also foster abductive insights.

When Iddo joined an advertising agency to understand the work of account planners—the advertising professionals who are tasked with producing the basic idea the campaign will center on and who are considered the agency's culture experts—he experienced such a moment. He worked alongside a team of planners who constructed a campaign for a hotel brand that centered on the notion of "life balance" as central to wellness. They worked on this idea for two weeks, collecting statistics and constructing elaborate PowerPoint presentations (decks) explaining it. The project seemed settled. In a presentation of the campaign, the agency's CEO, however, seemed unenthused. After skipping a couple of days, Iddo realized the campaign had radically changed on his return to the fieldsite:

Returning to the field two days after the meeting, I was sent the new deck. There, balance was much reduced, and the research support for it came neither from Iconoculture [a company that collates data into nuggets of wisdom about the state of "culture"] nor from this part of the consumer segmentation survey. Instead, it consisted of quotes from focus groups conducted by the planning team, and other parts of the segmentation survey. Balance was reconceptualized in the new deck as sustaining a healthy lifestyle, without overdoing it—a middle category between "lazy" and "crazy" that the planning and data analytics team constructed and positioned as the consumer segment that the brand should be targeting in order to further grow. Looking through the new deck at Patrick's [a mid-level planner] cubicle, I noted that I thought the definition of balance that we worked with was different. Without missing a beat or raising his head from the screen, Patrick shrugged, "Shobha [a senior planner] made it up" and continued working on the new deck.

Iddo experienced a moment of vertigo—of intense, embodied surprise. What he assumed were well-developed ideas based on survey evidence were simply shrugged off. Trying to understand what about it was so surprising, he realized that it was his entire training as an academic that militated against this relationship between evidence and ideas. It isn't that ideas don't change in academia, but a good part of our socialization into the academic world is about working through our ideas carefully and sticking to our guns based on evidence. This moment of surprise, which was grounded in the clash between academic training and what he felt was evidentiary carelessness in his field, ended up structuring a new set of research questions on the advertising professionals' relationship to data and to the ideas that they constructed. And contrasted with the way Iddo learned to treat data and ideas, it was a deeply positional surprise.

As this example reinforces, it's important to resist the temptation to fall into a biological or social determinism where some individual or group characteristics obliterate the complexity and intersectionality of both your biographical and intellectual identity.[31] While Iddo's status as a man, an immigrant, and White were important at some junctures in his research, his academic habits proved more relevant in this case. We see through gendered and racial lenses, but we also see through the spectacles of our theoretical and methodological training and alliances.

Thinking about these different elements of our biography, and their place in fostering different kinds of surprise, also means that it is imperative to diversify the qualitative research labor force to nurture new theoretical insights. Urban ethnography, for instance, has a disproportionately large body of research on poor African American communities subjected to various forms of violence and the collateral damage of this violence. These studies used to be conducted mainly (but not exclusively) by scholars who did not grow up in these neighborhoods. In reaction, Marcus Hunter and coauthors aim to rebalance the outsider perspectives by highlighting the creative, playful, and celebratory aspects of African American urban life, without ignoring the structural forces of oppression in the community.[32] Hunter's theorization of Black placemaking draws on an insider's knowledge and becomes surprising in light of a literature that privileges the assaults on Black communities.[33]

We ideally need *both* insiders and outsiders (and different kinds of each) to enrich the traditions we work in. Especially for outsiders, preconceived notions may stimulate analytical leads. For instance, in his study of homeless booksellers, Mitchell Duneier realized how cumbersome it was for these men to pee in public spaces. He could always enter a restaurant to use the bathroom, but the men he studied were regularly refused bathroom access. Duneier thus advises the researcher to "begin research with a humble commitment to being surprised by the things you learn in the field, and a constant awareness that your social position likely makes you blind to the very phenomena that might be useful to explain."[34]

But, but, but, what about . . . shortcuts, large-*N* studies, and excerpt analysis?

Thinking strategically about research design and paying careful attention to data collecting are critical to elicit surprises. At the same time, there are also research practices that may stymie surprises. We outline three such practices here. Each of these, we want to be clear, has given rise to good work. And yet these research practices, we find, are often reified, making it harder for researchers to craft abductive insights.

A. *Wouldn't audio and video recordings make this entire chapter moot because you have everything on tape anyway?* Well, no. The question suggests that with video you don't need to acquire an analytical sensibility; that the camera thinks for you. This is a seductive thought but unfortunately cameras have a feeble track record of writing articles or books. As a form of qualitative material gathering, video recording is raw. By relying on recordings, you only postpone the analytical work you will have to do in this book and you constrain yourself by not being able to steer a conversation or ask questions in the moment (especially if you turn on the camera and remove yourself from the scene). There is a place for video and audio recording in research, and for some scholars who pay careful attention to exact wording, pauses, and turns in conversation it is the research standard. Stefan used recordings extensively in his ethnographic study of genomic decision-making where a group of experts used highly technical but nuanced lingo to evaluate various genes. Together, we analyzed video recordings of racist encounters.[35] In both cases, without recording, the research would have missed too much. Still, for most qualitative researchers recording the interaction will be a shield: rather than acting in the moment, you act when watching the video post facto, safely in front of a computer screen. Therefore, when we teach ethnographic research methods, we insist that students take notes and rely on their observations because we want to push them to cultivate the kinds of research sensibilities that we explore here.

B. *What if I let some computer software analyze my data?* Over the past decades there has been an explosion of coding software for qualitative research. Specifically, Atlas.ti and NVivo emerged as powerful coding and memoing tools, explicitly designed with grounded theory precepts in mind. We do not, of course, have an opinion on which software works best. We are, however, struck by the fact that many seasoned qualitative researchers, and especially those who think most theoretically, do not actually rely much on software. This, we think, is not by chance, but has to do with the process of work. When we code with software, we split the text—field notes, interview transcripts, or other qualitative data—into siloed files. Even if we cross-code the data, we are propelled to make decisions quite early on in the research process. And while we are of course *able* to reread all the data in its rawer form, we tend not to. This results in what we call *excerpt analysis*, a mode of analysis that in practice uses excerpts as the relevant data units, even as it claims to use entire interviews or full sets of field notes as its data.

The problem is not that this research is somehow less real than immersing ourselves in the fuller data. Rather, the problem is that when we already excise excerpts from their context, we become blind to the way in which narratives develop and change in the course of an interview, or the way one ethnographic situation is related to others—precisely where interesting theoretical surprises often lurk. As one leading qualitative researcher told Iddo at a conference, visibly relieved after he told her that he too does not use software, "I just read my notes, like, fifty times."

Coding, especially in the grounded theory tradition, is great at cutting data up into small pieces, but sometimes what your analysis really needs is to synthesize observations, bring them together at a higher level of, for instance, structural analysis. If you want to use coding software, you should be aware of this danger, and regularly return to the unparsed data. Deploying such software may be more useful when you have a large research team working simultaneously on the same data fragments (but even then less so-phisticated data-sharing websites and apps remain an option).[36]

C. *Shouldn't I go for large-N qualitative research?* Another development in qualitative research over the last decade involves large-N qualitative research. This is research that has taken to heart the quantitative admonitions about the generalizability and representative power of qualitative research, and responded with surrender. Thus, increasingly, we receive articles to review that use 200 or 300 interviews as their data base. We have not, so far, been convinced that such big-N interview data fulfills its promise. Due to the volume of data, these studies inevitably gravitate to focus on the frequency of responses rather than the meaning of responses.[37]

Indeed, even if we leave more theoretical questions of inference aside, we think that such large-N qualitative projects are practically problematic. The problem is close to our unease with some of the uses of qualitative software. There is, quite simply, no way for a researcher to get to know 300 in-depth interviews well. The amount of data in ethnography can only be grasped because it features the same people, over often-similar situations. Informally surveying some of the most prominent interview methodologists in the US, we received different answers. Some said they could work with 70 interviews; others pegged it at 50. None could grasp 300 interviews. And so we must ask, what do people actually *do* with so much data? Our suspicion is that they either put it through a qualitative software program—they read each interview once or twice, and then code it, never to reread the whole interviews again—or that they look deeply at a subset of their interviews, and then conduct excerpt analysis with the rest of the data. Either way, we are thrown back to the pitfalls of excerpt analysis: most surprises do not come as we look at a social world cut into the byte size of excerpts. If our aim is surprise, large-N qualitative research is not something that we would recommend.

D. *And what about the recent fad of rapid ethnographic assessments?* You don't want to get us started on that topic. It does a number on our blood pressure.

Conclusions

Surprises assume that something in the data doesn't behave as it should based on what prevailing map or compass theories predict. Such insights often occur as we pore closely over our data while coding. Closely examining our observations, we realize that something doesn't add up but in a positive, theory-generative way. Too often, though, those moments of surprise are bittersweet. The "aha moment" and joy of a possible contribution are marred by our realization that we have been gathering insufficient or wrong data to capitalize on the surprise. We have one surprising observation, but not enough other observations for comparison or even to be sure we aren't reading too much into it and excluding alternative, plausible explanations. Especially in interview research, which is less iterative than ethnography, coming up short after the initial excitement of locating a surprise is a common risk. While paying attention to our gathered data during coding goes a long way to tease out surprises, you also need to ensure that you have solid grounds for comparison. It is in this sense that carefully designing a research project is imperative for abductive inference.

In order to set yourself up for surprises that call for abductive inferences, you thus need to make sure that you read and think about your data while in the field so that you can change questions and give yourself new marching orders. Even before you code your data, you need to ensure that the data you have will provide you not only with possibilities of surprise but with strong evidentiary grounds to develop these promising findings.

5: OPEN CODING

In the last two chapters, we explored how strategic reading of existing theories and deliberately tuning your research design maximizes the opportunities for being struck by surprising observations. These are necessary but insufficient conditions for abductive inference. We also need to thoroughly and carefully engage with our data while we are gathering it and afterwards. That grunt work is called "coding the data" in qualitative research parlance.

Why, of all terms, did qualitative researchers adopt the terminology of "coding" for analyzing observations? As with much in qualitative analysis, the term originates in the remarkable confluence of the qualitatively trained Chicago school sociologist Anselm Strauss and Barney Glaser, who was trained under the quantitative wizard Paul Lazarsfeld at Columbia. In an influential article, Glaser introduced the qualitative "coding" of data, transforming a common quantitative operation—of turning qualitative data commensurable with numerical codes such as ranking survey statements in an ordinal scale—into a qualitative rallying point.[1] In concise prose, Glaser proposed that we take the richness of our qualitative observations and reduce them by giving them more general, abstract terms, grouping disparate observational elements along conceptual lines. As we code, and this is the crucial insight, we do not aim to reduce the qualitative elements to a numerical frequency, but to a set of data elements that can be compared to each other to explore their analytical properties.

Regardless of your research goals, such qualitative coding is a key analytical activity. For us, it is a primary means of cultivating surprises that will require abductive inference. In many cases, what ends up as a key surprise does not register when you are in mid-interview, or in the back-and-forth of ethnographic observations. As we developed in *Abductive Analysis*, coding works as a way to distance yourself from the immediacy of your observations, while simultaneously familiarizing you with the materials and the variation in your data. A surprise is a misfit, an anomalous finding, an unexpected turn of events. It's not necessarily something that hits you over the head right away. In very formal settings such as state dinners, for example, a slight change might have deep symbolic meanings. The more familiar you are with the protocols and usual decorum at such dinners, the more likely you are to notice the discrepancy. Similarly, the more familiar you are with your data, the more likely you are to observe puzzling discrepancies. It is easy to accumulate transcriptions without remembering what happened in minute 40 of a two-hour interview, or to accumulate field notes and forget what struck you on a particular day. It all starts to blur. Coding encourages slow reading, a reacquainting with what you have, and pondering what your observations mean.

What does a code do? It labels a snippet of an observation as a particular "kind." Then, by putting other data instances under the conceptual umbrella of the code, you develop what this kind is about. With coding, you abstract away from observation to categorization. You interrogate the minute differences between observations, while temporarily suspending these differences by giving them a common name. The term you use implies that your observation is an instance of a category and that you may find other instances of this category or related categories in your materials. The label is inspired by your observations but transcends them at a level of abstraction. Labeling highlights issues salient within your research project; it highlights an analytical dimension and is thus different from a summary. Coding goes beyond the here and now of your observations, not just with the purpose of giving yourself new marching orders, but also to specify your project analytically.

Let's start with an example from Stefan's work. In transcriptions of doctors' interactions with the parents of teenagers living with epilepsy, the prospect of driving came up repeatedly. In order to learn to drive in California at age sixteen, a teenager has to be seizure free for six months, either on or off medication. Physicians, it turned out, hinted at this consequential age marker to keep teens on medications. Thus, for example, in the next fragment a physician invokes driving as a response to the mother's request to start tapering off her son's medications: "*So, I mean, it's like for me like I would probably wait for like another year or so until like next summer . . . because then you know we would, we'd be like a little bit over a year seizure free, at that point. . . . because then we're getting into age fifteen and stuff and then the driving is around the corner.*" A discussion of driving comes up 22 times in 149 transcripts. But what do you do with this realization? You could, perhaps, take all these instances together and look when and how the prospect of driving matters in epilepsy management—build a code that you call "driving and epilepsy."

That would not be coding; or, at least, not good coding. It would just be a summary statement that produces a tally of driving. A "driving and epilepsy" code would focus on a key word rather than on what actors are actually doing. It isn't that "driving and epilepsy" isn't relevant in these interactions, but that it is probably not an interesting grouping to compare data excerpts. The analytical concern is not driving per se but holding out the prospect of driving to keep teens on their meds. "Driving and epilepsy" myopically looks at a key word instead of thinking about what actors are up to. The other reason why this code falls short is that it fails to generalize the observation. How doctors speak about driving may be of some interest, but unless you are really into the sociology of transportation, the analytical potential isn't great.

Luckily, you don't have to code so narrowly. Rather than listing key words, you can ask other questions. You can focus on *who* the protagonists of the argument tend to be, thus constructing a code for something like "teen-centered arguments"; or else you can try to figure out what the doctors are *doing* when they mention driving, thus constructing a code about physicians' "defusing authority threats." In either case—and more are possible—snippets of talk about driving and epilepsy could be grouped with broader sets of instances. Depending on what analytical dimension you highlight with your code, the sets would be different. The former, for example, will include episodes when neurologists talk in general terms about the teenagers' quality of life, their medication preferences, and their aspirations. The latter, in contrast, may group driving snippets with talk about alternative medicine, patients' Internet searches, or concerns about medication reimbursement. The specific codes travel across the transcripts, illuminating and connecting seemingly unrelated utterances. Different codes provide different opportunities to interrogate the data, and are thus crucial moves in the analytic process. Like a photographer forcing herself to take pictures from different angles, a good exercise is to try to create as many coding datasets for one fragment to see what gets lumped together.

But what makes for a good code? Is there a way to make sure that we don't make codes like "driving and epilepsy"—or at least that we only construct such codes when that's where the analytic traction is? Sociologist Leigh Star tells the story of receiving a phone call from a colleague in the computer department who was worried about his student. This student wanted to do a qualitative research project but because no one in his department knew how to do such research, he was self-taught. He read that you begin coding word by word in one of Anselm Strauss's textbooks and he had spent the last months just coding through his interviews, producing reams of codes. His adviser was worried that this was a waste of time and wondered when the student could move on to the next level. You don't want to be coding mindlessly like the sorcerer's apprentice. It's a purposeful analytical activity.

Let's then clarify the aims of coding. Qualitative research books are filled with distinctions between different kinds of coding.[2] To simplify, we find it useful to distinguish between two coding activities. The first one, which we borrow from grounded theory, is a form of *open coding*. Whereas the next chapter will focus on *focused coding* and the importance of the *index case*, here we look at how to initially read through your observations and see what is going on. The main purpose of open coding is not to prematurely foreclose the analytical process given your interests, but to remain open to various theoretical possibilities for as long as possible. In other words, open coding helps render the taken-for-granted unfamiliar by pausing social life. Often you start by reading an observation and then thinking about what stands out in the reading: a turn of phrase that catches your attention, a contradiction, a strange reaction. These are good starting points for coding. You look at this fragment and then start interrogating it within a broader context.

And yet, as you may expect by now, we do *not* think that simply contemplating your data is an effective way to analyze. "Open coding" is a good name just as long as we think carefully about *to* where we are opening the coding. To subvert the metaphor of open coding, open coding isn't about letting our excerpts run freely and mindlessly in the wilderness. Rather, it is about opening different theoretical doors to see what vistas we find behind them.[3] Coding is never innocently atheoretical; the codes you come up with already speak to bodies of literature. Coding brings you closer to answering the organizing question of qualitative data analysis: what is my data a theoretical case of? Or, put differently, coding gives you an initial sense of the theoretical potential of your observations.

Even in the example above, both "teen-centered arguments" and "defusing authority threats" are already situated in relation to different literatures. The first theme speaks to a burgeoning literature on patient-centered care, which has encouraged clinicians to tailor their treatment recommendations to patients' preferences. How do clinicians take such preferences into consideration when their professional training and experience show them that treatments are superior to not treating? In this case, how does a physician convince a teen that taking antiepileptics may avoid permanent brain damage from uncontrolled seizures while still being sensitive to the teen's aversion to taking medication? Or in the second theme, how in an era where online searches, social media, and "Dr. Google" put medical knowledge at everyone's fingertips do physicans convey that they are experts in epilepsy treatment? How do they respond to threats to their professional expertise? This concept engages an extensive literature of how clients challenge professional authority and how professionals can counter such challenges. It is notable here that the physician does not try to defuse the teen's objections with doom and gloom biomedical scenarios but instead relies on an argument that may resonate with the teen's life-world and plays into a class-based expectation of normalness among a teen peer group. The neurologist uses a carrot rather than a stick—which could actually be a good way of conceptually splitting up such disarming of authority threats.

Our preexisting knowledge of theoretical maps and compasses does some of the important work of "opening" our coding. While sometimes you simply see the theory in your data, often it is easier to locate yourself within theories if you follow what actors are doing in field notes or how they construct their narratives in the interviews and then start reading theoretically based on these insights. Such reading, in turn, will spark more codes you can bring back to your data and expectations of what should be happening in your observations. Theories—even the most maplike of accounts—tell you how action is patterned in the world. And thus, disciplining yourself to look at such patterns in light of such theories is a helpful mode of provoking you to think theoretically.

To code openly, we tinker with the ancient rhetorical formula and interrogate our data asking: *who* did *what, when, where, how,* and *with what consequences.*[4] These elementary questions move us away from passive formulations. In any situation, or narrative, someone does something. With the *who* aspect of coding you restore implied agency. Then there is the *what.* What, for instance, are neurologists doing when they are talking about driving and epilepsy? What is the bigger aim? How does it fit in a sequence of activities? Next are the temporal sequences and the settings: the *when* and *where* of the analysis. If we are analyzing a snippet of interaction that occurred at a formal dinner party, for example, we need to take the intricacies of the ritual seriously. The same actors would act very differently at different times and in different settings—the scenes of social life deeply affect how people act together within them; the setting of a narrative is a crucial part of how it unfolds. And even more generally, as sociologist Daniel Silver put it, different settings have different moods that affect what can occur in them.[5] Think of the mood evoked by a classroom, a party, or a funeral.

How and *with what consequences* are trickier questions in coding. The question of *how* refers to the social mechanism through which people act. In the epilepsy example, the *how* is not simply "by *talking* about driving." That, again, would be a descriptive assessment that is technically correct but does not give you much analytical leverage (unless, for instance, physicians were to routinely resort to force to make patients take their meds, in which case talking might stand out). The answer to a *how* question needs to be more abstracted than a repetition or summary of the actors' words. Confronted with patients reluctant to swallow medications, physicians tend to persuade. So "persuasion" could be a general *how* code. We can do better, though, and capture the specifics of persuasion. The clinician makes a recommendation calling upon alternative futures. The same statement also focuses on the quality of a patient's current life and offers an incentive for seizure control. *Presenting alternative futures, confronting the patient with a snapshot of her current life*, and *incentivizing* are means to an end. Coding for *how* then lays the foundation for an exploration of social mechanisms, recurrent habitual ways of solving similar problems.[6]

Why not ask *why?*, as Kenneth Burke[7] (and the rhetoricians on whose shoulders he stood) would do? It isn't that *why* is not a good question to ask sometimes. For some research puzzles in some situations, it is a good question, especially when you are interested in people's self-rationalizations. But such justification is not the same as asking *why* in the existential or causal implied sense of the question. In fact, giving a reason is often precisely *how* people construct their narratives; in other words, *why* is a subcategory of *how* questions, but a subcategory with a specific and limited reach.[8] *How* questions, in contrast, open up queries to circumstances, doing things together, in specific places. Following in the footsteps of many constructionist sociologists—from C. Wright Mills to Howard Becker—we think that it is only at the end of inquiry, and only very tentatively, that we can answer a *why* question with any confidence and only in the sense that the luminous empirical details of how things came to be suggest an answer to why things are the way they are.[9]

Instead of asking *why*, then, we ask a different question—we ask *with what consequences*. You may have recognized the pragmatist resonances in the coding question. Consequences are critical to an abductive approach because it is through consequences that we know what kind of phenomenon we face. Coding for consequences then means either following interactions forward to examine how they affect what's to follow, or retrodicting—tracing interactions back in time to see how they crystallized the way they did.[10] In other words, much like conversation analysts who determine the meaning of an utterance by looking at the *next turn* of the conversation, we ask "how do actions shape, and how are they shaped by, previous actions?" We do not presume that interaction is simply an arena where action plays out, but instead try to see what happens when we take multiple iterations of ongoing meaning-making as our unit of analysis. This form of coding, which we have elsewhere termed *coding-in-motion*,[11] then supplants the question of *why* with a more emergent sense of how action (including talk) takes on meaning over time.

Let's work through some examples to make this more concrete.

Open coding sessions

So how do we code in practice? When we teach qualitative data analysis, we spend about half of the course on open coding. It gets you deeper into the field and farther out of your head. It also demystifies analysis. And pedagogically, such open coding works especially well with groups of peers looking at your observations. Your fellow researchers do not have similar attachments to your notes and experiences. They haven't yet traveled the distance you did as a researcher in getting to know your site or interlocutors and seeing the world from their perspective. The stakes are lower for them and therefore they tend to be less inhibited. They often read your notes differently, so can theorize observations in different ways. When you code in a group, the session forms its own interaction and people may play off each other, egging each other on, pushing each other to show in the observations whether an inference is warranted or challenging emerging interpretations. We have found that coding sessions almost always bring something thoughtful for the researcher—just as long as the data is strong enough, with rich ethnographic detail, and uninterrupted interview transcripts and just as long as the content matter isn't too technical.

Here are our ground rules for a groups coding session:

1. For a three-hour session, we ask two student-researchers to choose about 1.5 single-spaced pages of a particularly interesting or puzzling set of observations (whether field notes or interview transcripts). We discuss each researcher's notes in turn, spending about an hour on each one (we check the notes in advance to make sure they are appropriate for a coding session, asking for changes if the notes are too cryptic or an interview is too technical to be useful). For each class, we have also assigned a classical reading in qualitative sociology and we discuss this reading during the first hour. Everyone is thus already primed with some possibly relevant literature.

2. At the beginning of the session, everyone takes some time to read the notes and write any codes they can think of in the margin. At that point, the class members can ask simple clarification questions to the person whose notes they are coding. After the researcher clarifies, we ask them to be silent for the remainder of the session and take

notes of the discussion. Without this rule, some researchers can't help themselves correcting their peers with what is *really* going on. This tends to have a chilling effect on the discussion and stifles working imaginatively with the observations.

3. We open the discussion asking each student what stood out for them. Sometimes there is convergence, sometimes there is a variety of opinions. The advantage is that everyone has already spoken and hopefully will continue to contribute.

4. We write the different themes on the whiteboard and then make the decision to start with one of the themes. We focus on what the observations speak most clearly to in terms of the coding guidelines we presented above. From then on, we ask the students questions in order to develop the themes, sometimes in dialogue with the reading we have done, at other times with other scholarly work. We fill the board with arrows of how concepts relate to each other as the coding session progresses. At the end, we ask the researcher who has been biting her tongue for the hour what she has to add, what was useful, and we discuss promising next steps.

5. One final key step is, after the class ends, for the researcher to write down the codes in a memo format. The memo includes a short narrative on what we found in the observations and what the import of these codes could be. It's another in-between document that you can fill out as observations and coding progress. A good way to write these memos is to pick a number of illuminative quotes and then narrate the concepts in a paragraph format.

Below, we exemplify the potential of such open coding with a few examples from Stefan's class. Rather than focusing on each of the coding heuristics, we examine three; you can fill in the rest. So here we are. Imagine a group of about twelve to fifteen doctoral students in a small conference room facing a white board. We hand out a copy of the notes, give the students ten minutes to scribble codes in the margin, and then we are off. Woohoo!

Who

Alexandra (Alex) Tate[12] was conducting a research project about the communication between gynecologic oncology surgeons and their patients. She relied mostly on conversation analytical methods, meaning that she video-recorded the patient-doctor interactions but did not sit in on the meetings or write down her own observation notes. For the ethnography class, she added participant observation. She decided to shadow one of her surgeons, Dr. Chang, and write notes in ethnographic fashion. Prior to the following field note extract, Dr. Chang told Alex that she had a VIP (very important person) patient. Alex wondered whether that is an informal label for some patients, but Dr. Chang, eyebrows raised, explained that this is an official classification for powerful, wealthy patients in this Los Angeles–area hospital. She added that she would elaborate her thoughts about such patients one evening "over a glass of wine."

As we enter the room I see a woman sitting on the exam table and two women sitting on chairs nearby. One of the women sitting in the chairs has a hospital badge with the title "concierge" and is wearing a business suit and holding a stack of papers. The patient has an expensive-brand purse on her lap and her skin, hair, and nails look like she just came from the salon. The other woman sitting in the chair has a similarly pricey bag, although a different brand, and looks younger and more disheveled. The concierge stands up first and greets us at the door, "Hello Dr. Chang, this is Rena Daniels, Rena, this is your oncologist, Dr. Chang, and Dr. Chang, this is Rena's niece Rebecca." The concierge gestures her arms wide when she makes the introductions. Dr. Chang greets Rena with a wide smile and handshake and a hello. She introduces me as a Ph.D. student doing some "research with [her] group." The concierge looks confused by this, her brow furrowed and a small frown, and asks Rena if she is OK with my presence. Rena says of course she is. The concierge asks Rena whether she'd like her to stay in the room or wait for her outside and Rena, without skipping a beat, asks her to wait outside.

Once the concierge leaves, Dr. Chang brings the rolling stool over to Rena and sits squarely in front of her, blocking out her niece from the conversation. "I've had a chance to look at what Dr. Romano sent over for me," she begins, and moves into describing what Rena's diagnosis is, which she agrees with: an ovarian cyst. I understand a cyst to be benign, but Rena begins to show emotion the more Dr. Chang discusses the nature of the cyst and removing it via surgery. Dr. Chang picks up on this, and leans in closer to her. "Rena, this cyst is not cancerous. It's going to be OK, it's going to be fine." Rena's niece pipes in from behind Dr. Chang, "Really?" Rena shows relief on her face and then says that she "is so relieved to hear that!" She thought she was dealing with something serious because Dr. Romano says she had a "mass" on her ovary, which she thought was a tumor. "I was on WebMD and the American Cancer Society websites, looking to see what the survival rates were for cancer." Dr. Chang reassures her repeatedly that "it's really nothing" and sanctions her, "no more websites! those will just scare you." Once more details of the surgery are discussed—that it will be laparoscopic and easy healing for her—Rena looks pleased and signs off, "Yes, let's do it. I want to get this over with. Can we do it soon?" Dr. Chang says she doesn't

know what her schedule is like but she says to Rena, "But I'm sure your concierge
will help you out with all of that." They exchange thank-yous, Rena goes in to
hug Dr. Chang, who hugs her back and tells her again "It's gonna be OK."

When Stefan turned to the class and asked what they think the data is
about, one of them, a medical sociologist in training, had what sounded
like the perfect answer: this is about patient-doctor interaction and the return of benign testing results to a potential cancer patient. This kind of answer sounds great: it fits both the way clinicians and patients think of the
interaction and it also dovetails on a broad literature in medical sociology
looking at communication between patients and clinicians. Such an answer, however, does not analytically open up the observation. By defining
the case as a "doctor-patient interaction," the student ignored most of the
actors. Rather than different people, with shifting perspectives and positions, the situation is abstracted and oversimplified.

To open up the coding, Stefan then asked the class to put this seemingly
obvious thematization aside for now and think about the actors involved
in the exchange. A patient-doctor relationship presumes two parties with
clearly defined interests, but how many parties do we actually have in this
interaction? Thinking about it, a different student noted that she was struck
by the *insiders* and *outsiders* in the patient room. This was different. How far
can we go with our analysis if we look at the people in the room as insiders and outsiders? The class listed combinations of insiders and outsiders
based on various criteria. If the embodied experience of cancer fright was
the criterion for being an insider, then only Rena was the insider and everyone else was the outsider. If closeness to the patient was a sign of insiderness, then Rena and her niece were insiders, and the others were outsiders.

Here, then, we are beginning to get some analytical traction. The class
distinguished the categories of *insiders* and *outsiders* and then defined them
around various criteria, *embodied experience* and *closeness to the patient*, each
one producing different configurations of people. We can further open up
the observation by spelling out different ways that people in this setting
can be grouped.

The class then turned to *medical knowledge* as a differentiation of insiders
and outsiders. If an understanding of the condition made you an insider,
then Dr. Chang was the obvious insider. But maybe then WebMD and the
website of the American Cancer Society need to be thought of as insiders as
well because they bring different forms of medical knowledge to the situation. Also, if medical knowledge matters for being an insider, then what
we see in the interaction is *a shift where some outsiders become insiders*. By
redefining the suspicious mass into a cyst that can be removed, Dr. Chang

has turned some of the outsiders into insiders. The only outsider by this criterion is the concierge, whom Rena asked to leave the room. The point of turning outsiders into insiders opens up the analysis because it draws attention to a process and to the many ways that others may be implicated in the outcome of the tests. The class could imagine the presence of Rena's niece as part of a support system. However, if Rena had cancer and opted for genetic testing, not an implausible sequence of events for the wealthy with suspected breast cancer, the niece may also become implicated in a more direct way due to her kinship ties.

Using medical knowledge as a criterion of insiderness across the different individuals involved allows us to delineate some of the properties of how medical knowledge varies: it is associated with emotions of *worry* or *reassurance*, it can be more or less *certain*, it can lead to *interventions* or not. Some of these properties are already present in Alex's observation, others are logical possibilities. We note these possibilities because we are interested in variation: will these possibilities emerge in future observations? Specifying properties also points us to how people in the fragment *marked* insiderness and outsiderness: the inclusive arm gesture of the concierge during the introduction, the questions of whether some nonobvious insiders could stay, the location of the chair to lock out the niece and focus on Rena, leaning in while talking, repeated reassurances, and the hugs at the end. Thinking more abstractly, not only does the marking of inclusion rest on professional authority, but the physician underscores it through gestures, spatial arrangements, and body positioning.

Then there is the insiderness of a VIP in the hospital. We discussed whether the expensive bags Alex noted were sufficient attributes of VIP status but agreed that many people with expensive handbags would not necessarily be VIPs. Instead, the presence of a concierge confirms the special status of the patient. The concierge takes several actions relating to insiderness status: She introduces everyone. When told that Alex is an observer, the concierge also gives Rena the power to dismiss her. Every patient faced with student observers should have the opportunity to agree to their presence, but a concierge usually does not broach the request. Dr. Chang typically would have asked whether the patient is comfortable with Alex's presence. By asking the question, the concierge, however, confirms Rena's power to decide who can go and stay, a power Rena uses to dismiss the concierge from the room when Dr. Chang presents the results. Dr. Chang later invokes the concierge as the person to schedule the surgery.

Thinking about insiders and outsiders drew our attention to the people present who were neither patient nor doctor: a relative, a concierge, Internet resources, signs of wealth, and a sociologist-observer. If we view the situation as a patient-doctor interaction, we would largely ignore these others or make them subservient to the intricacies of the news delivery and reception. In line with an extensive literature, we would approach this situation as a dialogue between the "voice of medicine" and the "voice of the lifeworld," in which medical authorities expect "compliance" with recommendations and social scientists can restore "patient narratives" about "biographical disruptions."[13] The assumption that clinical settings are about patient-doctor interactions is foundational to the social study of medicine. A VIP patient could be one small wrinkle in this well-studied domain, allowing us to study how entitlement and respect for an ascribed social status change the interactional dynamics.

Coding the field note from the perspective of insiders and outsiders shifts this normalized way of looking at what happens in clinics. We not only are able to account for more people present in the room, but we are also able to examine shifting alliances and configurations of parties based on different criteria, some of which related to health, wellness, and medicine, but others which have to do with the social organization of the hospital or, in this case, the privileges of wealth and status. If Alex were to pursue this line of coding and analysis, she could write about how the medical interaction turns some outsiders into insiders and leaves others as outsiders. This could lead to a different grouping of people involved: sometimes doctors and patients are on the same side while at other times they are at odds, or sometimes health professionals disagree among each other and align with a patient. Clinicians, however, may be at an advantage in securing internal assent and leave alternative opinions outside.[14]

This line of coding may bring Alex's work into dialogue with the work on boundary formation within institutions and how these institutionally supported classifications signal *social worth*, which in a health care context may be consequential to the extent to which clinicians go all out to take life-saving measures.[15] For instance, Alex could engage Carol Heimer and Lisa Staffen's research on how clinical staff labels patients to exclude or rehabilitate them. The surprising finding in these researchers' work was that neonatal intensive care unit (NICU) staff was less likely to label members of disadvantaged groups because of the organizational dependency of the staff on parents to take their sick infants home and on the weak control of organizational borders. The institutional logic of the NICU was reintegrative rather than disintegrative, aimed at reforming rather than excluding "bad" parents.[16]

Breaking through the patient-doctor interaction frame also may alert us to the critical work of discharge planners, concierges, social workers, respiratory therapists, nursing aids, janitorial staff, administrators, safety inspectors, laboratory personnel, and others who constitute the social world of the hospital. Rather than situating this research in the literature where it seemingly belonged at first sight—patient-doctor interaction—Alex could instead engage the superb work of Janet Shim about cultural health capital. Shim distinguishes the explicit and often tacit skills that people bring to medical settings and lead them to be taken seriously as partners in the management of their health. She notes that these skills are not only unevenly distributed but also unevenly attributed. By implication, she suggests that cultural health capital signals a certain level of insiderness.[17]

When you read these notes, you will likely think that we left a lot of interesting stuff on the table—and that's just by focusing on the question of *who*'s doing the action, and how these positions are relationally structured. Indeed, we always run out of time in these sessions. That's a better problem to have than being stumped.

What

Nada Ramadan was a first-year graduate student in the sociology program when she decided to study an NGO whose mission is to provide services to Arabic-speaking Muslim refugees. Nada worked for the organization as a volunteer and was assigned to a class teaching English as a second language. The following field notes were presented the second time that she attended the site.

> *I enter the classroom and sit in the back. The teacher, Kristen, who is a pregnant White woman, writes different professions on the board. The class is full as last time, with around forty men and women attending. Unlike last class, which was conducted in a mix of Arabic and English by the substitute teacher, Kristen solely speaks to them in English. While Mr. Fuad would refer to the students by titles based on their age (Hajj for elderly) or based on the name of their first male child (Abu/Umm Mohamed—Father/Mother of Mohamed), Kristen called on the students by their first names only to answer the questions.*
>
> *Kristen asks the students to go over the different professions in pairs and walks towards me and we introduce ourselves. Kristen is excited to hear that I am here to help. She tells me that they have to finish administering exams from the district before the end of this week. She says these exams are important because they determine whether they will continue getting funding from the district. She gives me her handbook and shows me the test.*
>
> *There are two sections of the exam. One has different pictures and blanks underneath. The directions ask you to describe the pictures that demonstrate habits of a successful student. When looking at the pictures however, I notice that even I have difficulty understanding what the pictures mean. There are sev-*

eral photos of a girl studying, one of a group of students studying, and a binder.
[. . .] I am supposed to score the student on a scale of 0–3 on the greeting, their
name, the reason and dates of absence, when they will be returning, and a clos-
ing. "If you're not sure what to give them, give them the lower score. Having bad
scores shows that there is still need for the class."

  Kristen thanks me again for my help and walks to the front of the class and
continues the exercise with the class. She announces to the class that I will be
helping Mona administer the exam. She reminds them slowly that this is the
exercise they practiced last week. "Please make sure to do your best in the exam.
The district needs to see you are improving in order for us to continue this class."
She asks for someone to volunteer to take the test first.

  An overenthusiastic middle-aged man, Adel, walks over and joins me. I could
tell from his Arabic accent while speaking to another man that he was Iraqi. He
formally greets me in English. "How are you doing today ma'am?" I hand him
the test and ask him to fill out the first section with the pictures in English. He
responds, "OK ma'am. I would be happy to do that." He writes out what the pic-
tures are, accurately describing them to fit attributes of a successful student. We
continue on to the speaking portion of the exam. He speaks confidently, making
no mistakes. I compliment his English and he smiles and explains that he took
English during his primary and secondary. I assumed, "And university?" He re-
sponds, "No. I went to technical university but I took English there. I also trans-
lated for the American government during the occupation." He explains how he
was given a special visa for immigration after offering his services. I thank him
and call the next student based on the attendance sheet to take the test.

  Farah, an old Syrian woman, does not want to take the test and asks if she
can take it tomorrow. The rest of the class prods her to get it over with. Her book
is filled with markings and she has identified all the words she doesn't know in
her neat handwriting in Arabic. She slowly writes out the exercises and slowly
but perfectly leaves the voice message.

  The class ends and Rana, a program director, makes an announcement in
Arabic. "We said last time that you could bring something of sentimental value
from back home. If you brought something with you please come to the front to
take a picture." Five men and three women come up. Most of them have brought
prayer beads with them. One woman holds a small Quran. One Iraqi man,
who usually wears a suit to class, joins them wearing a traditional thobe and
a ghutra on his head (Bedouin dress). They line up and awkwardly hold their
belongings. Rana takes several pictures.

  A younger blonde woman who usually sits by a young man comes up to me
and asks me in Arabic if I am a teacher. I respond in Arabic "No. I am just helping
with the class." "Oh, you're Egyptian! We were trying to figure out where you are
from. We were thinking you were Lebanese or Syrian." Lamia tells me that they

*have moved to the United States three years ago but were living in Washington
D.C. before they came here. Two other women in hijab join her. I can tell that the
other woman is Syrian based on the tight way she ties her white hijab. "It doesn't
matter where we are from. We're all sisters here." I ask them how long they have
been attending. Lamia says she has been coming here for eight months. She explains that she had tried going to a community college for classes several times
but would not continue because it was too difficult. She likes coming here because there is always someone to explain concepts in Arabic. She also said that
she enjoys coming to this class because it is a chance for them to see each other.
"We're sad when it's the weekend because we don't get to see each other."*

Because Nada is at the very beginning of her research, Stefan asked the
class to imagine that they are the scientific advisory board to her project.
She has data that is an answer to some puzzle, and the class's job is to help
her figure out what puzzle she is dealing with. The students were encouraged to keep many different possibilities open, and start with making a list
of different elements that stood out. One student points out that this is a
site of ethnic blurring—students of many different ethnicities are brought
together because they are Muslim and Arabic speaking—and simultaneously ethnic pinning down. A second student who has worked with NGOs
highlights the constant struggle for resources. A third student noted that
while this is an English class, in fact there is a lot happening in terms of
building solidarity among people who don't seem to belong. Rather than
choosing between these themes, the class kept them all afloat under the
general banner of the unofficial activities that are going on in an "English
class" setting—the *what*.

The contrast between the official goal and what actually happens in a
setting gets at the *what* of the coding guide. Here, we are interested in what
participants do during the ESL class including learning English but also
going beyond that issue. To get there, the class initially divided the activities into two groups, *informal* and *official* activities. One official activity
is *educational testing*. But then the graduate students in class commented
on the irony that educational testing was tied to a *funding mandate*, which
can be considered a quintessential aspect of the American NGO life cycle.
This is different from the ESL students' informal socializing: it reflects the
organization's not-so-hidden agenda. This aspect of the unofficial organizational agenda was emphasized by the teacher's admonition to Nada to
give the students lower scores in order to show the need for further education and at the same time demonstrate improvement for the class. Testing
renders the students part of a common practical project within the nonprofit organization.

Then again, students seem to aim for *socializing* with other people coming from Arabic-speaking countries. This was clear at the end of the fragment: *Lamia also said that she enjoys coming to this class because it is a chance for them to see each other. "We're sad when it's the weekend because we don't get to see each other."* How do *assimilation* and *socializing with other Arabic-speaking immigrants* relate to each other? A student noted that the students in the English class were addressed by the teacher in one way (first names) but then turn around and addressed each other in the ways common to their country of origin. Was this a form of differentiation? Was it a form of solidarity? These are questions Nada could pursue in her subsequent observations at her field site.

The teacher plays on this tension by inviting students to bring something from their home country. It could signal a confirmation of such communitarian goals but the objects are used to make photographs, which, one student surmised, is instead used to gather resources. They create a *record of diversity* to signal the project of assimilation. The teachers engage in the parallel goals of keeping the organization funded and demonstrating its relevance. From the notes, we don't know much about the purpose of the objects. They could also be props to practice English with, to tell stories about. At this point, all we do is note questions that can be hopefully answered by future observations.

We turn to an interesting exchange in the field notes: *"A younger blonde woman who usually sits by a young man comes up to me and asks me in Arabic if I am a teacher. I respond in Arabic 'No. I am just helping with the class.' 'Oh, you're Egyptian! We were trying to figure out where you are from. We were thinking you were Lebanese or Syrian.'"* Here we can begin to ask about *consequences in action.* Nada's presence becomes an opportunity for elaborating the tension between the official and informal activities in the setting. Once Nada answers in Arabic, the woman deduces from Nada's accent that she is Egyptian. Doing so, she signals what she considers Nada's relevant membership category. When Nada answered, the woman could have made countless other comments: observed how nice her hair was, or asked for help with some school task. Instead, she focuses on her national background. If we assume that it is not a random turn in the conversation, *pinning down Nada's nationality* becomes significant in the interaction. In doing so, Nada is interactionally transformed into "one of us." And by doing this to the researcher, Lamia signals, at least in the moment, what she considers important.

We then returned to how some of the students used the class test as *performances.* The tests suggest differences in skill sets, as one would expect. But more happens. Adel, for example, takes the test as an opportunity to shine. On the other hand, *Farah, an old Syrian woman, does not want to take the test and asks if she can take it tomorrow. The rest of the class prods her to get it over with.* She gets the vote of confidence of the class, people rally around her—Syrians and non-Syrians alike. Here we see that the class is used as an opportunity to bring people together, of creating a solidarity that goes beyond ties based on one's nationality of origin.

The goal of a coding session early in a project is to give some possible directions as to what is going on in a field site. What could this possibly be a study of? In the end, the coding session shows that activities in this ESL class happen at many different levels: Ethnic ties and relations seem crucial as different Arabic speakers' nationalities both become relevant through friendship ties but also are transcended as a community of Arabic speakers emerges in situ. Then we also find the activities related to keeping a nonprofit going, of both testing and perhaps exhibiting diversity as playing out to different invisible audiences. Different literatures here begin to suggest themselves. The literature on pan-ethnicity in immigration;[18] how authenticity and organizational funding become intertwined in practice;[19] the creation of located communities, based on shared experiences.[20]

With what consequences?

Kaiting Zhou was studying Republican and Democratic grassroots mobilization among the elderly for the 2020 election when the COVID-19 pandemic struck and California instituted a stay-at-home order. It became difficult to break into tight political networks during quarantine. Pivoting to a different project, she decided to interview people about their dating experiences during the lockdown. Pandemics are not great for observational research but many people were eager to chat. Cooped up at home, interviews were a respite from the daily ennui. In a relatively short amount of time, Kaiting was able to interview fifty individuals about how social distancing affected starting a romantic relationship.

The following fragment is of a gay male couple who decided to begin dating after meeting only once in a coffee shop in person before the pandemic struck:

K: During the quarantine, at what point do you feel comfortable meeting each other in person? Cuz you were both so cautious, right?

D: Yeah. Yeah, he was particularly cautious. He works for his family business (in food manufacturing). We ended up—it was actually interesting—I just bought a condo. I was packing up, getting ready to move. He had just moved back in Janu-

ary. He grew up here. He asked "Oh, do you need any boxes?" I was like "I'd love to have some boxes," cuz I didn't have any and I was concerned where to get some—I actually live next to a moving supply store that was open, but it was nice to . . . becuz boxes are expensive!

K: Yes.

D: *It's stupid—And I was like "You know, if you give me those boxes . . ." it was like we are going to be breaking quarantine. He was like "Yeah I figured it's the time to break the seal." I was like "alright." It probably was like after three weeks? It was two weeks ago. How long we have been in quarantine now? Yeah, we probably have been chatting and doing Facetime dates for like a month, at that point. He didn't want to—I was down to meet up. I was like "whenever," cuz I'm not really leaving my place other than go to coffee shops and grocery stores, like, that's it. I don't see anyone. I go for runs. That's it. I don't come into contact with anybody. I was down to—but he works for his mum, and she is sixty-five, he was like "I don't want to put her at more risk than normal." I was like OK I'm gonna be totally respectful of that, and I let him call the shots on it. But I got to a point when I'm like "Can we meet up? Cuz I need to have sex, hahaha." This has been the longest I've gone haha. There was never really "OK when do we feel safe doing it" but it was like me moving and him having boxes and him giving me boxes was kinda like the excuse. So we never had to have that conversation about it.*

K: *So basically you were explicitly telling him, wanting to meet with him. And he basically was using giving you boxes as the way to say yes? Is that the correct way to understand it?*

D: *I think so. Cuz he had always been like, "If I don't work for my parents, absolutely, but I'm like seeing my mum every single day. She is approaching elderly." I get it . . . So it's like I respect that. But yeah I think that having an excuse for we don't necessarily have to be like "OK, we are breaking quarantine." Like fuck it type of, I think maybe it was something easier for him.*

Teaching over the Zoom interface, Stefan asked the students what they thought the data was about. The initial ideas picked up on the opening statement about "cautious" and conceptualized it as *risk measurement* in a romantic relationship. A different student added that the fragment reflected a *transition within relationships*, especially here the transition from a virtual to a physical date suffused by physical longing. A third student observed that it reflected the *changed meaning of a first date* during quarantine. The second idea was the broader one, and the class decided to develop that one. The students noted how the moving boxes constituted a flimsy excuse for breaking quarantine and getting together. Although there seemed to be little ambiguity about *what* the respondent wanted to happen ("*I need to have sex, hahaha*"), the quarantine made the alignment of physical contact and intimacy more delicate.

The quarantine period changed the *moral calculus* of dating: part of the moral equation was the risk of endangering one's mother and, perhaps even more difficult, asking another person to potentially endanger their parent in order to have sex. The students also noted another moral calculation contemplated by the respondent: we have been good for several weeks, i.e., it's now reward time. This seemed like a broader sentiment in American society when people grew tired of the social distancing.

The first theme, then, was about *what* was going on in the interview excerpt. The students noted that while the respondent was explicitly talking about dating, he was managing other aspects of a relationship and of *self*—he needed to present himself as a "good person." Even the explicit mention of sex is softened by the humorous laughter in the interview. The stakes of the first date were raised: in the context of social deprivation, it had become a stronger signifier of a budding relationship.

The students also noted how the boxes are used as a foil by both the respondent and, it appears, by his new partner. And here is where *consequences* emerge in the interview. Even if there is no ambiguity about where the relationship is going, the pandemic introduced a *sense of responsibility*. Yet the boxes act as *props* that allow them to move the relationship along. The boxes reintroduce ambiguity into the relationship—while it isn't the sex that is being negotiated through these props, the boxes seem to tip the scale, since it is not *only* about a sexual encounter, but also about helping a potential partner in need.

The question of ambiguity and sexuality could be re-tied to dating through the notion of *gift giving*. The giving of moving boxes was a kind of gift, and like all gifts, it cements a relationship:[21] *It's stupid—And I was like "You know, if you give me those boxes . . ." it was like we are going to be breaking quarantine. He was like "Yeah I figured it's the time to break the seal." I was like "alright." It probably was like after three weeks? It was two weeks ago. How long we have been in quarantine now? Yeah, we probably have been chatting and doing Facetime dates for like a month, at that point.* But it was a strange gift. While scholars often see sex as linked to gift giving, this case seems to show how the gift (the boxes) could become a way to justify a sexual encounter. Gift giving operated to make the encounter possible.

A student also wondered how *gendered* these explicit articulations were: a male gay couple may be able to make different risk calculations than a heterosexual, bisexual, or lesbian couple. As students noted, thinking about this form of ambiguity then is a useful starting point if Kaiting would want to compare different relationships. It may be that sex in gay relationships is negotiated more openly than in heterosexual relationships.[22] But this does not mean that the negotiations of self in these situations are any easier. The interview suggested, rather, that the site of ambiguity had moved from whether to have sex to presenting oneself as a sensitive future partner.

Staying with the issue of ambiguity and uncertainty, students noted that the wider context of the interview really matters here: the interview took place during a situation that is rife with both relational and moral uncertainty. There are no clear *cultural scripts* for how to deal with statewide quarantine and social isolation: *Cuz he had always been like, "If I don't work for my parents, absolutely, but I'm like seeing my mum every single day. She is approaching elderly." I get it . . . So it's like I respect that. But yeah I think that having an excuse for we don't necessarily have to be like "OK, we are breaking quarantine."* When there are so few scripts available, questions of what makes a person a good partner or a good son and how to balance these identities become troubled. When *is* the right time to break quarantine in order to pursue a new relationship? The cultural scripts need to be negotiated anew, if not reinvented. In that sense, maybe the interview excerpt was about how people construct new moral scripts. In that case, dating is part of a wider potential set of observations—creating moral selves under new circumstances. Perhaps it is the literature on events and unsettled times that is the relevant point of reference.[23]

Across these different ideas, the question of *what* in the open coding of this excerpt is linked to the question of *consequences*. While interviews are always told from one perspective, they often include rich processual depictions of the unfolding of social life. Drawing attention to these processual questions—even if they say more about how the respondent saw the world than about how things "really" unfolded—provides important directions as to the kinds of literatures and questions we can query.

Conclusion

Open coding may seem like a jump in the dark. You pray for a soft landing but you don't know what the impact will be until you find firmer footing in the literature. It may be tempting to just gather more data in the hope that the next interview or the next observation will be particularly revelatory or illustrative of what you decided the theory already should be saying. That's not how research works. Surprises need to be teased out of the observations you have now. The rhetorical pragmatist heuristics we outlined in this chapter are broad questions to make you reflect on your data, and some will be more salient than others. The trick of open coding is to allow yourself to open your observations in different directions, but to do so with some idea where you are opening a door *to*.

One more reflection.

Coding provides a different emotional satisfaction than does collecting observations. Some students feel that the two activities are at odds. You spent all this time gathering richly textured observations that capture the contradictions and nuances of social life. Coding closes some avenues even as it opens others. With its focus on abstract categorizing, coding necessarily reduces some of the richness of observing lives unfolding. This dynamic is jarring and often feels like an objectification of social life. If you think about the big stack of observations and the handful of quotes that end up in a book manuscript, the discrepancy between the effort to be comprehensive and the few sample quotes in the end product is disappointing. Especially because researchers opt into qualitative research to preserve the integrity of social worlds.

But at the end, this is the craft of social science. Reducing, purifying, and objectifying are critical components of doing science. Bruno Latour has shown the dynamics of reduction in a study of soil scientists trying to understand whether the savanna is advancing on the Amazon Boa Vista forest or is instead receding. The soil and botanical scientists trying to solve this puzzle took samples from the edge between savanna and forest "as silent witnesses."[24] These samples work as specimens and as guarantors for the claims the scientists want to make. They represent the forest with its wildlife, humidity, and noises among its most pertinent features for answering their questions. The scientists use the samples to get an overview, shuffle them around, and engage them with other samples to find patterns that are invisible within the forest itself. But these samples are no longer the forest. Latour writes, "In losing the forest, we gain knowledge of it."[25] He elaborates: "What we lose in matter through successive reductions of the soil, we regain hundredfold in the branching off to other forms that such reductions—written, calculated, and archival—make possible."[26] And: "Stage by stage, we lost locality, particularity, materiality, multiplicity, and continuity, such that in the end, there was scarcely anything left but a few leaves of paper. . . . But at each stage we have not only reduced, we have also gained or regained, since, with the same work of representation, we have been able to obtain much greater compatibility, standardization, text, calculation, circulation, and relative universality, such that by the end, inside the field report, we hold not only all of Boa Vista, but also the explanation of its dynamic."[27] Indeed, in the end the soil samples will become one data point in a table in an article, a figure standing in for a forest and savanna. The key issue here is that reductions allow for transformation and renewals; they lead, as Latour writes, to amplification. There is less resemblance, but we gain a transformed world. Less is more, but it needs to be the right "less."

A similar dynamic holds for qualitative research: reduction and abstraction allow for calculation, conceptualization, validation, argumentation, and theorization. This tradeoff is the promise of coding: when you abstract, you don't just reduce but also gain something. Analysis is then a process of guided transformations, and coding helps you move this process along. You actually already started this process of reduction of social life when you observed and interviewed in a focused manner, sustained by the kinds of issues ethnographic research is good at, and when you asked particular interview questions, even if they were wide ranging. You can still show your argument in a richly textured presentation rather than asserting it in a blunt manner. As we show in chapter 8, that's partly a matter of writing up. To spell out your argument, however, you need to know what to say and coding helps you to get there. As an experience, coding appeals to the thrill of puzzling things out, finding an opening in an ongoing scholarly conversation, and demonstrating with your materials what others missed or how things have changed. It's a different kind of pleasure.

6: FOCUSED CODING

Stefan was in his second year in the sociology Ph.D. program, tucked within the cornfields of central Illinois. He was working on an article that drew from his experience several years earlier studying terminally ill and dying cancer patients during a time when his mother unexpectedly experienced a life-altering stroke. The article grew out of a fieldwork methods[1] class Norman Denzin taught at the University of Illinois. The course required students to first tell a story from their own lives, then look for institutionalized ways of dealing with this issue, and, in a third move, link the personal experience to public representations. Norm had encouraged Stefan to integrate the research he had been doing during the day with his own experience at home during the evenings when he sat at his mother's bedside with his father and brothers. More than anything Stefan had observed on the oncology wards, his mother's life-threatening condition brought both the existential uncertainty and the search for reassurance into sharp relief. It had been a time when the academic and the personal flowed into each other in the most intense way.

Stefan wrote a draft based on countless rounds of grounded theory-style open coding. But it just didn't gel: he had a lot of topics listed, but no argument. The paper ended up being a heartfelt story, but what was sociologically interesting about it? Handing Norm a copy, Stefan asked him for some direction.

What follows shows the difference between *open* and *focused* coding. After the paper had been, as Norm put it, "marinating" for several weeks on his desk, Norm finally read it. He asked for some more field notes from the hospital observations to get a better sense of the scope and the detail of the data. When they met, Norm did not recommend that Stefan continue with the open coding process. Instead, Norm set Stefan on the road to focused coding: "This is what you are going to do. You are going to engage Glaser and Strauss's work on awareness contexts, and you are going to link your experience to their notion of open awareness. The point you want to make is that knowing that someone could be terminally ill, as in open awareness, is not enough for coming to terms with disease and mortality. You are going to talk about the tension between keeping up hope and knowing that it may end badly."[2]

Focused coding means that you settle upon a promising theme and then code within it. It can follow rounds of open coding and then it means throwing the analysis into a new gear: you have identified a promising theme and you develop the focus with a sustained exploration of variation. Or it can be a starting point for data analysis: some scholars, especially experienced qualitative researchers, rarely engage in wide-ranging open coding. Instead, as they collect data, they already gravitate to a promising theme based on their long-time experience analyzing similar data and familiarity with the literature. It doesn't mean that they immediately work out an entire analysis in their head, but they know, based on their familiarity with the literature, what *could be* a promising focus to develop. It also doesn't mean that the initial focus is what ends up as the main story of a finished analysis. Experienced researchers may not know exactly what the case *is* but what it *could be about*. They don't start at square one with open coding, but code in light of a theme they identified. In Stefan's case, Norm identified the theory of awareness contexts as the focus around which to analyze both sources of observations.

Where then is the abductive insight in focused coding? Didn't the surprises already evaporate when you figured out the organizing theme of your analysis? Focused coding starts with what you think the case is most likely about, and ends with a close examination of what you actually have. There is inevitably a space between expectation and reality. It is in this gap between what you thought you were seeing and what you find in your data that the analytical surprise lies. Unlike open coding, where we go deep into singular observations in order to come up with a number of possible themes, focused coding first identifies a broad theme and then seeks to deepen it while coding for variations among excerpts. The analytical momentum is reversed, but in both forms of coding the goal is to prepare the ground for data surprises while working closely with your observations.

How does it work? After identifying a possible organizing analytical theme, you read through your observations looking for relevant data that speak to this topic. Any ethnographic or interview excerpt that remotely fits into the theme goes into a file labeled with the subject. Cut and paste works well, but at least for Iddo, colored pencils work too. You are constructing a "proto-set," an initial set of observations that you will later winnow down. You keep notes about why you think these fragments are relevant to the theme while you're reading. Sets may follow the structure of the research project. Interview-based studies, for instance, especially those that are based on semistructured interview guides, will often probe themes within a cluster of questions. You can take advantage of this structure by creating a set of answers across interviews.[3] More often than not, your set will cross different ethnographic or interview moments. While you construct the set, you also start gathering literature pertinent to the theme you identified.

Looking over the data set you have constructed, you search for what we call an *index case* that anchors the analysis you are embarking on. In the simplest terms, an index case is an observational excerpt that forms the starting point for your analysis (in epidemiology, an index case or patient zero is the origin of an infection). It is the point around which variation will be structured. Practically speaking, an index case is the excerpt that seems to best capture or provoke a possible central theme in your study. So you choose the index case strategically. If you could use only one illustration of the main theme, this would be it.

The index case can be a striking observation, perhaps a casual comment that nevertheless suggests hard-won insights, maybe a contradiction that people have to reconcile, or a particularly neat unfolding of a sequence of actions that reflects what is at stake in your field site. You often already know what we are talking about when you have done research for a while. It's the event you mention to friends when you discuss your study, the one interview quote you will invariably put on a PowerPoint slide for a conference presentation. It is the observations that flash in your mind while your thoughts wander off. Usually, there will be some interaction between emergence and scholarly excitement: you are primed to appreciate certain themes because you have your finger on the pulse of a literature.

There are no hard-and-fast rules for how to find an index case. There is, however, a spectrum, which is also exemplified in the difference between how we work individually. Some researchers like to start with a "modal" excerpt around which variation is built—an excerpt that neatly captures the most common pattern in the data; others start with an "edge case" that makes the case in the strongest possible terms. Whether you move from the center of the set to its fringes or from the theoretical fringes to the center is up to you.

After you pick an index case, it is time to return to the whole proto-set you have constructed. You explore the substantive and analytical variation of the theme you are developing. Puzzling out focused coding is to decide which observations in the proto-set should be grouped together and which data fragments can be chucked aside. You shape the range of analytical properties when you wonder how broad or specific the observations are in order to be considered as part of a set—the scope of meaningful variation;

where they start and end, who is involved, and what the glue is that holds them together. With every data point you position against the index case, you will need to articulate the reasons why some observations belong. There is little added analytical value in finding exactly the same example. What you are looking for is variation: instances that resemble but are not identical to the index case. If the index case has all the elements of what you are interested in, you look for other observations that have most but not all elements. The difference forms the ground for theoretical exploration.

You start looking for patterns within the data variation. This helps you figure out whether some phenomena in the data are striking but too rare, or whether some excerpts are too ambiguous to be part of the analysis. While the frequency of a variation does not necessarily reflect its analytical importance, it matters whether something happened only once or appeared wherever you looked.

At this point, the analysis could go in different directions. You could decide that your set should be subdivided into different categories. Looking through your dataset, you find that there are, for instance, three different processes subsumed under the broad theme and that it would make more sense to give each more space. Deciding where each case belongs and articulating why it belongs there is part of focused coding because it specifies the analytical boundaries of the categories. Or, you can move on to further characterize the broad theme of the entire set. As we'll show below, you may want to revisit the original index case. Does it still fit the variation? Does it still serve as a good starting point for the analysis? Or, should you find a different index case?

Finally, more detailed coding begins when you fill out the details of the categories. As with open coding, the point is to come up with theoretically grounded abstractions of data fragments: words, sentences, paragraphs, or incidents. You look for concepts that capture the specificity of your notes on an abstract level. You start with the index case and lay out all the conceptual dimensions. The coding guide "who does what, when, where, how, and with what kind of consequences" may again prove its utility at this point. You take each case in turn and compare it to the index case. You first want to evaluate whether the concepts travel from the index observation to the next. You draw out conceptual characteristics by mapping similarities and differences between your observations, using the index case as your benchmark.

As a result of working with your data in focused coding you may start to develop an *argument* about how people make sense of their circumstances, how they relate to broader structural constraints, or how they resolve tensions. As we pointed out in our first book, this is a time to also start checking whether your observations support alternative explanations or arguments. We noted earlier the risk of buying into institutional self-selection. This could be an alternative explanation: is what you observe due to what people do or due to the kinds of people who are most likely to be at your site? To think about such alternative explanations, it may help to imagine yourself defending your findings to a skeptical audience: what would a pesky critic bring up as likely alternative explanations for your claims? These alternatives are not limitless: they are bound by what is plausible based on the literature and based on what's in your data. Obviously, you will not be able to address every alternative explanation and you may need to acknowledge that some alternatives are impossible to verify due to the limitations of your data. Even then, it's still better to have anticipated these alternatives.

Of course, this process is not linear. You will sometimes find yourself staring at the observations for days, trying to figure out which case can serve as an index case, and how positioning it as an index case shapes the analysis. You may sometimes find that what you thought was a great index case elides too much of the patterns you see to serve as a useful analytical anchor. You should also stop and check what others have written about your or related topics. The farther along you get and the more you start articulating the specific contribution you are going to make, the more extensive and closer your reading of the literature will be.

Sounds good, but again, where is the lifeblood of abductive analysis? Where is the surprise? As in open coding, working with your observations in such a systematic, detailed way allows a surprise to stand out. It's like raking lines in a Zen garden sandbox. Only when you do this systematically do you encounter the pebble that requires you to shift the direction of the sand. During focused coding, the surprise is in the gap between your theoretical expectations and the empirical details. Coding from one instance to the next creates expectations of what should happen across observations. That's when you become sensitized to something that stands out because it does not fit the pattern that you found. For that reason, outliers are precious because they require you to rethink why they do not fit what you would have expected; they require recalibration of what you have or a decision to put the outlier aside.[4]

As in open coding, focused coding will alert you to the holes in your data gathering and suggest new venues to get additional observations. This is a reason for interspersing data analysis and writing with returns to the field. You may want to fact-check some offhand comment or get the perspective of additional people on an issue that has gained prominence in your budding analysis. Coding gives you marching orders of what to pay attention to in your next interviews or visits to a site, another reason to start coding early on.

Focusing the codes

In the qualitative research class, we follow open with focused coding. At this point, the students have been observing in their field site for at least a couple of months. We ask them to select three fragments of their notes that speak to one theme and write a memo that lays out the similarities. Then, during the class period, we do *reverse coding*: we read the notes and collectively code them by comparing and contrasting the fragments. The students do not have access to the memo or the theme selected by the original researcher, their job is to collectively reconstruct it or to come up with something better. Inevitably, the focused coding in class is more extensive and detailed than the original memo of the ethnographer. Quite frequently, focused coding by the collectivity also shows that the original student saw things in the observations that were just not there. Students inevitably wonder whether they can do such coding by themselves. Of course they can. It's a matter of not rushing the coding and sitting with it for a while. Not being satisfied with the obvious gloss of what is happening in the observations but probing. At the same time, it helps to do it collectively. After the class ends, some students code together in a buddy system where they take turns looking over each other's observations.

To give a taste of how such focused coding and the index case operate over the lifetime of a project, and also how to work *differently* with focused coding, we explore two examples, taken from independent research projects that we were engaged in while writing this book. The first example demonstrates the basic steps of focused coding to create a curated analytical collection of data points. The second illustrates how index cases and analytical arguments transform over the course of analyzing data and bring home the point that mapping variation does not make an argument.

Example 1: prognostication

While writing an article with Tanya Stivers, Stefan decided to take note of the analysis as it really played out so we could use it for this book. Besides the process of focused coding, looking under the hood also shows how originally bad ideas might be transformed into better ones. Here we go: detours, dead ends, and all.

Tanya and Stefan were working with 149 video-recorded (due to Tanya's interest in using the video recordings for conversation analysis) and transcribed observations of clinic visits between pediatric neurologists and their child patients with their parents. The goal of this project was to capture a pressing and consequential communication phenomenon typical of contemporary patient-clinician interactions, similar to, for instance, the extensive literature on how clinicians convey bad news to patients. The project was intended as an accompaniment to a previous study on the return of genomic testing results, contrasting genomic with nongenetic test results. But in the pediatric neurology visits, the return of results was either not happening or, if it happened, was not particularly salient. They dropped that idea and looked for a way to take advantage of these interesting observations on their own merit.

Confined to economy seats on a five-hour plane ride back from a sociology conference, they made a list of possible themes based on their reading of the excerpts and many hours spent watching the videos over and over. One of the more promising themes was a distinct but still vague phenomenon: the increasing number of children who remain under medical management even though hope for a cure for their epilepsy seemed to have been abandoned. There may still have been a small chance that the patients would improve, but the physicians prepared the parents and patients for the news that the children would likely remain ill for the rest of their life. They needed a name. Everything they came up with sounded judgmental. Still, as a working concept, they decided to go with conditions defined as *unfixable* (we know, we know, it's still judgmental, just bear with us), because as a concept it carved out a process on sociological terms.

What stood out was not one particular luminous observation, but a sense that, across these clinic visits, a monumental transformation was happening: patients (and their parents) were gradually told that seizures would likely remain uncontrollable, even with the best medications, and may affect their lives in profound ways. What the transcripts showed was the transition from a patient who could hope for recovery to one who would likely be chronically disabled. Even before they had gone systematically through the observations, they settled on the initial *focus* of focused coding. From here on, the coding process was aimed at refining this theme.

After deciding that the transition from possibly curable to unfixable was a possible theme worth pursuing, Tanya and Stefan worked on two fronts: they started a reading list of research that spoke to the topic of fixability, e.g., therapeutic developments, specialties that deal with those kinds of patients, communication challenges, etc. The reading list showed that this particular transition to a chronic illness was not much explored in the literature but might be a productive theme because it linked to the literatures on potentiality, forecasting, and coming to terms with a change in health status (e.g., biographical disruption). The list provoked questions about who determines whether a patient is unfixable and whether some groups of patients fell under the category, such as terminally ill patients or people with congenital, permanent disabilities. These were analytical distinctions that would require a better handle on what the neurology observations showed.

To jumpstart their analysis, they then picked a sample of twenty transcripts and read them closely for any indication of the patient's status as fixable/curable/treatable and this is what they came up with:

Parents orient to *fixability* through questions about . . .
   Growing out of it
   It going away: no more seizures
   Being able to stop the medicine
   Seizures (or other behaviors) stopping
Physicians orient to *fixability* when they mention . . .
   Prognoses about the condition going away or not going away
   A stance towards stopping treatment in future
   Curative surgery
   Medication that can stop seizures (or other symptoms)
   Time period of being seizure free
Parents and physicians orient to a condition as *unfixable* when they . . .
   Focus on support groups, understanding the condition better
   Offer bright sides regarding knowledge
   Focus on supportive equipment and therapies
   Limit discussion of treatment to managing difficult behavior or pain
   Try to lower number of seizures or their severity

Reading through the conversations between neurologists and parents contained clues about the children's current health status in terms of fixability, but these clues were quite vague in that they were implied in the diagnosis or the treatment recommendation. The clinicians rarely explicitly stated what the child's future would hold. Instead, they insinuated and subtly conveyed a future with seizures. Parents, in turn, rarely asked outright what future awaited their children.

Tanya and Stefan found distinct patterns. There seemed to be different kinds of *trajectories* that patients follow within the clinic—a helpful clue from the literature. Social scientists have used the notion of trajectory to refer to a course of action or in more deliberate theoretical ways. Anselm Strauss, for instance, put trajectory at the center of his theory of social action, defining it both as the course of a phenomenon experienced over time and as the actions and interactions contributing to its evolution. He then notes that trajectories can be further unpacked to contain phases, collective projections of what the course should look like, and schemes or conscious designs to shape the interaction. Strauss uses the notion of *trajectory management* to refer to how people shape the course of a trajectory.[5]

That seemed promising. At this point, Tanya and Stefan could have looked for an index case but they already knew that they wanted to further divide the sample into different trajectories. It made more sense to find an index case for each trajectory. They decided to group the 149 transcripts according to how clinicians and parents orient to the issue of fixability. They had 132 visits for epilepsy (the others were for other neurological conditions) and in 108 of them clinicians and parents oriented to the future. About halfway down the classification exercise (it took weeks to go through these transcripts), they developed three trajectory categories:

1. In the mildest cases, the child's seizures are likely fixable, but some level of uncertainty remains because the child and parents are not out of the woods yet.
2. In more serious cases, the child's seizures are likely controllable but not entirely fixable. The child may require meds for the long run, or seizures may recur unexpectedly.
3. In the most serious cases, the child's seizures are likely unfixable; it is unclear whether time and meds will help.

They had 33 cases where clinicians conveyed a *likely fixable* future, and 24 cases in which parents and clinicians oriented to *possibly fixable* future. And then there were 12 cases where the conversation suggested that the seizures were increasingly difficult to control, which they called the *likely unfixable* trajectory: the category that sparked their initial interest.

They now had the broad themes distinguishing the trajectories from each other. Their next step was to look for similarities within each group. They printed out the parts of the transcript where the clinicians indicated how the patient was doing for each of the three trajectories and went through it looking for commonalities. This is where the *index case* came in. They looked for a case that best captures each specific trajectory: not necessarily a modal or ideal-typical case but a case that exemplified the trajectory in a way that renders the key analytical dimensions explicit. It's a case that is particularly evocative and representative of the analytical spectrum of each trajectory—one that Tanya and Stefan could show a reader and hope that they will immediately get it.

For the group of patients with likely unfixable disease progression, an interaction with a patient Tanya and Stefan called Gina became the index case because her visit with the neurologist contained extensive—if still guarded—discussion of what Gina's future held, a discussion that captured most of the key analytical dimensions of the transition to unfixability. Her mother was bilingual Spanish and English, but her father spoke mainly Spanish. Gina, who at the time of the visit was ten months old, had difficult-to-control seizures that developed while she was in early infancy, and she was on three medications. The neurologist suspected that a genetic condition caused the seizures; in this visit he reported that the child has an X-linked mutation in the gene *PCTH19* associated with "bad seizures" in girls. The neurologist explained the finding as causing "difficult to control, like the wrong seizures, many seizures in younger girls." He said that "*my hope is* down the road, down the road we can gradually decrease her medicine."

He advised the family: "Plan for now I'll tell you, so you know, this gene is associated with lots of seizures, so *it's possible, it's possible* that we can control a seizure very well while going down the medication. That's possible, *but another possibility is you know*, recurrence of the seizures. We really have to watch out for that. You know? Especially we are going down the medicine. I really need to make sure she's not having seizures. . . . You know, the brain, the body you know, I want to give her the best chance of development. We want to control seizures so that *she can develop as normal.*"

When the mother asked whether Gina will have seizures all her life, the neurologist answered that it varies but that the girls who have bad seizures will have problems with development, while girls with fewer seizures will have good cognition. He went over the list of medications and how he might want to taper them because too many medications is not good either, saying that "Topomax can come off if she's doing well." The mother picked up on the conditional phrasing: "If she's doing well." The neurologist agreed, "But I think it's too early to say what if."

Contrast this case with the index case for the likely fixable category. This involves a child who had a seizure on vacation in Romania. The neurologist qualified the occurrence of the seizure with tiredness of traveling and possibly disturbance during sleep (parasomnia): "But again because we didn't see anything on the EEG, that does drop that a little bit and kind of make me lean a little bit more towards the parasomnia. I think that's more likely. If it is parasomnia, you may have it a couple more times and usually you grow out of it. If it is a seizure, a focal seizure, and not the Rolandic, I would expect it to happen again." He added, "I think if they continue to happen, one thing you may want to do is do the EEG again." But he emphasized, "Chances are, this is just. . . . You may have another one or two and then it's going to go away." The mother concurred: "Yeah, because there's been three months between this one and the one before and he was fine. They've never happened during the day."

You can readily see the difference. In Gina's case, the neurologist was tentative, held out the possibility of modest goals (lowering or eliminating some drugs), highlighted the need for achieving better seizure control, located the seizures genetically, and hinted at cognitive decline. In the second case, the physician was much more reassuring. There could be one or two more seizures but they were likely triggered by exceptional environmental circumstances.

Yet thinking through index cases also brought up a plausible *alternative explanation* to account for the variation among observations. Maybe fixability reflected the biological severity of seizures, and the futures clinicians discussed with patients and their parents were straightforward in light of clinical signs. This would limit the project's *sociological* relevance because the observations simply captured different scripts that are fully predetermined by the kind, frequency, and nature of seizures. While still important to document, where was the surprise if physicians' assessments simply capture biological symptoms? It would be more surprising if there was a level of uncertainty about what the future holds for seizure patients, regardless of the seriousness of seizures. Then, parents and clinicians would have to negotiate what could still be done. We will come back to this possible alternative explanation.

Looking at their data across fixability trajectories, Tanya and Stefan found a discussion of what they ended up calling **the goals of treatment**, the **timing of when these goals were achieved**, and the **certainty that these goals were achievable**. That is, for each trajectory, distinct goals were set: the goal for a *fixable disease trajectory* was to be both medication and seizure free; for a *likely fixable trajectory* the goal was to be seizure free with continued use of medications; and for a *possibly unfixable disease* the goal was to decrease the seizure frequency and intensity while using a variety of medications. The more fixable a patient was considered, the more precise the time line for achieving the goal was and the fewer uncertainties there were that the goal would be achieved. In no transcript did physicians state the patient's fixability status explicitly or did parents ask about it directly. Yet all over the consultations were clues that indicated what future the child with epilepsy could expect. A prognosis was conveyed implicitly and this implicitness allowed parents and clinicians to rally behind slightly shifting goals. This was the surprising realization that emerged from closely working with the observations during focused coding.

This ended up being the main theme of the analysis Tanya and Stefan

	Likely fixable trajectory	*Unfixable trajectory*
Goal	The expectation was that the child would outgrow seizures: "it's going to go away."	"We want to control seizures so that she can develop as normal"; maybe in the future they could taper off one of the medications.
Timing and uncertainties	Distinct endpoint, few uncertainties that the goal will be reached. "But again because we didn't see anything on the EEG, that does drop that a little bit and kind of make me lean a little bit more towards the parasomnia. I think that's more likely. If it is parasomnia, you may have it a couple more times and usually you grow out of it. If it is a seizure, a focal seizure, and not the Rolandic, I would expect it to happen again."	Vague, unspecified, qualifiers: "But I think it's too early to say what if . . ."

pursued: children with epilepsy follow three different trajectories that map whether the child is likely to become seizure free or to have seizures for the foreseeable future. During clinic visits, clinicians and parents dropped clues about goals, timing, and uncertainties. These trajectories corresponded indeed to a limited extent to the severity of the seizures (the alternative explanation that the consultations simply reflected the patients' biological findings), but the diagnosis was not yet certain. For instance, one patient was diagnosed with Landau-Kleffner syndrome, a disorder characterized by the loss of language comprehension, loss of verbal expression, and seizures. Among children with this diagnosis, however, there was a wide range of symptom manifestations. About 70 percent, for instance, develop seizures that may vary in intensity. Thus, even with a serious diagnosis, parents and clinicians still face the task of mapping out a child-specific future trajectory.

Two more issues needed to fall into place. First, Tanya and Stefan mapped the variation in each group, and second, they refined their literature review in order to highlight the contribution of this paper and draw out more analytical dimensions.

They worked on both tasks at the same time. Going back to the three stacks of trajectories, they mapped all the different ways goals, timing, and uncertainties were discussed in the index case and compared this to the other cases in the group. This segment of the process was similar to the guided open coding explained in the previous chapter, so we will skip the details here.

Second, and building on the literature they started this project with on trajectories and illness experiences, they knew that sociologists have looked closely at the process of *diagnosing* and how the consequences of receiving a diagnosis reverberate individually and institutionally. The literature on *prognosis*, however, is not only more limited but also more focused on prognosticating the end of life. Because of the institutional incentives of hospice care, which is available for patients with a life-expectancy of six months or less, we know most about prognosis at the end of life. Physician-sociologist Nicholas Christakis pioneered this research when he examined how physicians inform patients about their terminal condition.[6] A read through a database of sociology articles showed that this literature has been stagnant. Many scholars mentioned prognosis as something patients face, but few delved into the interactional processes of foreshadowing a future head-on or conceptualized what prognosis does for people and the clinical management. This was surprising, because for patients much is at stake when disease disrupts their biographies in terms of what the future holds for them. Prognosis mattered for those with chronic illnesses because of the variation in how diseases may affect biographies.

In spite of incentives such as the Patient Self-Determination Act and Medicare reimbursement for hospice, even in terminal conditions prognoses were given mostly indirectly and remained positively biased. That last point stood out: there was a similar positive bias in the conversations between neurologists and their patients. This suggested that one of the rationales behind the indirect dropping of prognostic clues was to maintain a physician-patient working relationship, especially when the child's future grew increasingly bleak. Parents and children became gradually prepared for a life with seizures while some of the clues still emphasized hope for improvement.

In developing some of the dimensions of prognostication, Tanya and Stefan drew on Ann Mische's article on projects and possibilities.[7] Mische suggested a conceptual toolbox to examine how future projections become actionable in ongoing situations. Even if people act on partial or incomplete information, their perception of the consequences of their action might still matter as a self-fulfilling prophecy (which is also a major theme in Christakis's work on prognosis). She quoted Henri Desroche's notion that "hope is a rope" cast into an uncertain and shifting future horizon, implying that future projections may allow you to climb out of the present.[8] To help understand the different kinds of ropes people have available, Mische listed a number of characteristics of future projections: reach (focus on short-, middle- or long-term future), breadth (range of possibilities in future), clarity of the imagined futures, contingency (whether the future is fixed, flexible, uncertain, or dependent on unknowable circumstances), expandability (whether imagined futures are expanding or contracting), volition (how much control people have over their future), sociality (who is intertwined or implicated in the future), connectivity (the logic of connection between different people), and genre (utopian, instrumental, pragmatic, oppositional).

From this list, we immediately see that reach, breadth, clarity, contingency, expandability, and volition were relevant in the study of epilepsy prognostic trajectories. In fact, the entire dilemma facing parents and clinicians could be viewed as an issue of expandability: are the kids' imagined futures opening up or contracting? To determine whether they were on an improvement or deterioration track, we could pay attention to clarity: how definite the signs of the future are. Here, an interesting sentinel set of observations gained analytical relevance: kids whose seizures seemed under control sometimes slid back. The question was whether these unexpected seizures indicated a temporary setback explainable by unusual circumstances or instead a turning point signaling a different future.

The research's contribution then was to show how prognostication takes place during chronic illnesses when clinicians conveyed clues to cultivate hope while still avoiding unrealistic expectations for those on a downward trajectory. The analysis opened up a new research area not just in medical sociology but also in any area where future imaginaries are critical and spoke to a growing literature on potentiality, forecasting, and prognosis.

Example 2: managers and pro bono in the advertising industry

Stefan's research with Tanya demonstrates a relatively smooth process of focused coding. While the distance between the initial theorization and the resulting article reflects the analytical terrain traveled during focused coding, the analysis did not stray that far from the initial hunch that prognosis is highly relevant even if it occurs in an understated fashion. It is a mark of hard-won expertise, where researchers have honed a sense for what is interesting in their field notes, based on a detailed sense of the substantive maps of the subfield. It is, perhaps even more crucially, a case developed by two researchers who spent decades studying doctor-patient interaction and the medical field. They not only knew the theories, but also had a pretty strong feel for what goes on in the empirical case.

Some cases, however, are bumpier. Most of us aren't leading researchers in our subfields; most have not studied a research area for long enough. In the majority of cases, then, the distance between what we thought we would find and what we actually find in the field is greater. Complementing Stefan's case, we follow part of an interview research project conducted by Iddo and two students-turned-colleagues. We show how the index case, as the gravitational center of variation, changes over the course of the project, and how the theoretical points become clearer through such shifts. Although the research process was continuous, we parse it out below into two phases.

PHASE I: EMERGING THEMES AND FALSE STARTS

The entire research project emerged somewhat serendipitously when Iddo was conducting an ethnographic study of an advertising agency in New York. A few months into the fieldwork, Iddo realized that the agency took on large numbers of pro bono projects for nonprofits: from humanitarian campaigns for clean water, awareness campaigns for Parkinson's disease, to issues facing gay youth who are just coming out. As he prodded advertising professionals in the agency about this kind of work, he realized that he hadn't simply chanced on an outlier in the industry: most successful agencies performed such pro bono work. This was a layman's surprise—an industry known more for its cynicism was one in which people put an inordinate amount of time into "good causes."

This naïve moment of discovery gave rise to an interesting puzzle. Talking to people at the agency, Iddo was struck by a recurring contradiction in how people talked about pro bono. People discussed pro bono—which translates literally as "for the public good" (*pro bono publico*)—as a solution to a moral conundrum. An advertising professional articulated a common sentiment that pro bono work assuaged the "existential angst" of spending one's creative energies convincing people to buy one brand of toothpaste instead of another. But in the same interview, advertising professionals also talked about such work as a way to conduct meaningful *creative* work— work that they would be proud of as a showcase of advertising craft—as well as a way to get recognition from their peers and advance their careers. Pro bono work often won advertising awards, and these awards were critical in securing raises or moving up the corporate ladder. How did advertising professionals manage these different, potentially clashing, notions of the good?

This question was both empirically and theoretically interesting. Iddo had been immersed in the sociology of culture. He had been especially interested in *repertoire theory*—a strand of theorizing that argues that it is crucial to see how people pragmatically mobilize different culturally available tropes or bundles of meaning (rather than ascribing them to a uniform "culture"). And in a sociology of culture course he was teaching at the time, a French stream of research focused on how people access different "regimes" of meaning that are constantly available yet seem completely incommensurable with how they conceptualize different notions of worth. In the advertising world, it seems, he found a case in which the alignments and tensions of these different goods seemed contested. It was a perspicuous site for examining morally good work with a variety of goods at play reflecting different basic assumptions about what constituted *good work*. And perhaps most intriguing, the advertising agency was a place where juggling these goods mattered in tangible material and career ways.

Considering that pro bono work was only a small part of the agency's portfolio (2 to 5 percent), Iddo realized that participant observation wasn't the right way to understand this phenomenon. People did pro bono work intermittently, and often when they were out of the office. The agency also did not organize dedicated "pro bono teams." Without a group of people who can predictably be observed, ethnography was a limited method. If Iddo wanted a sense of how pro bono work operated in advertising more generally, he would need to talk to more people. A spinoff interview study he had not initially planned started taking shape. Iddo turned to two graduate students—Sonia Prelat and Shelly Ronen—and they accepted his invitation to join him on the project.[9] The trio interviewed seventy-three advertising professionals in successful New York agencies, a small slice of the advertising world but—due to their location, scale, and clients—a sample that covered a disproportionately important set of agencies.

While the research team was most interested in how rank-and-file workers in advertising—whom they term "advertising professionals"—navigated the different goods, they also interviewed a number of CEOs and top-level executives. They wanted to explore not only whether executives thought about pro bono differently from front-line professionals, but also how they decided which pro bono projects to accept. Moreover, they realized that a lot of the experienced advertising professionals occupied middle-tier executive positions. Out of the seventy-three interviews, eighteen were with high-level executives and twenty-three were with people who occupied middle-management positions—enough to explore variation across management experience levels.

Following organizational literature, the team wanted to leverage the interviews to see how advertising managers shape the projects. Such a research project builds upon scholarship about managers hiring the "right" people to negotiate different company priorities,[10] and a lot of literature about how managers' values affect how many corporate social responsibility projects they can handle. Moreover, the literature on social responsibility in companies stressed that such pro bono investments needed to align with the corporate bottom line. At least from a bird's eye view, corporate social responsibility was mostly a thin veneer for maximizing corporate profits.

These theoretical expectations emphasizing profit maximization shaped the initial index case for the study. A striking and "luminous" moment came during an interview with the North American CEO of one of the world's largest and best-known global agencies. Asked when he would decline a pro bono account, a part of the interview guide explicitly designed to get at "negative cases," the CEO replied that:

> A lot of very worthy not-for-profits, they may actually run counter to, perhaps, some of the interests of some of our clients. So that's another thing that we take into consideration. So, for example, if we work with [Big Oil company], and it is an excellent client of ours, and they do a lot of really great things from a business perspective. But let's say the agency were to go off and do a whole pro bono effort with like Greenpeace. You know, Greenpeace, they're active detractors from [Big Oil]. We can't have the agency developing advertising that slams [Big Oil]. That's like crazy. We just can't do that. [Big Oil] helps keep us employed and in business. There are occasions when you have to be smart about making sure that the interests of our client come first, which is why any pro bono cause that gets into taking a stand on issues or policies—issues, policies, or politics—we have to stay away from.

Here was both a politically charged and theoretically interesting finding, in line with what the organizational literature predicted would be happening. The statement that CEOs were controlling the flow of pro bono work to filter out what they deemed to be "political" projects seemed important in an era in which "welfare capitalism" relegated doing good to corporate entities. The interesting action was not in deciding *whether* to take on pro bono cases, but *which* cases to choose. Wary of overtly political campaigns that would be at odds with their current clients, this executive chose safe cases of depoliticized suffering.

This excerpt thus emerged as a promising *index case* around which to build the variation in managers' responses. Using it as a starting point, the team reread all the interviews with managers, looking for similar cases of opting out of specific kinds of pro bono work in an effort to keep clients happy and avoiding overtly political causes. But looking at the variation across the interviews, they realized that these quotes were few and far between. Two other CEOs spoke against overtly political work, but the others didn't. In fact, in reading the interviews carefully, the three CEOs wary of politicizing were the only politically conservative top managers in the sample. Instead of a common way for CEOs to strategize, an alternative explanation—that this was the way conservative CEOs managed the flow of pro bono work in a predominantly liberal industry—seemed increasingly plausible. Still more revelatory, the researchers realized that many CEOs and middle managers spoke positively about the political nature of the projects they accepted. While these three CEOs were still interesting cases, what began as an index case was increasingly understood as an *outlier*—it was an interesting variant, but not theoretically or empirically central.

As they read and reread the management interviews and compared them to the interviews with advertising professionals, other differences became more salient. Rather than a story about avoiding or courting politics in corporate social responsibility, there were more mundane organizational challenges that both top managers and middle managers needed to solve. Managers talked about pro bono work as a training ground for agency talent—a safe way to gain experience in a setting in which failure does not equal lost revenue. They detailed attempts to gauge just how much work the pro bono project would take away from the paid work for clients; they listed their attempts to leverage pro bono work as a means of recruiting and retaining talent in the agency; they even mentioned pro bono efforts as a way for the agency to manage its own brand. The failed index case sensitized the team to the importance of the choices managers make about which pro bono campaign to invest.

While the politicization failed as a substantive claim, it opened up a generative question. The variation, as is often the case, did not reveal a single spectrum upon which things vary but several interesting dimensions. A mapping of the variation in topics that arose in the case of managers' interviews, but did not come up in professionals' interviews, ended up looking something like what's illustrated in figure 1. Laying out this variation, inspired by Adele Clarke's mapping of topics,[11] provided a first overview of the different kinds of common themes in the data. These themes are already organized around a substantive question: the different ways in which top and middle management decide which projects to accept. Variation, however, is not a *theoretical* story, nor (on its own) a very interesting one. What the researchers teased out is a collection of strategies rather than an analytic narrative. Still, it allowed them to go back and look at the larger themes in their work and think about variation in terms of theory.

Pro-bono as
retention tool

Pro bono as
"safe" training grounds

Pro bono as
recruitment tool

Pro bono as
Corporate Social Responsibility

Avoiding politics in
Pro bono accounts

Pro bono as developing
proficiency in a new kind of brand

Workload issues: guessing
how time intensive pro bono is
and weighing against paid clients

FIGURE 1

PHASE II: CONSTRUCTING AN ANALYTIC THEME

The project's research ask was to examine the tensions between different notions of "the good." Advertising professionals blended morality, creativity, and the recognition and careers afforded by awards together in interviews. Moreover, in focusing on managers' decisions about which pro bono accounts to allow and which to block, the team had an analytic direction: managers directed the flow of pro bono projects. How did these managers' actions affect the ways advertising professionals navigated different goods?

The team returned to the managers' interviews to further tease out variation. The literature tends to portray perspectives between differently positioned actors as rife with tension: workers see the world in one way, managers in another. But if the question motivating the research is about the practical alignment of different goods for various stakeholders in the firm, then some of the managers' ways of picking among possible pro bono projects gains new theoretical relevance because prioritization of some projects over others would reveal how different goods would be balanced. Building upon the conceptual map, the research team began looking more closely at the themes of "retention" and "recruitment" of talent into agencies through offering pro bono work—two themes where managers referred to their need to choose pro bono projects judiciously.

Combing through the interviews, the researchers were struck by the way managers talked about how they imagined that recruitment and retention worked. The managing partner of one agency explained it in the following way:

*As I was saying about advertising, there but for the grace of God I'm not sure
where they would go. For some people we've been that agency within that industry. You know . . . really true believers in causes and in changing the world, and
in living a more virtuous life. . . . You know people like that. And they're twenty-
something and they live in Brooklyn, they're hipsters, they ride bikes, they're
vegans. You know these guys, right? . . . What happens if they leave is then they
split their life. They'll be freelance at a big agency selling who-cares-what. And
then they'll have their private lives. But at [this agency] we offer them the chance
to have an integrated life where they can be that person, or at least to a greater
degree. Nothing's perfect, but they can be here and still live by their code of ethics
as they define it in work as well as at home. And that's an unusual thing.*

Compared to the original index case, this interview was an outlier of a different sort. It came from an executive in one of the few agencies (of thirty-
seven) priding themselves for doing "cause-based work" as a prominent
part of their portfolio (20 to 30 percent instead of the usual 2 to 5 percent).

The index case is not necessarily an "average case" in the data. While
it is certainly possible to use a kind of ideal type of each category, much
like Tanya and Stefan did in their research, there are other factors that
motivate this choice: what renders an index case effective is that it makes a
theoretical point that clarifies other excerpts, and thus allows us to launch
a promising analytical line of coding. In this case, what makes this interview analytically fascinating is that the respondent was more cynical than
other managers. Relatively confident of his agency's moral merit, he could
afford to be extremely explicit about his moral calculus. Since the agency
let people fulfill a moral calling during their everyday work, they allowed
workers to integrate their ideals and their work life. By taking on specific
pro bono projects, the manager solved a moral dilemma *for his employees.*
Rather than interperspectival difference as a tension, it appeared as a way
to enable his employees (and especially the Brooklyn-bike-riding-vegan-
hipsters) to feel like they were doing good.

Reading more of the data through this analytical prism, the researchers realized that many managers explicitly talked about gauging whether
a specific pro bono project was morally exciting for their workers. Since
they needed workers to be invested in the project—partly because it would
require them to work nights and weekends with no pay—most managers
tested the waters for employee enthusiasm:

*Everybody's got their passions and everybody's got their interests, [and] we've
had to learn to . . . it's not just what I want to do as the CEO of the company,
because everybody has unconscious bias. We've learned to consider things based*

on the input from our entire management team. So what I may want, may be different from somebody else. Can we ignite the passion of our people? . . . So, if some really worthy causes are coming in here and saying "hey, we'd love for you to help us" and I've walked around this office and I've talked to people and I can't get them excited about it, I have to unfortunately go back and say, "look, I wish you luck but I can't offer you our creative firepower for this big effort."

Collecting different cases in which managers consulted their workers, as well as a few negative cases in which they didn't, provided the researchers with some confidence that they were on the right track. This led to another query of the data. If managers, for their own reasons, enabled the moral commitment of workers to do pro bono projects, did they also enable the other goods that workers were invested in: the creative license and the awards? It turns out that they did:

And at [this firm], it was definitely [the case that] the pro bono projects were a little like a fun valve for you. And especially when you—you just have these massive accounts. IBM has an entire floor [dedicated to the account]. And you work on that business for two or three years. And so to have that little tiny valve, where it's like okay for a month this year, instead of selling servers, you get to think about whatever, the American Red Cross, or even the Tribeca Film Festival, or something like that. It was just very attractive because all of a sudden you're like, "oh my God, I don't have to think anything about diapers for a little while, and just maybe do this fun project."

Or, more generally:

And I think it is definitely, for a big agency, a way to keep talent excited and feeling like they are getting to try on new responsibilities. And sometimes a nonprofit will give you a little bit more creative license and sometimes creatively take more risks than a giant Fortune 100 company might.

In these excerpts (and many others), managers took active steps to provide creative challenges and compensate for routine work on accounts that are either uninteresting or simply so routinized that they cease to be exciting. The pro bono work needed not only to be morally exciting but also to have potential to allow "great creative" as a way to keep talent in the company happy and interested—something that is especially important in a business that has about a 30 percent yearly employee turnover rate.

Middle managers and CEOs talked about creativity *and* morality in the same breath—about approving projects where they thought there was moral enthusiasm and where it allowed the workers to do stimulating work. While managers had their own understandings of the place of pro bono in the organization—i.e., as a tool to solve managerial problems—they also curated the experience of advertising professionals in their agencies. Instead of the list of themes generated in the figure above, Iddo, Sonia, and Shelly suddenly had an *analytic theme* that cut through a few of the substantive themes in the data, and that structured one of the book's key chapters—*how managers' curatorial practices facilitated advertising professionals' ability to successfully align different goods.*[12]

Moreover, once these pieces fell into place, the research team could return to other interview excerpts. Many managers talked in detail about how they try to streamline the interaction between the agency and the pro bono client in order to make sure that the work is efficient and not overly time consuming. For example, managers gravitated toward pro bono organizations that had clear lines of decision making because there was far less double-guessing and internal politics that could ensnare their employees. Advertising professionals, in turn, spoke about the pleasure of the actual work with the clients as one reason they enjoyed working on pro bono projects.

Organizing this emerging argument, a number of previous topics that the team identified congealed as in figure 2, which reveals an emerging empirical and theoretical story. While there was a wealth of research on how actors navigate different goods—both in sociology and in management literature—the team uncovered an important mechanism for how different goods were made to align in action. By focusing on *curatorial practices*

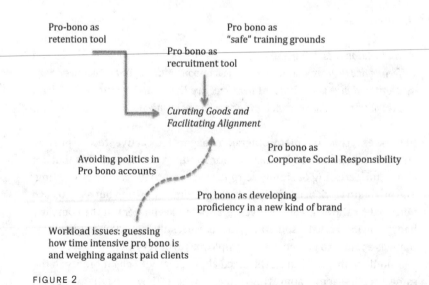

FIGURE 2

of managers, they explored these goods as an organizationally produced collective act. In order to understand how advertising professionals aligned different goods, the research team needed to expand their scope and note how the terms of navigation were set by managers—who were already anticipating the challenges that their employees might face. Both curation and *anticipation* became key to understanding how corporate social responsibility works in practice.

Conclusion

Taken together, open coding and focused coding cultivate data surprises and set up the empirical foundation for an analytical argument. And while different researchers may approach coding differently—choosing a different index case and moving iteratively in a research-specific rhythm—some commonality in the recursive relationship between index case selection and focused coding undergirds all abductive social science. In closing, we highlight two takeaway points about the craft of abductive analysis.

Initial work

You don't have to wait until you completely know what you will end up writing before you work through your research's variation. Both of our focused coding examples discuss data analysis at the end of data gathering, but there is no reason not to start focused coding earlier in the research project. In order to explore variation, however, you will need to have several data points that relate to the same index case. If not, open coding may be your better route.

Beginning with a striking finding, researchers can choose an index case without being completely wedded to it, and build variation around it. Working through such variation will help you assess two aspects of how you use your data. First, *are you cherry picking your observations?* That something is striking or surprising doesn't mean it matters analytically. In the advertising example, it seemed possible to mobilize the excerpts that centered on depoliticization of pro bono work and make a critique of "caring capitalism" that shows how offloading the good to private corporations depoliticizes the work. But looking through the entire corpus of interviews, this would have presented a skewed interpretation.

Second, *what is the thematic variation?* Variation in qualitative work is not primarily about the number of observations on a curve. Rather, in most cases researchers are confronted with different processes or narrative patterns that relate to their index case. Different answers to a common question; different solutions to a shared dilemma. Building out variation along multiple conceptual dimensions to avoid a narrow spectrum is crucial for moving beyond the index case. Thus, in the example above, while the researchers did need to know *how much* depoliticization was occurring in managers' interviews, the crucial move was in mapping the qualitative variation of *what kinds* of ends make for a good pro bono from a manager's perspective.

From substantive to analytic themes

Even as you explore variation, the endpoint is always about defining and specifying an analytic argument. *Variation in itself is not an analytic story.* While it may seem like a contribution to lay out the different ways in which a process occurs or the different narratives people produce, this cannot be the end of analysis, but an intermediate step in the intellectual research trajectory. We are not in the business of compiling lists. If the takeaway of your analysis is "we identified three themes in the interviews . . . ," you have more work ahead. A taxonomy of topics does not constitute an argument. In the neurology study, the analytical argument is that prognostication takes place implicitly during chronic illnesses when clinicians convey clues to cultivate hope while still avoiding unrealistic expectations for those on a downward trajectory. In the advertising project, the argument covers advertising managers' alignment of different organizational goals when choosing pro bono projects.

An analytic theme is a theme that tells a distinct empirical story while in dialogue with a theoretical literature. While the analytic theme is not yet the theoretical contribution, it foreshadows what this contribution could be. An analytic theme operates on a different level of aggregation than substantive variation. If they completely mirror each other, chances are that the analytic theme is a thinly theorized redescription of a substantive theme. This, as we have noted before, is bad theorizing.

7: CLUES ABOUT CLUES

We would love it if you could just glance at the social world and immediately see theoretical surprises—a world where the differences between the theoretical maps you construct and the maps folded up in your pocket jump out. Even with diligent research design preparation, note taking, transcription, and open and focused coding, it doesn't always work that way. Instead, you often need to hunt for clues of possible surprises. When you search for clues, what do you specifically look for? Since surprises emerge against a background of theoretical expectations, no one right answer exists. Different hunts, different habitats, different clues.

We can, however, point towards hunting grounds that we find theoretically generative. In our students' and our own experience, there are locations where surprises are more common. While there are no silver bullets for theorization, these sites constitute clues about clues—empirical hints suggestive of lurking theoretical surprises. *Tensions* in the data are one such water hole where clues abound. An expansive working definition of the kind of tension we are thinking about is a strained condition resulting from a variety of forces pulling actors, institutions, or organizations in different directions. In qualitative research, these opposing pull factors manifest themselves in different ways: people who make impossible choices between paths of action or find their desired path out of reach; reconcile opposing expectations; compromise, justify, or let go of aspirations; reorient their purpose; or try to move in different directions at once. We find tensions in interview transcripts and in fieldwork notes. Some tensions our interlocutors are aware of, others they gloss over. Some tensions occur within people's narratives, while others are found across different people's perspectives.

This is not to say that theoretical surprises only occur where tensions flourish. Perhaps it is exactly the stuff that is completely taken for granted and utterly unremarkable that ends up being the most theoretically fertile.[1] Yet moments of tension often alert you to aspects of the social worlds you study that you have not thought enough about. These moments are useful because they suggest a complexity hidden in the fabric of social worlds. This is yet another place where the principle of engagement comes to the fore—focusing on the tensions that the people you study work through helps you produce a better mapping of what goes on in their social world. Thus, what surprises you as a researcher and the tensions in the social world are often not the same, if you are looking for theoretical inspiration, starting off by focusing on tensions, mismatches, and glitches is a good opening bet.

The assumption we make—which we consider a basic uncontroversial theoretical assumption—is that there are no seamlessly coherent and homogeneous social worlds. In fact, even the plural of social world suggests potential for tension. Anthropologist and theorist Mary Douglas captured this keenly when she wrote about the structure of humor. Humor is a play on form where unresolved tensions are brought to the surface and toyed with. As Douglas saw it, humor only exists because the social world is riven with tensions. As she put it, "If there is no joke in the social structure, no other joking can appear." Jokes, she wrote, "are expressive of the social situations in which they occur."[2] A famous Soviet joke goes, "A man walks into a shop and asks, 'You wouldn't happen to have any fish, would you?' The shop assistant replies, 'You've got it wrong—ours is a butcher's shop. We don't have any meat. You're looking for the fish shop across the road. There they don't have any fish!'" What makes the joke so funny (to us, at least) is what makes it poignant—the tension between the bureaucratic efficiency and organization of life in the Soviet Union, and its complete disorganization, reflected in ongoing scarcity. The joke then plays in on a social tension.

To use a different theoretical language, social life is riddled with "sociological ambivalence": situations in which oppositions and tensions are woven into the fabric of the social world and people are pulled in different directions.[3] Ambivalence occurs due to opposing normative expectations related to a set of statuses or, more restrictively, to a specific position or social status. People living with dual nationalities, for instance, may experience the tension of clashing expectations depending on which nationality/friend group they engage. Stonequist's theory of the "marginal man" suspended between two cultures,[4] Hughes's writing on the contradictions of master status,[5] and Du Bois's notion of "double consciousness"—how Black people look at themselves through the eyes of Whites[6]—all center their analysis on such tensions.

At the beginning of *Doormen*, Peter Bearman writes that "this book focuses on this grammar—the unspoken rules that organize social interactions, shape decisions, and motivate behavior. One of the arguments of this book is that one can best see social grammar *by focusing on tensions and contradictions in interaction that appear when viewed from multiple standpoints, typically across levels*" (emphasis added).[7] He then proceeds to list seven such contradictions: e.g., getting a doorman job is both impossible and too easy; most doormen feel they are not racist but treat Black and other minorities coming to visit differently than White visitors; doormen claim they are part of the building's security but no doorman could recall doing anything security related. The book then uses these tensions as its organizational guide.

This chapter goes beyond research design to stack the deck in favor of surprises, and beyond coding to tease out such surprises. Here we focus on how you can interrogate your data in a theoretically generative way. It's about how to think as an empirical theorist.[8] Since tensions cover anything from slight misalignments to open conflict, they are particularly generative as a heuristic to tease out surprises in your observations. Attending to tensions also requires us to think about our data in a profoundly relational way. Something is in tension *with* something else. In this chapter, our mode of presentation is retrodictive; we draw from published examples and show how certain kinds of tensions became theoretically productive.

Incongruities in the collective act

The most immediate tensions that qualitative researchers come across— and often the most evocative—occur within the collective act, the process of living, doing things together. As social researchers, we study social worlds. That is, even when we conduct interviews with individuals, we are usually interested in more than an aggregate of personal decisions or attitudes. Instead, we wonder how any action, or even self, is partially defined by its relational position within webs of meanings and actions. We might think of these larger worlds in terms of "fields," "movements," "assemblages," or other theoretical terms—each with its own set of assumptions and theoretical heritage. You can pick your favorite. Regardless of your particular theoretical leanings, the phenomena of interest are defined by the intersection of different projects, as well as the creative moments in which novel modes of engaging in the world emerge in interaction.

Our assumption examining a social world is that it's rare that phenomena emerge through the seamless alignment of different people. Collective acts are made through disruptions and tensions no less than through careful alignment and consensus.[9] Indeed, the joke in the structure, as Douglas put it, is that often what looks from the outside as a coherent social reality is revealed as a mosaic of tensions between different people holding multiple positions. Methodologically, this means that we can lean into what is often one of the first things that qualitative researchers realize when they get into the field—that what looked from the outside to be monolithic is actually a complicated, tension-ridden social world.[10]

Of course, just as variation does not make an argument, showing that the world is complicated and tension ridden is not the endpoint of research. It can, however, be a useful starting clue to a research puzzle. We can start asking questions: Who experiences the tensions and who doesn't? And how? What are the social forces driving these tensions? Such questions may lead us to deepen our engagement with the patterning of the social world, as well as decenter some assumptions we may hold as naïve outsiders.

Consider the following examples.

A Fraught Embrace

A research project that showcases the value of focusing on tensions within the collective act is Ann Swidler and Susan Watkins's book *A Fraught Embrace*, a long-term study of the large-scale international effort to curb AIDS in Malawi, a small country in southeastern Africa.[11] The study—consisting of years of interviewing, observations, and document review—traces how different groups sustain the world of HIV international aid.

But the road to *A Fraught Embrace* was not straightforward, nor were the different perspectives of actors within the social world obviously analytically relevant. Rather, Swidler and Watkins slowly realized that the different international research projects that they observed—including their own—would have been impossible without intermediaries. When we interviewed Ann Swidler about the process of theorizing the book, she talked about an event that took place when they stayed in a Catholic center in a town in southern Malawi. It crystallized what their book would be about:

> There was that one really bizarre evening when this guy, who turns out to be a major . . . international criminal guy in his eighties, this Jim Humble who . . . invented the "Miracle Mineral Solution." And we were just totally taken aback by him. . . . But how did Jim Humble get there? How did Jim Humble who was trying to, in a sense, to rehabilitate his long career as a fraudster . . . by showing that his Miracle Mineral Solution cured AIDS. And so, he was running this totally unethical thing where he had found a local herbalist and he had thirty-six people and they were taking the Miracle Mineral Solution. I mean, it was horrible.[12] How did he get there and how could he be allowed to do this thing?
>
> The answer was he had gone to Nando's Chicken when he first got to Malawi. He didn't know and I guess he was totally unfamiliar with Africa. Didn't know

*what to eat. So he was eating what's the closest to Kentucky Fried Chicken, or
some kind of standard American fast food type chicken day after day. So, the guy
who worked there befriended him and said, "Oh, you know, what are you doing
here?" And he said, "Oh, I want to help people. I'm going to help cure AIDS," or
whatever. And the guy said, "Oh, why don't you go to my village?"*

And so he took him.

*And then we could say, "Gosh, how did we get here?" And that's where Susan
says, "Oh, I had this graduate student. . . ." And so, then we realized we too are
totally dependent on these people who help us reach the villages and who help
interpret what is going on.*

This moment of awakening structured their project. What was a practical
issue in the background—how outsiders get hooked up with the population—suddenly came to the foreground, both empirically and theoretically. And once the crucial importance and broad scope of these intermedi-
ary actors to broker social relationships came into focus, their project began
to fall into place. Their research attention turned to the people who they
knew best and spent the most time with—the people who both brought
them to where they were and whom they hired as research assistants.

In the resulting book, Swidler and Watkins showed that some of the
most important players of global health—beyond NGO elites (both in the
Western donor countries and in Malawi itself) and the poor villagers that
they targeted as aid recipients—were precisely this third group of brokers,
whom they call "interstitial elites." These were Malawians, usually with a
high school education, who connected NGO elites and villagers because
they knew where to go and who to talk to in Malawi. In essence, these
were the people who guided one group to another, and who translated the
dreams and needs of one group into the language of the other.[13]

This analytical reorientation allowed the authors to take observations
they had made over the years about repeated misunderstandings with
Malawians and what they had learned about what these interstitial elites
valued in their world, and turn them into the theoretical thread. Thus,
to take a telling example, the expectations of international donors often
didn't match the situation on the Malawian soil. International donors
presumed a general lack of knowledge about HIV. Yet even Malawians in
the poorest and most remote villages knew full well about the dangers of
AIDS and its modes of transmission. If anything, they overestimated risks
based on the constant barrage of information directed at them and their
experience of seeing their friends succumb to the virus. NGOs, however,
kept playing the public health card of inundating the airwaves and clinics
with health literacy. Was this then a waste of effort? Not quite. NGOs, as

the authors showed, provided critical services both to the villagers, who received some resources, and even more so to the interstitial elites who lead them there. Trainings that the NGOs offered were valuable, if not always for the reasons NGO bureaucrats imagined. As the authors put it: "Per diems and travel allowances may be the only source of cash that permits young people to contribute to their family's livelihood and to buy a new shirt for themselves. A second, and to us unexpected, advantage of training is that at the end participants are given what they consider to be a valuable credential: a certificate that they have completed a training in X."[14] In a hyper-credentialing society such as Malawi, these trainings allowed Malawians to both *get* something and *be* someone.

At the end, the fraught embrace that the authors depicted consists precisely of the tensions and structured misunderstandings among the groups making up the transnational field responding to a simmering pandemic. This central set of tensions had both theoretical and empirical ramifications. On an empirical level, it allowed the book to focus on the global world of AIDS aid in a truly novel way—showing the crucial role of overlooked interests. Theoretically, it outlined the import of what can be best described as a "global fantasy"—the dreams that global elites at large NGOs had about what Africa is like and what they can achieve; the dreams of a better life for villagers in Malawi; and, between them, the desperate hope for economic and identity mobility of these aspiring interstitial elites, who almost managed to lift themselves out of the poverty, but did so in an all too precarious way. Such a sociology of fantasy also went well beyond the Malawian case, or the world of NGOs more generally: it drew attention to how social phenomena are structured in the interstices between imaginaries and direct action.

Bringing it back to our coding scheme: we are exploring tensions in the "who" involved in the activity. Setting yourself up to examine such tensions has direct practical bearings for research design: both at the outset, and throughout the research process, interrogating how other people coproduce the phenomenon the researcher is interested in not only generates a better rounded picture of that social world but also alerts us to relational tensions (whether people are acutely aware of them or not). And these analytical tensions, in turn, can be important clues about where our theoretical maps need to be amended.

Tensions in time

The passage of time gives us another set of clues to tensions in social life. In interviews, people narrate different moments of their past and present, often at odds with each other; in ethnography, the close observation of time is an important tool to map change and ruptures. With the passing of time, tensions emerge because consistency is difficult to maintain, generating a wealth of sociological ambivalence. Such tensions reverberate as people find that what they cared about in one moment in their career seems trivial later on; tensions originate when people—such as the parents of children with seizures—try to proactively navigate the future. Tuning into these temporal tensions allows us to appreciate the dynamics of a world in motion, a world that is ridden with intractable dilemmas precisely because circumstances change; people grow if not wiser, at least older; and a pandemic scrambles a generation's life goals.

An interview-based example of the importance of temporal tensions as clues for theorizing can be found in a study of egg freezing. This technology, increasingly common in affluent countries, allows women to freeze their eggs when they are younger so that they can fertilize this egg at a later age, when they may want to become pregnant. The technology is promoted with the promise that women may lower the risk of their eggs aging over the life course and avoid potential complications for the fetus.

A temporal tension between present and future self is built into this biomedical technology: a tension between a woman's current age, relationship status, and career aspirations, and the aging of the body, gametes, and a future self. Eliza Brown and Mary Patrick uncovered through interviews with American women who decided to freeze their eggs that the tension between careers and the aging reproductive system was not the primary ambivalence in the interviews. As they read through transcripts, they were struck by the tension between *relational* time and *biological* time.[15] Their index case captured this dimension:

> Without the egg freezing, maybe I would date a guy or end up with a guy I shouldn't be, just because maybe he wanted a child and that's what we want, but in reality, I really . . . I just don't want to have a child with anyone. I actually would like to be . . . I want to be with the person that I want to be with and out of that have a child, and I think egg freezing will allow me to do that instead of doing it the other way.

The tension was between the ticking time of biological reproduction and the supposed timelessness of falling in love with Mr. Right. Instead of having to compromise with a less-than-perfect partner to father their children, the respondent opted for egg freezing to sustain the culturally expected putative timelessness of relational construction. This was, as Brown and Patrick put it, a "prominent pattern" in the data.[16]

These repeated variations of the tension between biological and romantic temporality mattered when the authors drew out the theoretical and empirical contours of the case. Thus, for example, Brown and Patrick could make sense of the ways in which women navigated the romantic relationships they entered—how they chose to tell (or not to tell) their partners about their egg freezing, how they often still felt like they failed to disentangle romantic time and biological age, how some decided to become single mothers and have their eggs fertilized by a sperm donor:

> I wanted to throw myself more into dating, and there was a relationship that I was hoping would work out, that ended up not working out. And I think as soon as, like that was part of it for me, like fuck, sorry I'm cursing, like: "fuck dating" . . . like I can't wait. I just felt like I needed to separate— there came a point after this relationship that I was hoping would work out and didn't, and I was just like, you know what, I need to separate these projects.

Starting from the tension between romantic and biological time, Brown and Patrick could also capture outliers in their data because the untangling of temporalities didn't offer the women what they hoped for. Building upon this core tension, they showed how other choices—such as becoming a single mother through sperm donation—became possible in ways that would otherwise be inconceivable.

Temporal tension in this context served two ends. First, it was a theoretical contribution in its own right. The authors made the case that studies of the life course need to consider the entangling and disentangling of different temporalities if researchers want to understand people's reproductive decisions. Second, temporal tensions constituted a gateway into the experience of egg freezing and how it shaped women's lives. In that sense, one of the important sources of the analytic power of their analysis was that by beginning with the temporal tensions, both researchers and the reader were thrust into the experiential world of these women.

Brown and Patrick's study was fortuitous. The theoretical tension that carried the narrative mapped onto women's lived tension. The ethnonarrative and the theoretical narrative seamlessly matched. In other research situations, however, the tensions emerge in the data without our interlocutors making much of them. Only some of the tensions in the social structure are made into jokes.

Such temporal tensions can also be witnessed in ethnographic work. Ethnography is partly predicated on the ability to stay with people for a longer period of time. This prolonged involvement in a community is not only about getting thicker description, being able to distinguish in more and more detail between a wink and a blink. It is also about observing people change. Putting different moments side by side in turn reveals some of the most theoretically interesting tensions. Yet these tensions are, in many ways, textual artifacts. The tensions we perceive on the page may not be felt by people acutely in their own life, since these moments are separated by years.

One case in which the ethnographer used change over time to powerful effect is Jooyoung Lee's *Blowin' Up*, an ethnography of aspiring rappers in South Central Los Angeles. Following his rapping friends over a period of five years, Lee was struck by how some relationships changed over time. At the early stages of the rappers' careers, they would come to rap in freestyle "cyphers" and "battles" on a street corner in South Central. Two young men would challenge each other to a rapping duel, egged on by an audience. Circling these battles, some (slightly) older rappers would mentor the young ones, teaching them how to spit rhymes. These men served as role models for many of the young rappers, who sought to emulate them and learn the craft from them. For example, in one exchange, when an aspiring rapper is booed off the stage:

> Shamir, a Project Blowed veteran, offered commentary in between rounds. He tells the second guy in the group, "you need to breathe! You can't get up here and spit sixteen bars in one breath! When your body tells you to, you need to breathe. [S]imple as that."[17]

While rappers spent a good amount of time preparing their lyrics and rhymes at home, the experience of the cypher, and the mentoring of veteran rappers, was critical to their fledgling careers. Rappers venturing into this world revered the old heads. And yet, as aspiring rappers tried to make it in the wider music industry, the mentoring of these veteran rappers became tinged with tensions. In a telling exchange, Lee described how an older rapper, once considered one of the best in South Central, berated an aspiring rapper for rhyming off beat. Instead of gratefully accepting the advice as he once used to, the aspirant ignored the putdown, saying this was how *he* did things now.

These kinds of tension form the backbone for Lee's analysis of rappers' career trajectories, and how over time the role of these veteran rappers changes from a mentor to emulate to a cautionary tale of the fate to avoid. These changes offer a window to explore the other ways in which people changed their relationship to rapping as they tried to finally make it in the music industry. Thus, the variation constructed within this set includes adapting some musical and lyrical sensitivities to align with what they imagined studios wanted their music to sound like, dressing differently, and attempting to expand their networks.

The theoretical payoff of attending to these temporal tensions between moments comes up in the relationship *between* excerpts gathered over a five-year observational period. Rather than starting with one excerpt, Lee contrasts several time points. The relationship between cases constituted the index case. The data set was then constructed around the different ways similar tensions repeat themselves over time and across cases. And while some of Lee's interlocutors reflected about how their views of the old heads changed over time, it was Lee's own sense of dissonance between data excerpts collected in different moments of time that initiated the construction of the set.

Whether built around a relationship between observations or around one tense observation, the basic idea is similar. By anchoring the set we construct around a temporal tension, we gain a deeper sense of the social dynamics—of a certain class of jokes in the structure—that prove theoretically generative.

Incongruities within and across situations

Lastly, another form of tension depends upon attending carefully to both inter- and intrasituational frictions for the same person. We each wear different hats. We embody multiple roles and identities, and each one of them may manifest itself in a social situation. Tensions and incongruities emerge not only between different people or over time, but also for the same person between and within different social situations.[18] Such incongruities where people have to reconcile who they are in the moment between and within situations may end up as some of the most important sets of clues that something interesting may be going on in your observations.

As we show, such incongruities can emerge in two distinct ways, which we lump together here for brevity. One is what goes on *between* situations. That is, rather than thinking about time as a relationship between two points in a life trajectory or the unfolding of history, we think about the nexus of time and space in which people go back and forth in their everyday lives. How we talk and act at home, at work, or in a Brooklyn café differs. Different situations elicit different performances and ways of being. And then, secondly, and especially important in interview contexts, are the tensions and incongruities that emerge *within* a single situation. Here, while time is still important—different modes of talking or reacting take place in different moments of the interview or interaction—our focus is again on the multiplicity of perspectives and ways of talking and acting that emerge even within a delimited situation.

Park and street: the meaning of violence

Let's think about how people shift among situations, sometimes leading them to make choices or reveal themselves in a different light. What people do and say in one situation in their everyday life is not the same as what they do in others. There are, as Trouille and Tavory noted, a host of good reasons to focus on such intersituational variations.[19] Here, we focus on how seeing how people define their world in one situation and keep it from spilling over into other parts of their life sheds light on the compartmentalized structure of their social world. Thus, to take one short example, Iddo observed that Orthodox Jewish men in Los Angeles who worked in jobs outside the community—those who didn't work as teachers in Orthodox schools, rabbis, or kosher supervisors—had to juggle very different selves. During their working hours, these people often had non-Orthodox friends and interests. Some, it turned out, were avid gun enthusiasts; others enjoyed thinking about office politics and had a deep knowledge of Dilbert cartoons. When these men and women came home, however, they often had to erase this other non-Jewish world. People took care *not* to talk about these interests and selves. As Iddo realized, being a good Orthodox Jew in this context often meant that other selves were erased. This became a generative theoretical insight. Rather than thinking about networks of relationships as something that can be drawn on a paper and thus somehow exist in a timeless fashion, he realized how important the *situational structure of networks* is for creating a dense moral environment. The communal accomplishment was not, in this case, creating a kind of institutional completeness and keeping people within the confines of the Orthodox world, but in making such ties situationally unspeakable.[20]

As another example, we can turn to David Trouille's ethnography of Latino immigrant networks and soccer playing in a park in Los Angeles.[21] He examined how through this play in a public space, immigrants found a place for themselves in their new country and intertwined leisure with both work and self-worth. The park, then, offered Trouille a strategic site to look at the work-leisure nexus. The park was also a place for partying, drinking alcohol, and sporadic violence. Every so often, skirmishes on the soccer field escalated into physical confrontations. As Trouille put it:

> I initially found this sporadic violence frightening and senseless, much as I had found certain aspects of the men's drinking at the park. Yet, to my

surprise, the men also talked about the park as a relatively "safe" place to fight, at least in terms of physical injuries.[22]

In order to understand the senseless violence, Trouille needed to leave the park. When he socialized with the men at bars after work, he saw much more threatening moments of violence and near violence—when the men were scared that they would be stabbed, for example, or when they started violence that could escalate unpredictably. When he told others in the park about hanging in these other places, they scolded him and told him how dangerous it was. The point, as Trouille realized, was that violence in the park, though still troubling, was predictable. It was a staging place for masculinity, but it was a relatively safe space. Others were always there to break up a fight and to make sure that things did not spin out of control. This intersituational variation was useful as a way to understand the meaning of violence in the soccer field, but also a hint about the importance of staged presentations of self that the soccer field afforded. In the larger context of Trouille's work, his understanding of safe violence provided him with a way to understand how leisure practices became important for the development of social relationships and for providing these immigrants with a sense of belonging.

Tensions within situations

Situational tensions do not need to occur at different moments in a trajectory or across locales but may emerge when people pushed along by the rhythms of life alternate meanings as their circumstances shift.

One goal of the interviewing craft is to bring out the tensions, incongruities, silences, and ambiguities of respondents' stories. Even if interviews are a relatively stable and coherent situation—where someone is sitting in one place and talking to one person—as interviewees move along their narratives, they often say very different things. These incongruities, in turn, can be elicited by the interviewer, but can also emerge when an interviewee seems to tell one story at one moment and a very different one in the next.

An example of an interviewer eliciting a tension can be found in Kathleen Gerson's *The Unfinished Revolution*, an interview study of the generation of children who experienced shifts in gendered division of labor at work and in the home. As Gerson showed, a clear majority of interviewees claimed that they saw an egalitarian division of labor as a relational ideal. And yet there were tensions in the interviews. Whereas most interviewees endorsed this ideal, they also talked at length about how hard it would be to actually foster such an egalitarian relationship. Thus, many of Gerson's interviewees also described a fallback position, the less-than-perfect relationship than the one they might hope for.[23]

Yet, Gerson asserted, the gap between ideals and fallbacks was an instructive one. Women's fallback position was mostly based on self-reliance—if they couldn't have it all, they would prioritize their work. As one of Gerson's interviewees put it: "I'm always conscious of trying to be responsible for myself. I fiercely fight for my independence. Any time I feel that someone's threatening that, my claws come out."[24] When men imagined their fallback position, they reverted to a traditionalist model in which they would be the breadwinners while their partner would stay at home. In other words, Gerson leveraged explicit intra-interview tensions in her respondents' narratives to show that focusing on the structure of the gap between egalitarian ideals and fallback positions reflected crucial differences in gendered expectations.

Researching against the grain

Focusing on tensions and incongruities, whether between participants or over time, between situations or within them, is also an exercise in developing a certain analytical sensitivity, or mood. For lack of a better term, we encourage you to become intellectually subversive. Every community tells a narrative about itself, a narrative grounded in tradition, branding, or presumed shared values. It's not difficult to figure out what the most general, *official* narrative is: an educational setting is about teaching students; health care is about treating patients; religion is about a belief system; journalism is about reporting the news; government is about governing. But is it the entire story? Often, the vocabularies and stories present neat pictures of different people moving together towards a shared goal; but even when they describe a tension between people or hard decisions, the way that a field understands itself often glosses over some of the most interesting things about that field.

Many social worlds and organizations have representatives whose task it is to generate impressions. When you go to Friendship Park at the US-Mexico border in San Diego, where a twenty-foot-tall steel wall border fence separates the two countries, you'll encounter US governmental border community liaison agents. The park is closed most days of the week, but on weekends small groups of people on the US side can speak through the tiny metal holes in the fence with people at the Mexican side for a couple of hours. Before allowing you forward, however, the liaison agents will talk to you about their perspective on why the fence is there and the agency's views on prioritizing security. Or to take a different setting, during college visits, prospective students and their parents will encounter guides with semiscripted narratives exulting the benefits of college. Once you're at the college, you may find that many of these touted virtues are not available or that the actual experience has little in common with these PR snapshots. Impressions are actively managed to be unified, coherent, and flattering. If there is a message that we want to send through this chapter, it is that going against the grain produces valuable clues about interesting things just below the surface.

To take a final example: Julia Bandini studied end-of-life decision making in intensive care units in some of the nation's most prestigious hospitals. Patients in these intensive care units were very sick and some of their vital functions had been taken over by machines, which was unsustainable in the long run. Patients either improved or the staff would need to make the difficult decision to withdraw or withhold care. They needed the consent of relatives to withdraw care because the decision to unhook ventilators and other life-sustaining technologies meant that patients will likely die. These were difficult conversations, and the staff often called in a bioethicist to facilitate the process of reaching agreement on a course of action. The staff would not want to act unilaterally because that would make the death, if not an instance of euthanasia, then at least physician-caused terminal sedation. The difference between appropriate or inappropriate dying rested on whether the staff had the family's buy-in. Most of the literature in this field was about the intricacies of these heart-rending and stressful decisions. Observers and insiders talked about how to deal with disagreements and how to bring the family to the right perspective. Observing these interactions and talking to the staff, Bandini—like others before her—discovered the drama of deciding when enough is enough.[25]

However, there was a surprising finding. When Bandini interviewed relatives three and six months after the ICU patient's death, the decision that preoccupied the staff was not the most salient aspect of the dying experience. What mattered more to relatives was that they acted in line with the patient's wishes expressed prior to the decision: many patients were clear that they wanted to avoid unnecessary suffering. Relatives also came back to small acts of caring such as bringing a pillow or toothbrush to a wife keeping a vigil next to her husband. Most of all, relatives appreciated that the time in the ICU helped them to prepare for a life without a partner or parent. While the decision to withhold care was part of the process, very few relatives spontaneously brought up the decision to withhold care when asked to tell their story of death in the ICU.[26]

This is a good example of how, as a researcher, you can play along or work against how a field has defined an issue–and a reminder that our principle of engagement does not mean deferring to respondents. It is not, in this case, a matter of finding tensions in what is presented as a unified or coherent situation or social world. Rather, the tensions and dilemmas that the field presents to the outside—and often to itself—are not the same as those that the researcher finds. If you stay within the parameters of how bioethicists and clinicians think about the decision, you would be limited in what you can say or even think. One is to do sociology *in* medicine where you bring sociological perspectives to bear on an issue that is clinically predefined as problematic. Here you would use sociological tools to explore the relatives' side, examine why relatives often disagree, and how one relative objecting to withdrawing care can lead to drawn out decision-making processes. There are advantages to such an approach: you have a clinical and bioethical audience and a body of literature you can speak to.

In contrast, you can contextualize the decision to withdraw care more broadly. This would be more akin to sociology *of* medicine.[27] Some scholars, for instance, have argued that some of the difficulties of these decisions to withhold or withdraw care reflect organizational issues such as the division of labor between nurses and doctors, who each have access to different pieces of knowledge.[28] They observed how bioethicists help smooth over such decisions without asking why these dilemmas keep recurring in intensive care units.[29] The role of bioethics in such family meetings is to mop up for clinicians because the meeting's goal is to get families to agree with a biomedical way of viewing the decision. You could critically analyze how the distribution of information, the opportunities for relatives to voice their opinions, and the arguments aimed at convincing relatives are staged towards guiding families towards the staff-preferred decision.[30] You could, for instance, problematize what shared decision-making actually looks like in end-of-life care. That's still working within the parameters of reaching a decision but putting the decision on a firmer social science domain.

Then there is the path of bracketing the relevance of deciding and instead taking the perspective of relatives to follow what they value. Rather than privileging any decision, you examine the experience of having a patient die in an ICU. The issue for relatives is not necessarily *how* a patient dies (which is what the staff focuses on) but *that a loved one dies*. Losing a family member is what's most important. Bandini's research showed that for some families, the decision to let go was indeed difficult and colored the dying experience, but she found that what families value most is whether the staff validated the decision the family reached. If staff members praised a decision, state that they would have made the same decision, or that the deteriorating health forced the decision, then family members felt re-assured and, much like Goffman showed in "On Cooling the Mark Out," such reassurance colored the grieving process.[31] Going against the grain allowed her to look at the interactions at the bedside and the stories fam-ilies told afterwards while setting aside the belief that the decision is the most salient aspect of end-of-life care.

The implication for qualitative researchers is the need to bracket the sanctioned idioms and public narratives of groups and institutions. Even as they are thoughtful depictions of some tensions and dilemmas, they are often those of particular people in that social world. Howard Becker noted that sociologists should "doubt everything anyone in power tells you."[32] Leigh Star encouraged her students to ask who benefits from this fram-ing.[33] Generalizing, you should doubt the official definitions of the order of things, since those accounts speak precisely to the dilemmas and tensions felt by those with the most power to shape the social world's definition— even if they may not profit from it, such definitions are grounded in only some persons' experiences, and your contribution is to reveal who is served and what is silenced in that process.

Conclusions

In themselves, tensions are not necessarily *theoretically* instructive. But when you are grasping for a handle on your data, the jokes in the structure are often analytically provocative.[34] The cases we outlined in this chapter are ones in which these tensions ended up constructing the researcher's theoretical and empirical story.

Getting what's funny about the joke in the structure is a way of ensuring that you get a deeper sense of the social world you are studying. A tension means that there is a struggle, a clash, an uneasy meeting point between different elements within the social worlds we study. In that sense, there is something similar between tensions and surprises. This may look counter-intuitive. A surprise is a narrative turning point,[35] while a tension often makes us stop in our tracks. And yet, a turning point often relies on our ability to stop for a while. Surprises and tensions are structural cousins.

Erving Goffman once said that you know you are in the field when "you feel you could settle down, and forget about being a sociologist.... You should be able to engage in the same body rhythms, rate of movement, tap-ping of the feet, that sort of thing, as the people around you. Those are the real tests of penetrating a group."[36] We think that this is a low bar. We would like to suggest, instead, that you know you are in a field when you start finding the jokes genuinely funny. When you are getting the tensions and unstated dilemmas that make things funny, you're in a good place. Explicitly attending to such tensions and incongruities provides us with better sketches of the field. And better sketches of the field are more interesting to compare both to our theoretical maps and to the directions our compasses point us to.

8: WRITING IT DOWN, WRITING IT UP

"What does the ethnographer do?"—[s]he writes.
CLIFFORD GEERTZ, *The Interpretation of Cultures*

The founders of grounded theory reminded qualitative researchers that analysis does not begin when you put your audiorecorder back in a drawer and have a pile of data neatly stacked on your desk. Analysis starts the moment you do your first interview or write up your initial field notes. You constantly take stock of what you have, give yourself marching orders for additional questions to ask, and code those first data points to stay on top of your research—spinning off analytical memos to work through your emerging theoretical thoughts. Even more, you may want to build in breaks in data gathering: observe for six months, take a monthlong pause to spend time analyzing, then return to the field for an additional round of data gathering. As we have argued throughout the book, you constrain your analysis and foreclose some of the most important avenues you could have otherwise taken if you only start analyzing your observations after everything is collected.

Our argument in this chapter is that qualitative analysis also does not end when you have refined your coding scheme and written memos summarizing how your analytical thoughts intervene in the literature. The abductive research cycle to separate the unpromising from the promising theoretical leads is most visible during the process of gathering and coding observations. There will come a point in a research project, however, when you feel that you have the analytical story down. Your data reaches a saturation point: you can pretty much predict what the next respondent will tell you, it's a slight variation of a story you have heard before. You have already accounted for it. Data analysis seemingly done, you are ready to pick up your coding and memos to write up the study for publication.

While you may think you are ready to wrap up, abductive analysis continues during the research write-up. It carries over in two ways. First, analysis resides in the writing itself. Writing is not a mop-up chore at the end of a research project. To write is to make countless choices of what pieces of evidence to present; what metaphors are most convincing; whose narrative voice to use; whether to develop a scene, a setting, a concept, or a theme; and what transformations in your main characters will carry a theoretical arc. All these choices are analytical; they animate theoretical points. Scientific writing is a form of persuasion but, especially in theoretical articles, that aspect is often glossed over and bracketed as incidental. pure force of ideas should carry the day. But as any novelist or poet can tell you, how you write is intrinsically constitutive of your message.

Second, exposing your work to your peers during the publication process will reveal surprises that you did not know you had and make you realize that some of the surprises you thought you discovered are actually not all that surprising or novel. Having someone else look at your data, your claims, and your intended theoretical contributions in the context of anonymous peer review may force you to go back and recalibrate your analysis. If you were to take a researcher's data analysis when they felt they were finished with coding and ready to write an article and compare that analysis to what ends up being published, the difference is often astounding. The original analysis occasionally offers a bare-bones outline that was further refined and elaborated in the write-up but often there is even less continuity: the published analysis is completely different. Tremendously important analytical work is done during the writing process but it falls outside the purview of most methodology books. While authors thank reviewers for helpful comments during the review process in their acknowledgments, no methods section explains how the dreaded *reviewer* 2—a moniker for the nitpicky anonymous reviewer—actually shaped what was published.

This chapter examines how the process of writing up research and actively engaging a community of inquiry throws your research for an additional abductive loop by scrapping and refining emergent theorizations. Fussing with codes at your desk is one thing, but incorporating coding in an article that will have to go through the eyes of peer reviewers is a different issue. Imagining your colleagues reading your writing tends to sharpen the pen. Some theoretical insights, even though they looked great when you were alone with your thoughts, will quickly dissolve, while others solidify through these encounters.

An abductive write-up

An abductive manuscript provides the opportunity to use the process of theory development to organize the write-up. What we are advocating is *rhetorical abduction*:[1] the deliberate use of language and rhetorical devices to express the data theory surprise, a presentation style that doesn't jump straight to denouement but takes advantage of the sequencing of theory discovery to structure and convey the argument. This requires you to think of abduction not just as a logic of scientific inference but also as a narrative structure and set of resources that can be used to organize a qualitative research write-up. But, and this is the important part, there is a cognitive feedback loop: the narrative organization, in turn, likely will prompt further abductive tinkering. While you draft your findings to reach and engage an audience, you also develop new analytical insights.

This leap is in line with Peirce scholars who argue that abductive reasoning is not confined to science but also structures other kinds of narratives. The most obvious example is the detective story where a Sherlock Holmes, Hercule Poirot, or Auguste Dupin abducts from clues left behind that the person who is the most likely suspect is actually innocent and that another character is guilty of the crime.[2] Expanding on this literature, James Liszka and Genie Babb argued that abductive thinking is inherent to any plot that connects events in a way to elicit surprise from readers.[3] Abduction works as a narrative device to organize a text, both as a construction by the author and as a reading experience by an audience. A competent author organizes a plot to evoke surprise and encourage an abductive response in the readers, which, if effective, provokes modification of knowledge of what the reader thought they knew about the world. While not obviously predictable to the reader, the plot needs to be comprehensible and plausible.[4]

Drawing on the work of literary scholar Wolfgang Iser, Liszka and Babb stated that author and reader participate in a game of the imagination, with the author guiding the reader by the signs of the text to convey critical thought. This means that the text does not completely spell out solutions to conflict but provokes the reader to connect the dots (in rhetoric this is called *reticence* and refers to the device of deliberately breaking off speech to make the reader pause and finish the thought).[5] The author introduces disruptions, surprises, and anomalies that encourage realizations on the reader's part. Liszka and Babb dealt with fiction writing, but the narrative organization can be extended to qualitative research writing.

Rhetorical abduction can be mobilized as a narrative device to organize a text. As authors, we begin with what we knew or thought we knew about a topic, then introduce the surprise, followed by the new theorization. It's a variation on one of the oldest Aristotelian narrative formats that constitutes the foundation of countless movies and books: set-up, conflict, catharsis. Yet qualitative texts rarely emulate the detective story by gradually introducing clues and aiming for a big reveal at the end of the text. As Becker has already pointed out, social science prefers showcasing the plot up front in a text and working with evidence, theory, and insights to compel a reader to change their mind.[6] An abstract and introduction usually give the plot away. It takes a maverick to breach this ingrained format.

One such maverick is historian Carlo Ginzburg. In a masterful paper, he analyzed a story about a harangue during a seventeenth-century uprising against Spanish settlers of the Mariana Islands as typical of the genre of the "noble savage," with its roots going into antiquity. So why would we believe that the text is authentic and not a projection of the Jesuit author who never even visited the Mariana Islands? After showing in detail how the author of the text recycled ideas, and even turns of phrase, at the end of his essay Ginzburg points out that the text's author used yearly letters from Jesuit missionaries to construct the speech. In a footnote in the Jesuits' text, the author expresses puzzlement at the reference to Spaniards introducing "rats, mice, flies, mosquitoes and all those small animals that exist only to plague us?" Even though, as Ginzburg reveals in his article's final paragraph, the author ridiculed this belief, ecologists have since shown that Spanish colonizers did in fact unknowingly import these pests from island to island, with devastating effects. Ginzburg wrote as a detective puzzle, throwing readers off with tangents about the history of harangues, to reveal that even in such a contrived genre, one can find kernels of historical voices that go against the grain: "Behind the smooth rhetoric," he wrote, "we hear at least a different, dissonant untamed voice: an alien voice, coming from a place outside the text."[7]

It is thus possible to appropriate the detective narrative, but it may require textual experimentation more fitting to an essay than a journal article. Still, even if the typical journal format works against a denouement in the final paragraph, we can take advantage of the narrative form of abductive surprises, even for journal articles. It is easier in books, where in order to sustain a narrative arc spanning several chapters, the author will inevitably need to build in some tension or puzzle that will be resolved later.

How does rhetorical abduction then work in practice? Here we focus on the presentation of data and the link between data and theory.

Writing through variation

"One sunny Sunday morning in January of 2007, I walked towards the front doors of the City Mosque to begin what would end up being three and a half years of fieldwork in the mosque's Muslim community. Though I did not know it at the time, I would end up working most intensively with a group of young Muslim men whom I here call the 'Legendz,' after the name of their sometimes active hip hop group."[8] This beginning of John O'Brien's ethnography of teenage Muslim boys growing up post-9/11 is what Atkinson, drawing from literary theory, refers to as the format of *verisimilitude*.[9] Qualitative researchers aspire to convince readers of the observed facts: an I-was-here textual effect.[10] These eyewitness reports depend on discursive conventions to give the impression that the text conforms to an observed reality. Qualitative research persuades through a combination of demonstration (e.g., excerpts of field notes or interview transcripts) and analytical commentary.[11]

This causes a practical problem in writing up data: how much of the documentation can you show? One of the attractions of qualitative research is that you capture more of the complexity of social life: everything seems interrelated, empirically and theoretically. You build deep relationships with respondents and informants and feel an obligation to do justice to the privilege of witnessing their lives. So much data and so many ideas, but so little space to write. How do you squeeze this complexity into an 8,000-word article, which, after you take out references, an introduction, conclusion, and methods section, is actually much closer to 5,000 words? How do you stay true to all the work you have done and still reach your audience?

Here is the painful truth of qualitative research: ultimately, your loyalty is to your readers. It is not going to matter if you capture the full complexity of your analysis or the richness of your data if you can only do it in an article of 23,000 words or a book of 600 pages. Almost no journal will review your work, acquisition editors will ignore your emails, and few readers will make it through your writing. This means that to get published the readers will need to miss out on some of your respondents' amazing experiences. That's painful, but in writing less often begets more. If your goal is to please each one of your respondents with your writing, it's going to be a painful process that will likely end up in paralysis because no text can truly do justice to the wealth of an even temporarily shared life. What it means instead is that you think foremost about writing as an act of communication; a means of engaging and persuading an audience. And considering that your writing will go through anonymous peer review, you should imagine convincing a skeptical audience. Your writing needs to be one step ahead of the skeptics, to anticipate and disarm their objections before they can even articulate them while reading your analysis.

OK, but you are still staring at a 746-page pile of transcripts and field notes. How to reduce this to the three pages of quotes and excerpts that will constitute the empirical basis of your article? We realize that you may feel protective of all these carefully curated and coded interview insights, but in the end you have to be ruthless and only use the one quote that will move the argument forward. If you have two or three that make the same point, you usually just need to let the weaker ones go.[12] You proffer the exemplar as an iconic representation of a set of observations within the social world you studied.

To make rhetorical abduction work, the chapters on open and focused coding should inform how to cull the vast amount of data to support an argument. A good place to start your write-up is the index case, and then you pay attention to the internal or comparative variation in your data. You want to go for the most evocative, luminous, and striking observations or interview stories. And as we noted, the exemplars should be theoretically stimulating rather than statistically typical. The chosen data fragments are not representative in any statistical sense, but are theoretically concentrated evocations that prepare readers for a subsequent argument.

In abductive analysis, the researcher presents the luminous data excerpt as a microcosm of a pattern they have found in the social world but then— through commentary or additional empirical detail—shows that the data also points to something unexplained in the literature. To work with data is to construct a theoretical puzzle. Considering your goal of evoking an abductive surprise in your readers, you want to arrange data fragments to demonstrate a contrast. A common rhetorical device in abductive writing is *juxtaposition*. A surprise is surprising in contrast to what is expected. So as a writer, you first want to prime your audience's expectations: what other scholars take for granted, what the majority or at least some of your respondents think, the usual way of processing in which people solve problems. In light of that context, something unexpected happens: people don't behave in what seems to be the way they should, the usual course of action or proposed solution does not produce the expected results, there is a tension in the literature that needs explaining. It's important that you pause at the surprise and really work it out empirically without skimping on detail. This will give you the analytical space to develop the abductive inferences that explain the surprise and draw out its consequences. You question the relationship between the familiar and the new through both the textual arrangement and the data selection. Basically, what it comes down to is reconstructing what struck you as surprising about your data when you were doing the analysis.

Except in most cases it doesn't really work out that neatly. When you review your data to pick that one interview quote or that stellar field note, you will realize that the simple act of reducing the empirical material to its most telling moments changes the analysis. Your previous rounds of coding depended on being able to work through many examples and map their variations. The write-up forces you to select only a few exemplars and to edit them down to fit the word limit of a journal article. It requires you to arrange the notes and quotes in a narrative order. It requires you to edit down the quote, and in doing so, its meaning changes.[13] Here is a warning against editing interview quotes for readability: one of Bonilla-Silva's influential theoretical insights of colorblind racism rested on attending to college students' hesitation, squirming, and fumbling when asked personal questions about race.[14] With edited transcripts, these pauses and evasive answers could have disappeared.

Or the surprise you thought was mind blowing is actually not as surprising once you turn it into pixels on your computer screen. Writing for an imaginary audience likely will show you that what you thought you had doesn't fit as well. The image that comes to mind is doing a do-it-yourself plumbing job. In your mind, you had thought the project through and then you went out and gathered all the parts. But once you squeeze yourself under the sink, you see that you miss a key piece of equipment and that the ones you have don't really fit. So off you go back to the store. Similarly, when you go from what you had planned for an analysis to the actual write-up, you realize that it doesn't really fit as well. *And you have this realization because of the writing process.* So you have to go back to reading more literature, more coding, or even returning to the field to figure out what it is you can claim persuasively. The act of writing then may prompt another abductive analytical cycle.

On terminology

A key writing challenge facing qualitative researchers is to link observations to pertinent theoretical ideas. Remember the organizing question of abductive data analysis: *what is the data a theoretical case of?* This requires that your observations exemplify theoretically relevant themes. Another means of achieving rhetorical abduction is to conceptualize your insights in ways that support their innovative theoretical message.

Quite regularly, a reviewer asks an author proposing a conceptual innovation whether we really need another term in social science. These disciplines are indeed saturated with people who put everyday terms in scare quotes and present them as conceptual breakthroughs although they do nothing more than contribute to a cornucopia of slight variants. Anselm Strauss and his coauthors had an affinity for adding nouns as adjectives in front of the word "work" so we have a book with chapters about "machine work," "safety work," "comfort work," "sentimental work," and "articulation work" in hospitals to refer to what the staff did and simply "the work of patients" for the other party.[15] More recently, we have a proliferation of "citizenship," which includes traumatic, carceral, sexual, political, biopolitical, liminal, legal, biological, and other forms of citizenship to denote the relationship of how people can make claims on the state and are legitimately recognized by state actors. A similar conceptual cottage industry exists with the prefix of "bio-" as in biomedicalization, biovalue, biosociality, biopolitical, etc. Many of these concepts only move the theoretical goalposts marginally: they are slight variations on a well-established theme, sufficiently recognizable to insiders not to ruffle any feathers.

A reviewer skeptical of new terms where existing ones do the job has a point. In many cases you can make a theoretical contribution without inventing new language. If you can stick to the existing vocabulary, this is probably better for everyone. But there are moments where a term can do important work, as the notion of habitus did for Bourdieu's theory of social inequality. In the first article where we suggested the term abductive analysis, the version that we sent for publication didn't use abductive analysis. Instead we fumbled around with a discussion of modified grounded theory, even though we were clearly moving farther and farther away from grounded theory. We didn't think that we needed our own label. The reviewers disagreed, and one of them tasked us to find a name for our approach. An appropriate term makes your idea graspable in one moment. Instead of going through an explanation, you have a term. In phenomenological jargon, what could only be captured in a multistep "polythetical" way can now be understood in one "monothetical" go. It thus allows you to build off this packaged insight rather than reconstructing it every time it is used. This in turn makes it easier to develop the theoretical point further later on.

If you do think that the process or point you are making merits a new term, the onus is on you. Your challenge is to make the case that this terminology captures something or works out a puzzle that has stumped others. This is a high bar to clear, and the new concept or theoretical extension needs to merit its reason for existence.

The best terminology captures what you want it to say without requiring additional explanation. Theories are infused by metaphor and synecdoche. In synecdoche, parts stand for the whole, such as *the gavel* for *the law*, and in metaphor we understand one kind of thing in terms of another, through comparison or analogy.[16] Social science writing is more likely to be innovative with fresh imagery than with worn-down metaphors. You invite being ignored if your writing is clichéd. You will also turn off readers when your concept is a grating neologism. You will confuse readers when you adopt an everyday concept but give it a different meaning. Every time you use the concept, you will need to realign the readers' more obvious interpretation. Better to pick a concept that implies its meaning in a more straightforward manner. You also tip your hand semiotically with the metaphors you pick. Whether theory, for instance, is viewed as *constructed*, *extended*, or *discovered* implies a different set of processes, agency, modes of inference, and relationships to the past. In a study that has withstood the passing of time, anthropologist Emily Martin reviewed the metaphors that medical textbooks used to describe the birthing process, noting how mechanical labor metaphors prevail: the pregnant woman's body is discussed as a machine, with the uterus producing a baby, labor taking place in stages with assigned rates of progress, and the physician representing a mechanic implementing interventions to improve the rate of productivity.[17] These metaphors matter in real life for women giving birth because they distribute agency and responsibility in the birthing process.[18]

Strong conceptual innovations not only add a semantic meaning, but they may also demonstrate a theoretical shift through their vocabulary. Matthew Desmond argues that relational ethnography requires a relational language, in the same way that processual sociology requires a language eschewing essentialist terms.[19] "Many urban ethnographers accept poverty as a given," Desmond writes, "as opposed to treating it as an active project involving people far removed from the gritty street corner where the fieldworker has chosen to plant himself or herself. Poverty is not a thing; it is a relation. And it is not just a relation between past and present, nor only between 'macro structures' and 'micro settings'; it is a relation between winners and losers, extractors and the extracted, discipliners and the disciplined—all bound together in real time."[20]

Desmond's point is that qualitative researchers forfeit their game when they talk about poverty as a given rather than as something that some people experience and others maintain because it is profitable. Building on insights from ethnomethodology, Desmond asserts that the story lies exactly in the collective action, the relationship between, in his case, landlords and tenants producing enduring class and race inequities. Jack Katz gives an example that anticipates Desmond's insight: "Thus an owner who is said to 'have an apartment building' does not really have any thing; he is benefitting from being in a mesh of relationships that include the income earning behavior of tenants, the ongoing processes that sustain the courts that will have to enforce his demands for payment, the daily dressing into uniforms of the officials who will chase out squatters, etc. What the owner has is no thing but a beneficial relationship to others' doings, doings which in their evolving, interactive interrelatings throw off material rewards to the owner."[21] Questioning what it means to be an "owner" opens up a wealth of institutional and social relationships that would have been glossed by the shorthand of "owner."

Your conceptual language then should consistently support the analytical points you are making. To play it safe, it may be tempting to drown your hard-won data in academese. You can squeeze the life out of relational thinking, for instance, by reducing the nuances of a tenant-landlord relationship to social network lingo that emphasizes nodes, edges, ego's alters, alter-alter edges, etc. This, however, would play against the strength of qualitative methods in getting close to social life as it is lived.

Thinking through the implications of conceptualizing during the writing process may lead to revisions of the analysis and engage another round of abductive inferencing. Once you write it down and integrate the data, the theoretical innovation that you have been pursuing may not come out right. Remember the article on the subtle signs of prognosis during neurology consultations that we wrote about in chapter 6? Well, if you check the published version,[22] you will see that the specific trajectories Tanya and Stefan used for months to organize their analysis (likely fixable, possibly fixable, and likely unfixable trajectories) are not in the final version. What happened? During the writing process (including the reviewing process), it became obvious that there was no way to shake the stigmatizing connotation of a term like *unfixable*. The term inevitably was morally charged, which overshadowed the analytical work the concept needed to accomplish. After double-fitting different concepts, they agreed that *fixable* best captures the first trajectory, where the child is looking to a medication- and seizure-free future, while *treatable* matches the second one, where the seizures may be treated if the right combination of medications can be found, but for the near future the child would remain medicated. In the third trajectory, the issue at stake is whether the seizures would ever be managed with medical treatment. Therefore, in the final and published version, they refer to *fixable, treatable,* and *manageable trajectories.* The final version thus dropped the term *unfixable*, which had anchored the entire analytical process. The renamed categories lost a sense of continuity (being located on one conceptual axis), but the concepts also capture something aspirational for each trajectory, which is in line with the optimistic tenor of the indirect prognostic discussion. These are fundamental changes: the main concepts have been changed and consequently the link between the concepts is modified.

Peer review as abductive engagement

An abductive write-up of research calls for an intertwining of content and style: an explicit analysis supported by an implicit analysis embedded in the text, both at the level of data presentation and at the level of theorizing, forged by clear and tight writing. But it still depends on readers being persuaded by what you've written. A theory always remains tentative, but it is somewhat safer when a community of peers has reached an agreement to its utility. As Peirce beautifully put it, "Science is not standing upon the bedrock of fact. It is walking upon a bog, and can only say, this ground seems to hold for the present. Here I will stay till it begins to give way."[23] Whether you will be able to hold your ground or sink quickly into the bog depends on how your peers evaluate your writing and whether you can overcome their skepticism. In contemporary science, one of the main ways the community of inquiry expresses itself is through the peer-reviewed publishing process.

In this section, we show that the review process may launch new abductive thinking. To reach your coveted audience, you have to sneak past a gatekeeper: anonymous reviewer 2.

Reviewers for a journal anticipate the review's reading by an editor making a publishing decision. It's a purposeful evaluative communicative practice with its own loose norms of length, detail, and appropriate targets. It is also linked to very practical concerns. Book and journal editors are usually under constant pressure to reject manuscripts—they get dozens to hundreds of submissions and can only publish a small fraction of them. Reviewers are, to put it counterintuitively, the editors' first line of defense *against* prospective authors. Authors and reviewers negotiate relationships in the triangle of published work, editorial decision making, and the review.

In spite of their critical role, we know surprisingly little about how reviewers review. One rare glance of this gatekeeping in action is a study by Stefan Hirschauer of editorial decision making at a generalist German sociology journal when he was one of the editors. This journal was unique because it held regular editorial board meetings where the five editors made joint decisions based on reviews. Hirschauer, with permission, took notes of the evaluation process and had access to the reviews and votes from the journal archive. Asking someone to review a manuscript is an imposition, and reviewers hope for a pleasant experience but remain wary that they may be disappointed. Hirschauer was struck by reviewers' transfer of their joy or suffering when reading a manuscript to the evaluation of the manuscript.[24] Bodily language seeps into the review: reading was fun/torturous/infuriating/a joy/palatable. This reflects not just the intellectual insights gained from reading but the experience of working through an overwrought or easily flowing manuscript. This is another reason not only to keep content and writing style consistent but to make it an engaging experience. And, if there was ever any doubt, to forgo smothering writing in academese.

You intend your text as a unified set of allies supporting your argument, but Hirschauer observed that it was easy for reviewers to poke holes in the lineup. Anything in your text can be used against you and the entire argument, even if it is just a small slip into bombastic language or a grammar mistake. Out of context, it casts suspicion on the entire project. Moreover, the criteria for evaluation are not universally agreed upon by a community of inquiry. Rather than thinking about criteria as reasons for accepting or rejecting work, it is useful to think about them much as some ethnomethodologically inspired neoinstitutionalists view rules—as resources that are rhetorically mobilized and become operative arguments to either reject or make the case for a specific decision. Everyone who has published regularly will grouse about the capriciousness of the review process.

And yet, even if criteria are often used as modes of justification for decisions made for other reasons, the review process isn't completely unpredictable. In social science writing, it is theoretical framing and theoretical contributions that often trip up researchers. In her observations of grant panels, Michèle Lamont found that 75 percent of the panelists mentioned that the connection between theory and data analysis is an important aspect of grant proposals.[25] In a study of the role of peer review in published quantitative papers, Misha Teplitskiy compared papers presented at the American Sociological Association meetings and their publication in two major general sociology journals: *American Sociological Review* and *Social Forces*. He found that the nature of the data analysis was altered relatively modestly while the theoretical framing often changed substantively. "This finding suggests that a chief achievement of peer review may be to provoke authors to adjust their theoretical framing while leaving the bulk of the data analysis intact."[26] In other words, the theoretical framing for quantitative papers is collectively negotiated during peer review.

What about qualitative research?

Rather than speculating about the general review of qualitative articles, let us focus on an example of qualitative work published in one of sociology's two flagship journals. Publishing a qualitative article in *American Sociological Review* or *American Journal of Sociology* is challenging. These journals oscillate on how open the rotating cast of editors is to qualitative research. This makes Kimberly Kay Hoang's 2018 article in *ASR*, "Risky Investments: How Local and Foreign Investors Finesse Corruption-Rife Emerging Markets," a remarkable feat.[27] The theoretical contribution of this article, however, changed drastically through the review process to the point that

Hoang told us that it emerged out of a dialogue between her and the reviewers. She was kind enough to share with us the originally submitted manuscript, the reviews she received along the way, and her revisions. Her journey, far from unique, shows how the analysis, theoretical framing, and contribution to scholarship can be transformed during the review process.

The basic topic, at least, remained the same: Hoang interviewed different investors in Vietnam's emerging real estate market and focused on the kind of social relationships required to make a deal. In both versions of the article she looked at three kinds of commercial real estate investors—local developers, foreign East Asian investors, and Western investors—and their relationships with local government officials. Already from the beginning, her research contained several abductive moments. For instance, considering the high financial stakes of investing in emerging markets, Hoang expected foreign investors to play a major role in the real estate business, but foreign investors came in at a later stage: local actors dominated the land acquisition and early development stage of the real estate market. This required Hoang to adjust her sampling strategy to capture a more diverse group of investors. The most important impetus for abductive change to the analysis, however, came through the review process.

The first submitted version of the article linked social network theory to the notion of the relational work of economic transactions. From social network theory, Hoang took the notion of brokers who bridge two actors with no direct ties to each other and can gain advantage and financial benefit from controlling information. While network analysis is able to map brokers, Hoang argued that this approach does not reveal the substantive content of the social ties, how people broker deals, and the broader cultural and structural arrangements that affect the process of deal brokering. Enter relational work. This concept examines how people manage interpersonal economic relations and singles out the social ties between people or groups, economic transactions across those ties, various media of exchange, and the social moralized meanings associated with these ties as distinguishing characteristics.[28] Building on her earlier research of relational work among Vietnamese sex workers in bars,[29] her intended contribution was to build out the notion of relational work by specifying the variation in deal brokering strategies in the real estate market and the conditions that produce this variation.

To that end, she proposed three ideal types of investors—insiders, outsiders, and peripheral market actors—and argued that they used different deal-brokering styles (direct, mediated, and indirect) that reflected their position in the Vietnamese real estate market. Hoang specified five structural conditions that influenced the possibility of brokering: the global and

local legal context, exchange frequency, exchange quantity, length of relationship, and access to information.

Drawing upon twelve months of ethnography between 2009 and 2016
and seventy-eight interviews, she compared how local developers, investors from East Asia, and European-American investors sealed commercial
real estate deals in Vietnam. She showed how government officials and
local developers developed close friendships based on gifts and favors, including bribery. They avoided the legal system because the person with
the best connections to judges would always prevail in conflicts anyway.
She cited Lainer-Vos's work[30] to support her observation that payoffs were
spread out over time and presented as expensive purses or tickets that
could be exchanged for money at a later time in order to blur the line between gift giving and bribery. Then she turned to the Western investors
and showed how they were bound by their legal systems in Europe or the
US that rendered bribery illegal. Westerners rarely moved to Vietnam.
They had a short investment timeline dictated by the cycles of the stock
market to show profits quickly. They made relatively few deals and almost
never developed a project in the early phases. They created a buffer of local
intermediaries, such as public relations agencies and lawyers, to connect
them with local developers and officials for permits and approvals, in effect
outsourcing bribery and corruption.

In between those two groups are the East Asian developers, such as
South Koreans, who developed direct relationships with central government officials: they spoke the language, they married politically connected
Vietnamese partners, and they participated in the gift and favor exchanges.
Their timeframe was also more focused on the long term than the Westerners': they moved their families to Vietnam and hired locally connected
individuals—university-educated sons and daughters of the local elite—
whom they invited to invest in their projects. If these investments would go
awry, they would take the local officials with them. Hoang concluded that
the three groups of investors work as brokers but they do so differently, and
the value of her ethnographic work was that it typified the kinds of brokering along five structural dimensions.

Hoang sent the article to *ASR*, anxiously awaiting the reviewers' evalua-
tions of her manuscript. The verdict was mixed. While the reviewers loved
her close qualitative research and saw tremendous potential in the analysis, they considered the manuscript "misframed." As the editors put it in
their letter, "readers are telling you that you are barking at the wrong conceptual tree." The reviewers did not consider "relational work" a theoretical
framework that leads to propositions and predictions. Hoang's proposed

extension of relational work was then evaluated as not much of a theoretical contribution.

In a rare unanimous vote, the three reviewers recommended that Hoang elaborate the work of Gabriel Rossman and Dan Lainer-Vos, which she had minimally engaged in the original version, on the management of disreputable trades through blurring practices. This would be a change in focus from deal brokering to an analysis of bribery and corruption in an emerging market. In fact, the editor and the reviewers didn't think that the groups that Hoang defined as brokers did much brokerage at all and, even worse, just pointing out variation in how brokering took place was not a sufficient warrant for publication. Hoang would need to show how the different deal-making strategies explained outcomes, the different real estate deals. The *ASR* editors issued a *revise and resubmit* but noted that the paper might not make it because it required a radical overhaul of the original submission.[31] They warned that if the manuscript spoke just to economic sociology, they would reject it: they needed something with crossover appeal.

Few scholars decline an opportunity to revise from *ASR* and Hoang grabbed the chance. She told us that she ended up spending three months reading the work of Rossman and Lainer-Vos, mulling over how it could apply to her work, and what she could add with her research. Rossman delineated three strategies people use to obfuscate disreputable or illegal exchanges: gift giving, bundling (mixed reputable and less reputable deals in one package), and brokerage (finding a third party to accept responsibility for the exchange).[32] These strategies offered actors plausible deniability if a bribe is investigated. It's a very different, much more focused framework on the kind of exchange she discussed, in effect turning a minor point in her manuscript into its major theoretical and empirical theme. Just reading this new literature was not enough, however. Hoang realized that because she had not gathered her data with this framework around bribery and corruption in mind, she would need to ask her respondents different questions. She ended up returning to Vietnam for additional research and conducting additional interviews (the published paper is based on a hundred interviews) to query her respondents about why they chose one deal-making strategy over another. This, in turn, required a reanalysis of both her old and her new observations.

In the published version of the article (there was a second round of reviews after which the paper was conditionally accepted, but the footprint of the published version was set after the first round of reviews), Hoang defined her contribution as advancing Rossman's "line of work by addressing a novel set of questions, specifically when an actor might choose one strategy of obfuscation over another, and how actors' relationships with state officials might influence their different strategies."[33] The article was about the management of risky investments, why different actors might choose one deal-making strategy over another in developing countries. Hoang argued that the choice of strategy depends on the proximity between the investor and the state officials approving investments. She redefined the structural factors from the earlier version to legal/regulatory context, social ties, cultural matching, and stage of investment.[34] Combining both components, she argued that where relationships between investors and state officials are close, relational obfuscation takes the form of gift giving. If relationships are distant, they were more likely to rely on brokerage. If investors don't have direct access to state officials but rely on arm's-length ties through political elites' family members, then all three obfuscation strategies will be used.

We can further observe how the analysis shifted by mapping her index case (even though that's not a term she used) in the section on Vietnamese real estate developers across drafts. In the original version, the motivating analytical insight was that local developers developed a trust relationship with key government officials. Hoang showed that over and over again, her Vietnamese respondents explained that their livelihood depended on close relationships: "It's all about who you know in this country." Trust was monetized: the local developers gave monetary gifts in exchange for building permits.

In the published version the index case, and with it the analysis, had shifted. The point about establishing trusting personal relationships with key officials was a jumping-off point for an in-depth exploration of how local developers needed to bribe a revolving cast of government officials to obtain building licenses, pass monthly inspections, and settle government investigations. The index case was different: a building executive pulls out a photograph of his team with local officials holding hands at a signing, the final result of countless gifts along the way. Hoang drew attention to the fact that the most senior members of the firm cemented their relationship symbolically with a handshake in the picture. Hoang marshaled her respondents' explanations of the benefits (lower tax rates and permits, prevailing in conflicts) and financial opportunities (getting land for cheap) of bribing government officials. The analysis also dwelled on the cultivation of the right personalized gifts for specific officials (knowing what kind of luxury purse a daughter of a government official desires). The steady trickle of highly coveted gifts not only covered up outright bribes but personalized the relationships. Government connections through gift giving bypassed the legal system to settle disputes. This analysis then elaborated

Rossman's and Lainer-Vos's accounts of blurring practices between gifts, bribes, and market exchange. Hoang showed how gift giving establishes long-term advantageous business relationships while protecting both parties from reputational risks and jail time.

Comparing the analysis in both versions, there was very little overlap: only a couple of quotes carried over. The most telling sign of how much the manuscript changed is an unobtrusive measure: the original version had 81 references, the published one had 77. Only 16 references (or about 20 percent) remained the same! It's a completely different paper engaging different theoretical literatures, putting a different index case at its core, marshaling and analyzing data differently, and making a different contribution. The review process showed that what Hoang thought was the surprise at the center of her analysis actually masked a different surprise in light of a literature she only had touched on in passing in the initial version. The review process then generated a complete overhaul of the analysis, prompting a new abductive analytical cycle.

We don't want to give the impression that reviewers are always right and that you should cave to them. When reviewers make suggestions for additional data analysis or theoretical reframing, they put you in a tough spot. They are gatekeepers, and ignoring their comments may doom publication in that journal, but bending over backwards to accommodate them may lead to a distorted paper. The review process seems to insert a level of conservativeness in a body of scholarship, especially in tradition-rich fields. This may work against the goal of abductive reasoning to stimulate theoretically innovative insights. How can you do creative theoretical work if you have to sneak past the gatekeepers who may be looking for an analysis that corresponds to their expectations? Doesn't such a system reward incremental change? Indeed, as Thomas Kuhn explained, there is an essential tension in science: adhering to a research tradition increases the probability for publication but forgoes opportunities for originality.[35] It's a reliable career path. Taking a higher-risk strategy may lead to higher rejection rates.

However, that same review process also allows for radical shifts in a body of knowledge. And this is not because such papers manage to fool reviewers but often because the findings and theoretical contributions are truly groundbreaking. Rather than holding novelty back, reviewers and editors may actually react excitedly when reading something that changes the basic assumptions in their field, is methodologically ambitious, or solves a recalcitrant puzzle. These are the manuscripts where reviewers write that they can't wait to see the paper in print, or where the editor solicits a commentary to highlight the originality of the insights. Or alternatively, reviewers give the green light for a publication somewhat reluctantly, but a group of readers recognizes that the implications are absolutely stunning and start sharing and promoting the ideas. While we will never know how many revolutionary papers never made it to publication, some do. If a more creative strategy succeeds, it may also have greater payoff. Innovation is a risky gamble. In a study of 6.5 million abstracts in biomedicine, Foster and coauthors found indeed that innovative strategies are rare but gather higher career and scientific rewards.[36]

Here, we can see why submitting articles for publication may lead to an additional abductive loop. Editors and reviewers, as representatives of a community of intellectual stakeholders and gatekeepers to publication, have a constitutive role in shaping an analysis. As early observer of science Ludwik Fleck noted, scientific experience is not just individual but collective.[37] Qualitative researchers engage in thought styles detailing what constitutes convincing evidence, causal claims, and the appropriate literature to cite. You participate in a disciplinary culture filled with tacit, unwritten rules,[38] and engagement with gatekeepers marks your work.

Articles and books

Our chapter so far has mostly assumed that you are writing an article rather than a book. There are some good reasons for this assumption: qualitative researchers write many more articles than books, articles take a smaller bite out of your data, and writing articles occupies the bulk of most academic careers. Books are involved projects, and their writing process usually takes much longer. This book, for example, took us five years from the moment we began to really write until its publication.[39]

As we write this book, we are both serving as journal editors[40] and we may publish an interesting article that speaks to a small niche readership. Book publishers don't have that luxury.[41] They need the book to reach a book-buying audience (among the most desired books are those that will be adopted in classrooms). When you send them your proposal, they will look up the sales figures of similar books and gauge whether this is a worthy investment of their time and reputation. You don't have that many shots at book publishing: the sales figures of your first book may determine whether a publisher will be interested in publishing with you again.

Books are also much more network reliant than are peer-reviewed articles. The reasons for this are mostly practical: it is harder to get reviewers to offer detailed comments on a whole manuscript. This, in turn, means that a book editor has to make harder choices about which manuscripts she would even send out for review than does a journal editor. While a journal editor may send out a paper even when they are skeptical about its chances to pass the trials of a review, book editors usually do not. And so although book editors read the manuscripts they receive, this means that they have to use other heuristics for their decisions. Reputation becomes one; a connection to an author that the editor trusts, who can vouch for the manuscript, is another. Most academic book publishers are risk averse: even though they are inundated with book proposals, they actually have trouble finding enough books to publish because few manuscripts have the potential to reach a broad academic audience.[42]

Lastly, books are more idiosyncratic than articles. Journal articles are a well-circumscribed genre. You have a lot of freedom within the confines of the genre, but you better have an introduction, a literature review, a methods section, two or three findings, and a conclusion. Very few articles break this mold. The creativity of journal article writing is a lot like the creativity of writing a classical haiku. You know how many lines and syllables are going to be there, you know that there needs to be an allusion to the season, the rest is up to you. Books are more akin to modern poetry. There are still many conventions you may follow, but the form is easier to break. Annemarie Mol's book *The Body Multiple*, for instance, is split into two on every page with a more ethnographic top part and a more theoretical engagement at the bottom of the page.[43] More than articles, books live by the motto "show, don't tell."

That being said, after writing a number of books and reviewing many others, we can say that there are certain ways in which books can produce surprises differently than do journal articles. There are many books that are built like a series of articles. Iddo still remembers that as a new assistant professor, he asked a student he worked with to read his dissertation with an eye to publication. The student came back a few weeks later and gleefully told Iddo that the only thing holding the chapters together was the glue on the cover. He had a point. But this is why qualitative dissertations are not yet books (and why it took Iddo six additional years to get from his dissertation to the book). A good book has a wide narrative arc. What happens in chapter three may reverberate in chapter six; what is a minor puzzle in chapter four may come to the fore in chapter five. A good book has been storyboarded for thematic and narrative development and the author will create a reverse outline to make sure that every paragraph, every section, and every chapter contributes to the central message.

In that regard, a book provides a writer with more space to define puzzles and with the possibility of constructing a more elaborate solution architecture. Such theoretical puzzles are one way to draw readers in. There is the opportunity to relate multiple theoretical puzzles to each other. In that sense, the analytic structure of a book is a little like that of a crossword puzzle, where solutions to one part of the puzzle set the stage and shape the solution to others.[44] A book also allows the abductive writer to have a nested structure of puzzles—where the solution to smaller puzzles becomes part of the solution of a larger puzzle.

Got readers?

Let's assume your article or book sees the light of day. What now? In the best-case scenario, readers will pick it up and engage with it. In spite of your careful negotiation with reviewers, you have even less control over how your work will be received.[45] You can promote your research on social media and in department talks, but eventually your work will be recycled into ongoing conversations in ways that you may either like or consider unpleasant.

A way to understand this iterative process of how public exposure reveals the potential of abductive inferences is to extend Ian Hacking's looping theory. Hacking started from the observation that science creates categories of people.[46] When scientists invent new categories, as, for instance, when psychiatrists introduce an ADHD diagnosis for fidgety children, we "make up" people. There always have been ants-in-their-pants kids in schools, but a label of ADHD put these children under medical surveillance as a distinct category, introducing common symptoms, treatments, and monitoring. The way these children understand themselves and the way others view them changed once the ADHD label became widely applied. In that sense, a category constitutes a new human kind with shared characteristics. Scientific categories like suicidal people, undocumented immigrants, or geniuses help us to define, study, understand, emulate, or control people, and, also for these reasons, individuals and social movements may resist labels, which, as Erving Goffman pointed out, inadvertently confirms these labels as well (because reacting against a label requires acknowledging the existence of that label).[47]

Such scientific categories don't stick automatically and uniformly: people act on them. They appropriate and leverage them for their own goals, they rally around them, and in the process they change the categories. Additionally, a scientific investigation changes those people: it involves the accumulation of knowledge about kinds of people, a process of sorting them through institutions, the emergence of new experts and forms of expertise, and a refinement of categories. Scientific classifications are thus moving targets, even though a label abstracts specific properties. Hacking referred to these iterative and recursive effects of labels through their application and use as looping effects. The label loops back onto itself, changing what we understand the boundaries and characteristics of what it means to be a particular human kind.

As Daniel Navon elaborated, looping is not limited to human kinds: when geneticists associate a disease with a genetic mutation, the resulting research may lead to a radical revision of the nature of the disease.[48] The disease category "wanders" and acquires on its journey new properties: it changes how people understand themselves and how experts understand them, and it changes our understanding of the incidence of disease in a population.[49]

We can take this mode of reasoning one step further: what Hacking's dynamic nominalism highlights is that naming things is consequential; there is no knowledge that is independent of its conditions of creation and immune to looping effects. Instead, through engagement and use, categories change over time.

The same transformative looping effects apply to innovative qualitative data analysis. Conceptualizing is an instance of naming, labeling, and abstracting pertinent properties. Theorizing means arranging concepts into a narrative argument that explains why and how things are the way they are. Such theories, however, are living things; they exist in whether and how they are contextualized, how portable they are, how they inform other people's research. The worst fate for the work of qualitative researchers, or any researcher for that matter, is being ignored. A theory that does not find an audience is a lifeless artifact.

Wrap-up

The write-up of research is an often-overlooked process of qualitative data analysis where the author facing a computer screen and keyboard makes countless decisions about data selection, presentation, terming, organization, structuring, and theoretical engagement. Each of these decisions is consequential in the sense that the writing itself may support or obfuscate the theoretical contribution. We have argued for rhetorical abduction, an organizing of the text that conveys the surprising findings by juxtaposing the surprise against the background of expectations based on earlier theoretical work. Writing an argument down and spelling out the theoretical implications of empirical surprises is a moment of truth for a fledgling theoretical innovation. Once written, certain ideas may not be as innovative as they were in your mind, or you may realize that you should shore up your argument with a piling of different readings. Maybe you need to go back and fill in some gaps you assumed in your analysis and figure out how your respondents view the events you are writing about. Writing means inserting yourself in a community of inquiry and may prompt an additional round of abductive analyzing.

When your article or book is sent out for review, another abductive analytical cycle may be required when reviewers do not buy either your data, your surprise, your theoretical framing, or your contribution. Entire data sections may demand revision. In some cases, the final version of a theoretical argument emerges as a joint accomplishment between author, reviewer, and editors.

The process of writing up research allows you to adjust the theory based on what you anticipate your audience will take away in that critical time period before you finalize a version. Your aspiration is, to put it in semiotic terms, to have a transparent sign: one that conveys its meaning with little extra information and independent of its empirical origins. Writing things up and receiving feedback shows how transparent your work is. Of course, signs are always multivocal, but your aim is to limit the interpretative range. The back-and-forth of the publishing process gives you an inkling as to whether your writing will find an audience and allows you to loop back.[50] So write well.

9: ABDUCTION IN ACTION

Heaven's Gate was a Christian UFO cult led by a charismatic leader. Its members believed that when the comet Hale-Bopp passed Earth, it was followed by a space ship. If members left their bodies, which they referred to as vessels, a UFO would take their souls to an extra-human level of existence, leading to their salvation and ascendance into the kingdom of heaven. Five months before thirty-nine members took phenobarbital mixed with apple sauce in an act of mass suicide in 1987, they purchased alien abduction insurance that would cover up to fifty members and would pay out $10 million per person. The insurance covered abduction, impregnation, and death by aliens. Alien abduction insurance is indeed a thing (albeit a gimmick): one company sold more than 30,000 policies. It even paid out a claim, yet only at $1/year for ten million years.[1]

That's not the kind of abductive insurance that this book can offer. If only it were this simple. If insurance is about hedging against the risk of loss, in qualitative research the risk is that your research efforts are all for naught—that you spend all this time gathering and analyzing data but have little to show for it. While no approach can guarantee that you would be able to contribute something of value to the disciplinary debates in your field, we believe it should be a rare outcome. If you read widely both within and beyond your subfield, and if you work carefully to bring out your data's surprises in data collection, analysis, and writing, you should be able to make a contribution. This book outlines ways in which you can design and conduct your research project to insure yourself against futile research efforts by creating favorable circumstances for the occurrence of data-theory surprises.

Our departure points are that we do research to find out things we don't know or aren't certain about, that an important facet of every research is its theoretical contribution, and that we want to play to the methodological strengths of qualitative research to aid in theory construction. We cannot overemphasize these starting points: if your research goal is to collect some illustrative quotes to prove your favorite theoretician right or to support an ideological agenda, we are at cross-purposes. Our research craft aims to discover something unanticipated. We look for analytical patterns in a corpus of data in light of existing literatures.

Let's recall what happens during analysis. The goal of qualitative data analysis is coming up with an answer to the question *what is this data a theoretical case of?* Abductive analysis is a scientific logic of inference aimed at theory construction that involves a recursive process of moving between data and theories. An abductive inference makes a preliminary guess of what kind of case you have when surprising or unexpected findings occur. As Peirce pointed out, abductive reasoning by itself is insufficient: there simply are too many possible inferences you can come up with that may account for data surprises. An abductive inference therefore is a hypothesis on probation.

As a constitutive part of an iterative research cycle, abductive analysis jump-starts both inductive and deductive forms of reasoning. Induction looks for generalizations, patterns, outliers, and salient themes in the data to test the abductive inference, while deduction specifies the hypotheses to gather more data. Induction gives us confidence in a theory based on the accumulation of new observations; deduction tells us what to expect based on a theory. The development of the theory occurs through fitting the class of empirical phenomena to which the new theory applies and reshaping the theoretical scope to make it better suited for the cluster of empirical phenomena we theoretically lump together. The result will be a new theoretical argument, emerging in abductive analysis through the dialogue between data and an amalgam of existing and new conceptualizations.

The recursive and iterative nature of abductive analysis not only generates but also culls possible theoretical leads. Although some abductive inferences are productive, there are many more dead ends and false starts than good ideas that culminate in theory construction. You weed out abductive leads primarily through the process of testing the emergent abductive hypothesis with new observations to further shape the fit between the theoretical framework developed and the observations explained by your account. Researchers deliberately aim to gather negative cases to progressively redefine the phenomenon to be explained in order to make it fit the explanatory theoretical factors.

Our approach focuses on moments of abductive inference as the pivot point in the inferential seesaw of induction and deduction. We hold that abductive inference can be cultivated both theoretically and practically. The purpose of this book, and of abductive analysis more generally, has been to stack the deck in favor of theory construction by shuffling the cards so that theoretical surprises are more likely to turn up. Theoretical innovations do not pop up unexpectedly out of nowhere but need theoretical and methodological cultivation. Theoretically, you gather conceptual maps that may provide direction for your research, and you try out different theoretical compasses to navigate your project—both theories that are specific to your subfield and tell you what to substantively expect, and theories that tell you how social life is organized more generally. Often, you may be more inspired by theoretical tracts that at first sight have little to do with what you are finding because they make you wonder about similarities and differences. In the data analysis class, we may read a theoretical article on internet communities and then go around to pick out ideas that may be relevant for projects that have little to do with either a virtual world or community. In media training, this is called bridging. Whatever question a reporter asks, you segue your answer to the points you want to make. In research you don't have talking points, but you have data that needs to speak up. So you look for what may help you get theoretical traction wherever you find it, not just within your friendly theory. Everett Hughes once pointed out that you may learn about prostitutes by studying psychiatrists; both have to be careful not to become attached to people who come to them with intimate problems, and both are privy to discrediting information about their clients.[2] The stronger and deeper the theoretical points in your readings, the more likely you'll be inspired.

Moving from reading to design, we argue that working abductively requires us not only to look at our observations differently, but also to collect them in novel ways so that surprises are allowed to emerge in the data. If we want to organize our work to allow and even encourage surprises, we need to think carefully about the interplay between the openness of our work—which provides avenues for surprise—and our ability to construct meaningful variation later on. Ethnographic observations are finely tuned to reveal social mechanisms across situations but are often too scattered to provide a coherent narrative. Interviews give insight into personal and collective perspectives but become closed off too quickly, and thus close off avenues for surprise.

For ethnographies, then, the challenge is to focus the project because there is an endless variation of things to observe, even in one scene, and often a paralyzing choice of where and with whom to spend time. Focused field notes push description as far as it goes, avoiding glossy imputations and staying close to the observed interactional sequences. Analytical field notes tip us off to social processes, frictions, and collective actions. Being sensitive to the purpose of field notes to move a line of reasoning along may require you to focus your observations on particular questions for clarification and elaboration that emerge on a daily basis. You give yourself marching orders of what to look for next, pursuing a budding theme. For interviews, the challenge is to defocus our interview guide enough to allow for surprises, and to take care that we defocus our interview guide in similar ways across interviews, so that we are not stuck with evocative excerpts that we cannot evaluate since we realize too late that we asked the wrong questions. A surprising research finding without variation is analytically frustrating—without a sense of the theme's saliency our analysis is stifled.

Coding techniques are what most people associate with data analysis in qualitative research, but coding only makes sense if you are well equipped with theories and have stellar observations. Coding is mired in mysticism: while there are as many ways to code as there are qualitative data analysis books, they all promise analytical enlightenment.[3] That should signal that there is not one invariably correct way of coding data fragments. Moreover, it suggests that coding is insufficient to constitute data analysis. You need a strong theoretical foundation, luminous data, and a sense of direction. Coding, though, helps you to situate yourself on various theoretical maps. In essence, coding is nothing more than a systematic process of slow reading and reflecting on what you have in your observations and how they allow you to make larger arguments.

We outlined two ways of coding that may make sense for different projects or for the same project at different stages of analysis. The first one, our pragmatist-inspired version of open coding, is a process of interrogating your observations with "who does what, when, where, and with what consequences" that allows you to trace the relevant actors, processes, outcomes, and actions. Such traces allow you to discover patterns and search out variation in your data. It's a good way to figure out what you have in your data, as well as allowing you to test the strengths of your interviews and observations. Such coding alternates with more developed focused coding, which happens when you develop a good sense of a promising theme in your data. Then you single out an index case that captures that theme and go systematically through your observations to find related cases.

In either coding process, showing variation in a phenomenon, developing a taxonomy of manifestations, or slicing data into ever finer bits does not make a theory. As Kieran Healy noted, adding small variations to an existing theory is often counterproductive because the point of theorizing is to abstract the details from a variety of different things or events to create an explanatory generalization.[4] Theorizing goes across cases and it places a bet on what matters; adding more variables or details hedges the theory with particulars. A good theory is often simple: it cannot capture everything to everyone. In fact, if it tries to do that, it slowly turns into description. Some of the most enduring ideas of classic social theorists are not their nuanced discussions but their account of elementary social processes or recurring tensions.

In order to deepen your understanding of the social world you study and as a way to unearth possible surprises, one promising avenue is to seek out tensions among people, situations, or processes. Building on the notion of the principle of engagement—that we need to take the concerns of the people we study seriously—we argue that such tensions are places where incongruities among moments, situations, actors, or institutions come to the fore. Focusing on such tensions helps us see how power is yielded and where biographical dilemmas emerge as patterns of social life. Attending to tensions gives you insight into the specifics of the social fields we study: how people generate and respond to problems.

Chapter 8 may be the most unexpected. We argued that writing an analysis up for publication is itself an analytical act. The choice of narrative voice, decisions of which data fragments to foreground, how to build up a character a reader may care about, how you decide to respond to reviewers, what audience you aim to engage: all this does analytical work. Your words are the little dots of a pointillist painting that create an analytical image. Each word, sentence, paragraph guides the reader to a different analytical impression. It matters, for instance, to talk about tensions rather than control. These metaphors invoke different associations and have different theoretical affordances. Exposing your work to readers is, as Latour pointed out, a trial of analytical strength.[5] This metaphor fits in the sense that exposing your writing to reviewers and general readers culls ideas and theories. Some will spread through citations across disciplines, others will flourish in specialized circles, and still others will wither away in digital libraries.

Abductive analysis implodes the difference between theory discovery and justification in social research. Above all, this means that you need to do research differently. Our position implies that your observations are not fully contained by the theories you know. Observations bump up against your conceptual apparatus and in this friction lies the opportunity for surprise. Another consequence is that research requires both forethought and flexibility: in an overly flexible method like ethnography, you may need to build in some constraints to avoid a scatterplot of unrelated observations, while for an interviewing study, you may want to push more on flexibility and not lock in questions once you sense a promising theme. In other words, you need to design your research differently, carefully alternating between moments of focusing and defocusing; you need to think differently about where you build observational variation. You may, we suggest, even have to read and write differently.

What surprise? What theory?

If social science is a kind of conversation, this book is in the genre of *how to become a better conversation partner*. Except, of course, that the answer is much harder than such guides would make it look. It takes years of dedication—of reading, of researching, of working with data, of writing and rewriting—to be able to enter a theoretical conversation and recount more than a fading echo of somebody else's tale.

Surprises are theoretical conversation starters, but they are insufficient to become an engaging conversationalist. You may still end up with fluffy small talk, squandering a catchy opening line. Surprises provide you with a space to broach a topic and ideally open up the dialogue for others to listen to what you are about to say. The conversation flows from how you build upon the surprise. Theorizing makes the difference between chit-chat, witty banter, and a rousing, life-changing speech. There are limits to how conversation books can teach you how to be a better conversationalist. This book has been mum about what will normalize your surprising observation. We told you about how to talk more persuasively, but we didn't give you surefire scripts that will work every time to enliven a conversation. In other words, we did not tell you what your theory should look like. In part this is because different people theorize differently. Some theories are strictly middle-range theories within specific fields, opening your subfield up somewhat guardedly and feeling more comfortable talking to peers. Others will theorize in broader strokes, flitting from subfield to subfield, but perhaps arriving at their destination battered by engaging a wide array of interlocutors.

A final thought. While we don't give you a checklist of what a good theory should look like, we advocate for theories that open up the research of others to surprises rather than shushing them down. If a theory propels you to simply redescribe everything that you see in its terms, then your theory may be a good narrative device, but it is not good theory to research with. Indeed, the history of sociology is strewn with theories that have become ossified into grand narratives—that have become so general or vague that they have produced cottage industries of exemplifications, but precious few surprises. Theories are always a work in progress. You'll never have the final word.

APPENDIX: FROM QUALITATIVE TO COMPUTATIONAL ABDUCTIVE ANALYSIS

Is abductive analysis purely a qualitative approach? We hope not. While we conduct qualitative research, and the approach we have developed is geared towards the kind of work we know best, we hope that this approach can also help other researchers make sense of their data. We would therefore like to sketch the possible value of abductive analysis for quantitative research, and especially branches of quantitative analysis that currently fall under the general umbrella of computational social science.[1] We want to shine some light on the topic in the hope that others will carry this torch forward.[2] The point is this: there is nothing in abductive inference that makes it uniquely compatible with qualitative research. While we have been thinking about different ways to work through qualitative methods, at its core abductive analysis offers a novel theorization for a surprising research finding. Surprises occur in qualitative and quantitative research and theorizations may flow from all kinds of methods.

And yet it is not mysterious that much quantitative research is still under the spell of a deductive model of inference, even if reality often strays from deduction. Survey research in particular constrains many research possibilities. While there are crucial pilot stages to any good survey where plenty of abduction can happen, there really *is* a separation between the context of discovery and the context of justification in much survey-based research. This is not primarily an epistemological choice, but a practical one. There is simply little room for experimentation with "defocusing" questions to see what happens when the practicalities of running a survey are so foreboding. Moreover, survey research is one place where multiple researchers use the same generic database. This means that most researchers *cannot* change anything about the survey they use. Different people collected the data, and the questions they ask and their theoretical sensitivities are likely different from your own.

Yet survey-based research is only one mode of conducting quantitative work. Over the past decade or so there has been an explosion of computational methods, with techniques as different as topic modeling, sentiment analysis, and other natural language processing approaches developed to analyze the deluge of digital data.[3] These data (e.g., points of sale, geolocation data, social media scrapings, CCTV recordings) are not explicitly created for social science research and as such present new challenges and opportunities. There are a few things about this computational turn that drives researchers away from deduction. First, since the logic of most of this research is that of population studies rather than sampling and statistical inference, there is no practical impetus to think deductively. Indeed, when you are dealing with the population, a seductive thought is to imagine that you can be a pure inductive researcher and put your hope in "seeing what emerges from the data." This is related to a second part of the allure of these new computational methods: that we let the algorithms that we employ at least partially define our analytical categories and sets.[4] The technique relies on the notion that a computer can generate collections of text based on the cooccurrence of words within specific documents. While what we do with these sets (and, crucially, their number) is left for interpretation, such methods do not mesh comfortably with strong deductive approaches.

How should these data and method opportunities be analyzed? Some scholars in computational sociology, Laura Nelson in particular, have advocated for adapting grounded theory to computational sociology. She proposes a three-step procedure: The first, pattern detection, involves inductive computational exploration of text, using techniques such as unsupervised machine learning and word scores to help researchers see novel patterns in their data. The second, pattern refinement, returns to an interpretive engagement with the data through qualitative deep reading. The third, pattern confirmation, assesses the inductively identified patterns using further computational and natural language processing techniques.[5] While this mode of inference allows researchers to examine whether a signal exists in their data, it does not tell them whether the signal is theoretically worth pursuing. Therefore, an abductive approach, where the unsupervised machine learning is focused on a theoretically possibly interesting topic and the deep reading occurs in light of the literature, will likely be more productive and help researchers appreciate the data they have.

Indeed, other computational sociologists have gravitated towards abduction. Some of the questions facing computational sociologists are very similar to those we posed in this book: how can we stack machine learning and pattern recognition in favor of theoretically relevant data surprises?

And much as with the relation between abductive analysis and grounded theory, the idea that categories emerge from the data through some sort of immaculate conception is quickly dispelled when you work with computational data. To take a simple example—the question of how many categories to allow in a topic-modeling study is a deeply theoretical and interpretive question. Not to mention that the flexibility of computational methods allows people to shift registers and methods as different surprises emerge within their work.[6]

We have been talking so far about the value of *abductive inference*, rather than the value of *abductive analysis*. Karell and Freedman develop an abductive computational approach that defamiliarizes the concepts under study to expose their puzzling aspects. Resolving these puzzles through an iterative movement between a widening body of empirical material and further analyses paves the way for novel theory construction. They provide an example. In their study of political radicalism, Karell and Freedman noted that the existing literature agrees that radicalism entails opposition to sociopolitical systems and powerful organizations or institutions. This can take the form of championing vanishing traditions, justifying violence against innocents, or pursuing nonviolent extra-institutional action. Studying over two decades of radical discourse in Afghanistan, they found, consistent with the literature, a rhetoric of subversion that evoked a historical fight against powerful external enemies. They also discovered, however, a second body of discursive radicalism that did not fit the literature. The rhetoric of reversion drew upon the notions of everyday morality to uproot undesirable developments in the personal and local contexts.[7]

This surprising finding relied not only on a comprehensive corpus of materials produced by Afghani mujahideen organizations between 1979 and 2001, but also on the adaptation of topic modeling to defamiliarize existing theoretical concepts[8] and generate new observations that a coding strategy modeled on existing theories and literature would have missed. Five of the ten topics consisted of words around war and international conflicts, consistent with the familiar rhetoric of subversion. Two of the remaining topics comprised words that are associated with local economic issues and private life.[9] To make sense of these results, Karell and Freedman took a closer look at documents that are associated with these words and consulted additional social scientific theories about the ability of social discourses to foster social relationships. This led them to interpret the topics as "a sociotemporally intimate gaze, stitching together concepts of morality, the everyday, and the personal and local to challenge members of radicals' own groups and communities, as well as the radicals themselves."[10]

This novel work is exciting but only the beginning of how an abductive scientific logic may travel within computational sociology. In an emerging field that is marked by an explosion of new measurement techniques, algorithms, and data sources, creative theorization could redraw not only research practice but the boundaries of traditional social science disciplines.

ACKNOWLEDGMENTS

This book inevitably builds on the work of others; one of our goals is to introduce a new generation to some of the great work of ethnographic pioneers. The voice of Jack Katz resonates in these pages. When rereading Howard Becker's book *Tricks of the Trade*,[1] we noticed that several ideas Jack taught can be found in Howie's book. Howie was one of Jack's Ph.D. advisers. Howie, in turn, cited his own teacher, Everett Hughes, for many of these insights. Another stream of influence can be found in chapter 3. Stefan learned the dynamics of group coding from Leigh Star, who organized sessions around the living room table in her house in Champaign-Urbana. Leigh, in turn, practiced these sessions with Anselm Strauss. Anselm was also a student of Everett Hughes. While we stand on the shoulders of an inbred family pedigree, each one of us puts a different emphasis on the material.

Stefan would like to thank several generations of graduate students cycling through the two-course ethnography sequence at Brandeis and UCLA. Several of their projects appear in this book. Each one of them received an opportunity to read the material presented here, make changes, and decide whether they wanted to have the material included. All of them agreed in writing. Beyond these more direct influences, Stefan thanks Caroline Tietbohl, Neil Gong, Amy Zhou, Terrell Winder, Laura Orrico, Pamela Prickett, John O'Brien, Forrest Stuart, Chinyere Osuji, Rocio Rosales, Nazgol Ghandnoosh, Ana Muñiz, Tara McKay, Hyeyoung Nelson, Yiling Hung, Sarah Lakhani, Mirian Martinez-Aranda, Kyle Nelson, Eduardo Duran, Ian Gray, and Sara Johnsen for sharing their intellectual journeys.

Iddo would like to thank his students at NYU and The New School, and especially Eliza Brown, Sam Dinger, Sonia Prelat, and Liz Ziff. Thinking through their work, and about how to best advise them, has been (and still is) one of the best parts of the job.

We thank Pamela Prickett, Tanya Stivers, Forrest Stuart, Terrell Winder, Kaiting Zhou, and Catherine Crooke for comments on the different chapters. We also thank Ann Swidler and Seth Abrutyn for talking through their work with us, and Kimberly Hoang for sharing many drafts of her article and explaining her publishing journey.

We have been thrilled with the support we received from Elizabeth Branch Dyson and her crew at the University of Chicago Press. Elizabeth carefully read our manuscript, engaged with the big and small ideas, and, for at least half a day, considered taking up qualitative research. In the end, she didn't, which is also a good outcome because sociology needs supportive and enthusiastic editors. We also thank the two anonymous reviewers for their feedback.

Stefan wants to apologize to Iddo's daughters Eliana and Amalya for interrupting their play, story, and bath time with phone calls to their father. His own family was blissfully unaware this book was written.

NOTES

Chapter 1

1. This book had as its working title *Surprise! Abductive Analysis in Action*, which captures the centrality of surprises as its organizing theme. The marketing team at the University of Chicago Press requested that we change the title to something that is more friendly to the Amazon search algorithms.
2. Shi and Evans 2019.
3. Merton 1968, 158 (our emphasis).
4. Tavory and Timmermans 2014.
5. Locke 2007; Reichertz 2007; Strubing 2007.
6. Ottolenghi 2011, 12.
7. This qualification is important. In contemporary logic of science, induction is a logic of evidentiary support. The idea is that the more you find similar results, the more support you have for a theory to be true. It is thus not part of theory discovery but of theory testing.

   In grounded theory, induction suggests that you build theory out of observations. It has been used to make an argument for theory discovery in qualitative research. And it has been very successful, to the point that many now define induction in the grounded theory way. We will indicate when we use the grounded theory or the more conventional understanding of induction.

   Here is an example to show the difference: We have the hypothesis that all ravens are black and then we go collecting observations of ravens. We observe 3,049 ravens and they are all black. In the traditional philosophy of science, this would be using an inductive logic to give us confidence in our hypothesis.

   Grounded theory would have you go into nature and observe all kinds of birds. You notice a pattern of black birds, many of which are ravens. So you come up with the theory that ravens are black. Grounded theory presents this as a form of theory discovery. This is still different from abduction, where a surprise emerges against a backdrop of familiarity with existing theories.
8. Wacquant 2002, 1524.
9. Paterniti et al. 2010; Schoenberg 1997.
10. Suchman 1987.
11. Pager 2003.
12. https://sociology.princeton.edu/devah-pager-memorial.

13. Lareau 2003.
14. Katz 1997.
15. Duneier 1999; Desmond 2016; McMillan Cottom 2019.
16. Star and Griesemer 1989.
17. Swedberg 2014.
18. Abbott 2004; Becker 1998.
19. Burke 1945.

Chapter 2

1. Grounded theory was built on an inductive model where researchers were encouraged to ignore what others had written or thought and instead let theory emerge from observations through a process of coding and memo writing. While the methodological steps have been proven useful, holding on to induction remains a barrier to theory development. The truth is that precious little theory came out of grounded theory research. Indeed, induction provides more facts but little extra theory.

   The extended case method as interpreted in sociology, in contrast, is overly committed to a singular theoretical project and does not provide much methodological guidance on working with observations. The goal of the extended case method is to build upon an existing theory, working much closer to a deductive form of reasoning where the researcher views observations through the lenses of a strong theoretical framework—usually a variation of a Marxist theme. In particular, the reliance on a deus ex machina, the god who would restore order at the end of Greek plays, in the form of structural factors as the final explanation of any study, is deeply problematic. Burawoy is adamant that these structural factors are not directly observable during fieldwork but can be postulated on theoretical grounds. Like grounded theory's assumption that data begets theory, structuralism as imperceptible final causes constitutes another form of magical thinking inserted in qualitative data analysis. See chapter 1 of Tavory and Timmermans 2014.

2. The researcher likely misunderstands in vivo codes; 141 is an amazingly high number.

3. Tavory and Timmermans 2019, 532.

4. Burawoy 2019, 51.

5. Hartshorne, Weiss, and Burks 1931–1958, 5.117. This collection is hereinafter referred to as *CP*.

6. *CP* 7.219.

7. See our appendix. However, if you are reading this endnote, you've already gone beyond the appendix and you might well have seen that we address it there. This is a self-defeating endnote. But without the endnote, you might not have seen the appendix. So the endnote is necessary after all. Aagh.

8. Peirce offered some criteria for a good abductive inference: it is *testable*, should

explain the puzzling observations, and is *economical*, meaning that among all the countless possible hypotheses, it is worth pursuing. These criteria are quite generic and not specific to qualitative research.

9. Small 2009.
10. Katz 1997.
11. Pescosolido et al. 2008; Thoits 2011; Link and Phelan 2001, 2014.
12. Abrutyn and Mueller 2016.
13. Mears 2017.
14. For a different understanding of focused coding consistent with the grounded theory tradition, see Charmaz 2014.
15. Tavory and Timmermans 2013.
16. Abend, Petre, and Sauder 2013.
17. Jeopardy question in the Apples category of July 10, 2007, available at http://www.j-archive.com/showgame.php?game_id=1951.
18. Portes and Zhou 1993.
19. Jiménez and Horowitz 2013.
20. Portes and Rumbaut 2001.
21. Bonilla-Silva 2003; Omi and Winant 2015.
22. Alba and Nee 1997.
23. Katz 2001, 2002a.
24. Katz 2002a, 73.
25. Robertson 2002; Reyes 2020.
26. *CP* 8.343.
27. For our own examples of using Peirce's semiotics, see Tavory and Timmermans 2021; Timmermans and Stivers 2017; Timmermans and Tavory 2020.

    The semiotic process is also useful as a way to think about doing research. As a researcher, you signify a set of observations for an audience. The observations, in turn, will limit the kinds of inferences you can draw. You don't know what kind of effect you will produce for those readers, but you imagine your interlocutors having certain understandings and interests in your topic. You anticipate what they may think. It's an unusual kind of signification act in the sense that you will not have much feedback on what you did until after the article or book has been published. And, of course, you have to get the writing past some gatekeepers such as editors and reviewers. At the same time, while writing and deciding whom to engage, your project itself interprets the work of others. It helps to think about doing qualitative research as a process of communicating where it matters that you know as much about the interpreters and range of likely interpretants as about your research site.
28. Becker 1973.
29. Venkatesh 2000; Bourgois 1996.
30. Willis 1977.
31. Merton 1968.
32. Mancillas 2017.

Chapter 3

1. Latour 1987, 33.
2. Davis 1971.
3. Abend 2008.
4. And yes, we know no map is like any other map. Cartography is a field rife with new technical and theoretical developments. Peirce, for instance, worked at the U.S. Coast and Geodetic Survey and developed a new quincuncial projection of the globe. Peirce 1879.
5. Tavory and Timmermans 2009.
6. Strauss 1969, 10; Schoenberg 1997.
7. Henwood and Pidgeon 2003.
8. Timmermans and Tavory 2020.
9. Katz 2015.
10. Meyers 2014.
11. Brubaker and Cooper 2000.
12. Clarke and Star 2008.
13. Menjívar 2000.
14. Jerolmack and Walker 2018.
15. Becker 1982.
16. In fact, the influence between Star and Latour (who pioneered actor-network theory) was mutual, with Star introducing Latour to pragmatist ideas. Bowker et al. 2015.
17. Star and Griesemer 1989, 393.
18. Brand and Jax 2007.
19. Swedberg 2012.

Chapter 4

1. Pasteur 1939, 131.
2. There is some common sense: if you do a project about the pregnancy experience and only interview six couples, many readers will wonder why such a low number since pregnant women are not hard to come by. If, instead, you interview six European ministers of justice, this could be a tremendous accomplishment since every country only has one such minister. A study of how to become a lawyer could require you to follow a cohort of law school students through three years of education and their first jobs. Other phenomena have a short lifespan or touch upon many diffuse and dispersed sites: trying to get a sense of the whole phenomenon will require quick visits and cold-calling a lot of people. Adding more analytical variation to your study will likely increase the time spent interviewing or observing. There are no hard-and-fast rules. See also Lareau 2021.
3. Jerolmack and Khan 2014; Lamont and Swidler 2014; Pugh 2013; Vaisey 2014; Gerson and Damaske 2020.

4. Rinaldo and Guhin 2019; Tavory 2020.

5. Krause 2021.

6. Charles Bosk shared our sense that there was no real definitive average number of interviews to strive for. However, he told his students that an even number such as forty would be a bit too neat and recommended that they always stop at an uneven number. Forty-one would suggest that you just found an extra respondent but aimed to stop at forty. Of course, thirty-nine may suggest that you fell one respondent short of your aim of forty.

7. Small 2009.

8. Geertz 1973, 30.

9. Winder 2015.

10. Nelson 2021.

11. Hooker 1957.

12. We thank one of the reviewers for pointing us to this example.

13. Small 2009. See also the literature on theoretical sampling in grounded theory, e.g., Glaser and Strauss 1967; Charmaz 2014.

14. We work the idea of sequential comparison out in Tavory and Timmermans 2020.

15. Ragin and Becker 1992.

16. Bearman 2005, 263.

17. Gerson and Damaske 2020; Lamont and Swidler 2014.

18. Swedberg 2014.

19. Tavory and Poulin 2012.

20. This section complements Emerson, Fretz, and Shaw 2011.

21. Glaser and Strauss 1967.

22. Katz 1975.

23. Bosk 2008.

24. Jerolmack and Murphy 2017.

25. Duneier 2011.

26. Nippert-Eng 2015.

27. Stuart 2016.

28. Schutz and Luckmann 1973.

29. Katz 2001.

30. Timmermans and Tavory 2012.

31. Robertson 2002; Reyes 2020.

32. Hunter et al. 2016.

33. Hunter and Robinson 2018.

34. Duneier 2004, 100.

35. Timmermans and Tavory 2020.

36. Speaking of data-sharing websites, when did you last back up your data? It would be a real bummer if you lost it all.

37. Lareau 2012.

Chapter 5

1. Glaser 1965.
2. E.g., Saldaña 2015.
3. Pena-Alves 2019; Simmel 1994.
4. Abbott 2004, 104–106; Burke 1925.
5. Silver 2011.
6. Tavory and Timmermans 2013; Gross 2009; Lichterman and Reed 2014.
7. Burke 1945.
8. Scott and Lyman 1968; Mills 1963.
9. Katz 2001, 2002a.
10. Katz 2002b.
11. Tavory and Timmermans 2017.
12. All names of researchers refer to real participants. We recorded the coding sessions. Everyone in the classroom was aware of the recordings and that they could be used for this book. If we used a recorded session, we gave the text to the researcher and gave them the opportunity to respond or request that the session not be included in the book. The names of the people in the field notes are pseudonyms picked by the students who wrote the field notes.
13. Mishler 1984.
14. Anspach 1993.
15. Roth 1972; Timmermans 1999.
16. Heimer and Staffen 1998.
17. Shim 2010.
18. Lopez and Espiritu 1990; Okamoto and Mora 2014.
19. Eliasoph 2013.
20. Fine 2012.
21. Mauss 1954.
22. Green 2008.
23. Swidler 1986; Wagner-Pacifici 2017.
24. Latour 1999, 34.
25. Latour 1999, 38.
26. Latour 1999, 55.
27. Latour 1999, 70–71.

Chapter 6

1. When Norm moved to communication studies, the sociology department asked Stefan to teach fieldwork methods. Ten minutes into the very first lecture, a student stood up, apologized, and said that she had misinterpreted the course title. She was expecting a course about working in fields, an agricultural sociology course. Since then, Stefan has been partial to the term "ethnography" over "fieldwork methods," even though the latter term is more popular among some Chicago sociologists.

2. Norm, it turns out, knew exactly what he was talking about. See Timmermans 1994.
3. Deterding and Waters 2018.
4. Lakatos 1978.
5. Strauss 1993.
6. Christakis 1999.
7. Mische 2009.
8. Mische 2009, 694.
9. Sonia was emerging as an interview methodologist and was interested in how people think about worth in her work on small business entrepreneurs in Argentina; Shelly conducted both interviews and ethnographic fieldwork in the sex toy industry in the USA, and was deeply immersed in theoretical work about how people think about the worth of what they do, particularly in a stigmatized industry.
10. Battilana and Dorado 2010.
11. Clarke, Friese, and Washburn 2018.
12. Tavory, Prelat, and Ronen 2022.

Chapter 7

1. Zerubavel 2018.
2. Douglas 1968, 366.
3. Merton and Barber 1963.
4. Stonequist 1937.
5. Hughes 1971.
6. Du Bois 1994.
7. Bearman 2005, 4.
8. The anchor is attending to tensions but, of course, tensions are not the only such route. We could have written a chapter about strengthening your theoretical muscles with an exploration of unintended consequences, for instance.
9. Tavory and Fine 2020.
10. Tavory 2019.
11. Swidler and Watkins 2017.
12. And of course, Humble would later promote his "miracle mineral" as a cure for COVID-19 as well: https://www.fda.gov/inspections-compliance-enforcement -and-criminal-investigations/warning-letters/genesis-2-church-606459 -04082020.
13. Epstein 2007.
14. Swidler and Watkins 2017, 231.
15. Brown and Patrick 2018.
16. Brown and Patrick 2018, 968.
17. Lee 2016, 65.
18. Although we realize that time and situations are inextricably linked, we find it useful to distinguish between them for heuristic purposes.
19. Trouille and Tavory 2019.

20. Tavory 2016.
21. Trouille and Tavory 2019; Trouille 2021.
22. Trouille 2021, 128.
23. Gerson 2010; Gerson and Damaske 2020.
24. Gerson 2010, 126.
25. Bandini 2020.
26. This also underscores our point in chapter 4 of asking defocusing questions. Julia could have asked specifically about the decision to withhold treatment, but by asking broader questions of how relatives reflected back on the time in the ICU, she allowed them to tell her what was truly salient.
27. Straus 1957.
28. Anspach 1993.
29. Chambliss 1996.
30. Kaufman 2005.
31. Goffman 1952.
32. Becker 1998, 91.
33. Star 1991.
34. To use different language, we are not interested here in forwarding a "hermeneutics of suspicion." Ricoeur 1971.
35. Tobin 2018.
36. Goffman 1989.

Chapter 8

1. We are inspired by Edmondson 1984.
2. Sebeok and Umiker-Sebeok 1983.
3. Liszka and Babb 2019.
4. Or, as we put it in the last chapter of *Abductive Analysis*, the argument of a qualitative article needs to convey a fit between theory and data, plausibility of the findings, and theoretical relevance (an answer to the *so what?* question).
5. Edmondson 1984, 26.
6. Becker 1986.
7. Ginzburg 1999, 83.
8. O'Brien 2017, xi.
9. Atkinson 1990.
10. Geertz 1988.
11. Atkinson 1990.
12. Lofland 1974. If it helps, you can hum the annoying *Frozen* song as you do so: "Let it go, let it go. . . ."
13. Lareau 2012.
14. Bonilla-Silva and Forman 2000.
15. Strauss et al. 1985.
16. Lakoff and Johnson 1980.
17. Martin 1987.

18. After writing this passage, Stefan went to buy persimmons and cauliflower at a farmer's market in Santa Monica. A man wandered around the stalls with a T-shirt that said "Metaphors be with you." A rare moment of convergence between work and nonwork life.
19. Desmond 2014.
20. Desmond 2014, 568.
21. Katz 2012, 130.
22. Timmermans and Stivers 2018.
23. *CP* 5.589.
24. Hirschauer 2010. For more on gatekeeping, see Clayman and Reisner 1998.
25. Lamont 2009, 182.
26. Teplitskiy 2015, 266.
27. Hoang 2018.
28. Bandelj 2012; Zelizer 2005.
29. Hoang 2015.
30. Lainer-Vos 2013.
31. We wish editors would stop telling authors that their papers may not make it. It's demoralizing advice that doesn't help the author.
32. Rossman 2014. See also Schilke and Rossman 2018.
33. Hoang 2018, 658.
34. Hoang also engages the sociology of development literature in the revision, but here we focus on the major theme.
35. Kuhn 1962.
36. Foster, Rzhetsky, and Evans 2015.

    As an aside, here is a bit of career advice: your goal should not be to have a manuscript accepted after the first round of reviews. Your goal should be to write a manuscript that is good enough for a revise and resubmit. You would use the reviewer's comments to finalize the analysis. Aiming for an immediate acceptance likely means that you were overwriting the analysis.

    Learning to handle rejection is part of the game. Most graduate students are terrified of getting a rejection but the good news about a rejection is that at least you have a paper you can resubmit.
37. Fleck 1979 [1935].
38. Knorr-Cetina 1999.
39. When colleagues tell us they want to write a book, we tell them that books are extremely time consuming and there is an opportunity cost: while you write a book, there are many other things you will not be doing. First-time book authors also are not guaranteed that they will find a publisher. The bar should therefore be very high before you embark on a book-writing journey.
40. Stefan of *Social Science and Medicine*; Iddo of *Sociological Theory*.
41. Publishers have some ways to lower their risks. In some instances, even academic presses (and not just predatory presses) will ask authors to offset some of the cost of publishing by subsidizing the publication process.
42. Some publishers, even some academic ones, will publish pretty much anything

but price the book super expensive. They make their money by selling a few copies to libraries across the world. It's frustrating because your book will be out of reach for most readers and the cost will make classroom adoption prohibitively expensive.

43. Mol 2002.

44. Haack 1997.

45. Except that throughout the writing process you have selected readers, and then after publication they choose you. You probably have already been imagining them all this time as an army of invisible buddies reading over your shoulder, when you read the literature, when you zoomed in on themes, when you developed theorizations that are portable to other research projects. Try to imagine what will resonate with them. If you want to write something that will be used in classrooms, you need to engage not just the professor but also relate your topic to the concerns of undergraduates: what will animate them out of their social media slumber and stir up debate? If you write for the experts in your field, the task is different: there you insert yourself into an ongoing dialogue that shows familiarity with theoretical nuances of interest to that community. For a general sociology audience, you need to address something that crosses subareas and speaks to broadly shared concerns. Each audience is different. Don't just write in the hope of finding an audience. You need to consciously decide who you are writing for and then write for them. Academics make a living from writing, sort of. We have safety nets; even if we didn't write or no one read our work, we often are still fine. To get you focused, imagine that the safety nets are gone and your livelihood depends on your ability to write things that find an audience.

46. Hacking 1991, 2007a, 2007b.

47. Goffman 1963.

48. Navon 2011.

49. Hacking 1998; Paul 1997.

50. One take-home message of this chapter is that you should seek out the opinions of others before you send your text into the world: do some test runs by asking peers and friends to read your material, ask advisers and mentors for feedback when you get stuck or have doubts about what you are writing, and take reviews seriously even if you feel that the reader completely misread the paper. That a misreading is possible shows that, at a minimum, you should try to make your argument clearer. Since everyone looks for readers of their work, you should be part of a set of exchange relationships: start a writing group, organize a workshop on your book manuscript, and then pay it forward to the next group of scholars by commenting on their work. The key is to find the right kind of reader, one who can appreciate a messy draft for the little hidden gems and give you the encouragement and direction to polish those.

Chapter 9

1. https://www.canadianunderwriter.ca/citb/alien-abduction-insurance-costs -just-9-99/.
2. Hughes 1971 [1945].
3. Saldaña 2015.
4. Healy 2017.
5. Latour 1987. But wait a minute. "Trial of strength" sounds a bit intense. Where does this metaphor come from? Trials of strength were popular in ancient Sparta, where Plutarch reported that young men from the age of infants were exposed to elements, meat, and darkness to cultivate their spirit. (This fits the theme that you should know where your metaphors—such as trials of strength—originate and what meaning they carry. In fact, Plutarch writes about "trials of strength and wit" because the Spartans also valued a quick mind.)

Appendix

1. Bail 2014; Salganik 2018.
2. Brandt and Timmermans 2021.
3. Salganik 2018.
4. Mohr et al. 2020.
5. Nelson 2017.
6. Mohr et al. 2020.
7. Karell and Freedman 2019.
8. Karell and Freedman 2019, 722.
9. Karell and Freedman 2019, 733.
10. Karell and Freedman 2019, 734.

Acknowledgments

1. Becker 1998.

BIBLIOGRAPHY

Abbott, A. 2004. *Methods of Discovery: Heuristics of the Social Sciences*. New York: Norton.

Abend, G. 2008. "The Meaning of 'Theory.'" *Sociological Theory* 26 (2): 173–199.

Abend, G., C. Petre, and M. Sauder. 2013. "Styles of Causal Thought: An Empirical Investigation." *American Journal of Sociology* 119: 602–654.

Abrutyn, S., and A. S. Mueller. 2016. "When Too Much Integration and Regulation Hurts: Reenvisioning Durkheim's Altruistic Suicide." *Society and Mental Health* 6 (1): 56–71. doi: 10.1177/2156869315604346.

Alba, R., and V. Nee. 1997. "Rethinking Assimilation Theory for a New Era of Immigration." *International Migration Review* 31 (4): 826–874. doi: 10.2307/2547416.

Anspach, R. 1993. *Deciding Who Lives: Fateful Choices in the Intensive Care Nursery*. Berkeley: University of California Press.

Atkinson, P. 1990. *The Ethnographic Imagination: Textual Constructions of Reality*. New York: Routledge.

Bail, C. A. 2014. "The Cultural Environment: Measuring Culture with Big Data." *Theory and Society* 43 (3–4): 465–482. doi: 10.1007/s11186-014-9216-5.

Bandelj, N. 2012. "Relational Work and Economic Sociology." *Politics & Society* 40 (2): 175–201. doi: 10.1177/0032329212441597.

Bandini, J. I. 2020. "Negotiating the 'Buffet' of Choice: Advances in Technology and End-of-Life Decision-Making in the Intensive Care Unit Setting." *Sociology of Health and Illness* 42 (4): 877–891. doi: 10.1111/1467-9566.13068.

Battilana, J., and S. Dorado. 2010. "Building Sustainable Hybrid Organizations: The Case of Commercial Microfinance Organizations." *Academy of Management Journal* 53 (6): 1419–1440. doi: 10.5465/Amj.2010.57318391.

Bearman, P. 2005. *Doormen*. Chicago: University of Chicago Press.

Becker, E. 1973. *The Denial of Death*. New York: Free Press.

Becker, H. S. 1982. *Art Worlds*. Berkeley: University of California Press.

Becker, H. S. 1986. *Writing for Social Scientists: How to Start and Finish Your Thesis, Book, or Article*. Chicago: University of Chicago Press.

Becker, H. S. 1998. *Tricks of the Trade: How to Think about Your Research While You're Doing It*. Chicago: University of Chicago Press.

Bonilla-Silva, E. 2003. *Racism without Racists: Colorblind Racism and Persistence of Racial Inequality in the United States*. 4th ed. Lanham, MD: Rowman and Littlefield.

Bonilla-Silva, E., and T. A. Forman. 2000. "I Am Not Racist But . . .': Mapping White Students' Racial Ideology in the United States." *Discourse and Society* (1): 50–85.

Bosk, C. L. 2008. *What Would You Do? Juggling Bioethics and Ethnography*. Chicago: University of Chicago Press.

Bourgois, P. 1996. *In Search of Respect: Selling Crack in El Barrio*. Cambridge: Cambridge University Press.

Bowker, G. C., S. Timmermans, A. E. Clarke, and E. Balka. 2015. *Boundary Objects and Beyond: Working with Leigh Star, Infrastructures*. Cambridge, MA: MIT Press.

Brand, F. S., and K. Jax. 2007. "Focusing the Meaning(s) of Resilience: Resilience as a Boundary Object." *Ecology and Society* 12 (1): 23–39.

Brandt, P., and S. Timmermans. 2021. "Abductive Logic of Inquiry for Quantitative Research in the Digital Age." *Sociological Science* 8: 191–210.

Brown, E., and M. Patrick. 2018. "Time, Anticipation, and the Life Course: Egg Freezing as Temporally Disentangling Romance and Reproduction." *American Sociological Review* 83 (5): 959–982. doi: 10.1177/0003122418796807.

Brubaker, R., and F. Cooper. 2000. "Beyond 'Identity.'" *Theory and Society* 29 (1): 1–47. doi: 10.1023/A:1007068714468.

Burawoy, M. 2019. "Empiricism and Its Fallacies." *Contexts* 18 (1): 47–53.

Burke, K. 1925. "Psychology and Form." *Dial* 79:34–46.

Burke, K. 1945. *A Grammar of Motives*. London: Prentice-Hall.

Chambliss, D. F. 1996. *Beyond Caring: Hospitals, Nurses, and the Social Organization of Ethics*. Chicago: University of Chicago Press.

Charmaz, K. 2014. *Constructing Grounded Theory*. 2nd ed. Thousand Oaks: SAGE.

Christakis, N. A. 1999. *Death Foretold: Prophecy and Prognosis in Medical Care*. Chicago: University of Chicago Press.

Clarke, A., C. Friese, and R. S. Washburn. 2018. *Situational Analysis: Grounded Theory After the Postmodern Turn*. Los Angeles: SAGE.

Clarke, A., and S. L. Star. 2008. "Social Worlds/Arenas as a Theory-Methods Package." In *Handbook of Science and Technology*, edited by E. J. Hackett, O. Amsterdamska, M. Lynch, and J. Wajcman. Cambridge, MA: MIT Press.

Clayman, S. E., and A. Reisner. 1998. "Gatekeeping in Action: Editorial Conferences and Assessments of Newsworthiness." *American Sociological Review* 63 (2): 178–199. doi: 10.2307/2657322.

Davis, M. S. "That's interesting! Towards a Phenomenology of Sociology and a Sociology of Phenomenology." *Philosophy of the Social Sciences* 1, no. 2 (1971): 309–344.

Desmond, M. 2014. "Relational Ethnography." *Theory and Society* 43 (5): 547–579.

Desmond, M. 2016. *Evicted: Poverty and Profit in the American City*. New York: Crown.

Deterding, N. M., and M. C. Waters. 2018. "Flexible Coding of In-Depth Interviews: A Twenty-First-Century Approach." *Sociological Methods and Research* 50 (2):1–32.

Douglas, M. 1968. "Social Control of Cognition: Some Factors in Joke Perception." *Man* 3 (3): 361–376. doi: 10.2307/2798875.

Du Bois, W. E. B. 1994 [1903]. *The Souls of Black Folk*. Mineola, NY: Dover.

Duneier, M. 1999. *Sidewalk*. New York: Farrar, Straus, and Giroux.

Duneier, M. 2011. "How Not to Lie with Ethnography." *Sociological Methodology* 41:1–11. doi: 10.1111/j.1467-9531.2011.01249.x.

Duneier, M. 2004. "Three Rules I Go By in My Ethnographic Research on Race and Racism." In *Researching Race and Racism*, edited by M. Bulmer and J. Solomos, 92–102. New York: Routledge.

Edmondson, R. 1984. *Rhetoric in Sociology*. London: MacMillan.

Eliasoph, N. 2013. *Making Volunteers: Civic Life after Welfare's End*. Princeton: Princeton University Press.

Emerson, R. M., R. I. Fretz, and L. L. Shaw. 2011. *Writing Ethnographic Fieldnotes*. 2nd ed. Chicago: University of Chicago Press.

Epstein, S. 2007. *Inclusion: The Politics of Difference in Medical Research*. Chicago: University of Chicago Press.

Fine, G. A. 2012. *Tiny Publics: A Theory of Group Action and Culture*. New York: Russell Sage Foundation.

Fleck, L. 1979 [1935]. *Genesis and Development of a Scientific Fact*. Chicago: University of Chicago Press.

Foster, J. G., A. Rzhetsky, and J. A. Evans. 2015. "Tradition and Innovation in Scientists' Research Strategies." *American Sociological Review* 80 (5): 875–908. doi: 10.1177/0003122415601618.

Geertz, C. 1973. *The Interpretation of Cultures: Selected Essays*. New York: Basic Books.

Geertz, C. 1988. *Works and Lives: The Anthropologist as Author*. Stanford: Stanford University Press.

Gerson, K. 2010. *The Unfinished Revolution: How a New Generation Is Reshaping Family, Work, and Gender in America*. Oxford: Oxford University Press.

Gerson, K., and S. Damaske. 2020. *The Science and Art of Interviewing*. New York: Oxford University Press.

Ginzburg, C. 1999. *History, Rhetoric, and Proof*. Hanover: University Press of New England.

Glaser, B. G. 1965. "The Constant Comparative Method of Qualitative-Analysis." *Social Problems* 12 (4): 436–445. doi: 10.1525/sp.1965.12.4.03a00070.

Glaser, B. G., and A. L. Strauss. 1967. *The Discovery of Grounded Theory*. New York: Aldine.

Goffman, E. 1952. "On Cooling the Mark Out: Some Aspects of Adaptation to Failure." *Psychiatry* 15 (4): 451–463. doi: 10.1080/00332747.1952.11022896.

Goffman, E. 1963. *Stigma: Notes on the Management of Spoiled Identity*. New York: Touchstone.

Goffman, E. 1989. "On Fieldwork." *Journal of Contemporary Ethnography* 18 (2): 123–132.

Green, A. I. 2008. "The Social Organization of Desire: The Sexual Fields Approach." *Sociological Theory* 26 (1): 25–50. doi: 10.1111/j.1467-9558.2008.00317.x.

Gross, N. 2009. "A Pragmatist Theory of Social Mechanisms." *American Sociological Review* 74 (June): 358–379.

Haack, S. 1997. "The Puzzle of 'Scientific Method' (Quine and Philosophical Meta-phor)." *Revue Internationale de Philosophie* 51 (202): 495–505.

Hacking, I. 1991. "The Making and Molding of Child Abuse." *Critical Inquiry* 17:253–288.

Hacking, I. 1998. *Mad Travelers: Reflections on the Reality of Transient Mental Illnesses.* Charlottesville: University Press of Virginia.

Hacking, I. 2007a. "Kinds of People: Moving Targets." *Proceedings of the British Academy* 151:285–318.

Hacking, I. 2007b. "Making Up People." In *Beyond the Body Proper: Reading the Anthropology of Material Life*, edited by M. Lock and J. Farquhar, 150–163. Durham: Duke University Press.

Hartshorne, C., P. Weiss, and A. Burks. 1931–1958. *Collected Papers of Charles Sanders Peirce.* 8 vols. Cambridge, MA: Harvard University Press.

Healy, K. 2017. "Fuck Nuance." *Sociological Theory* 35 (2): 118–127. doi: 10.1177/0735275117709046.

Heimer, C. A., and L. R. Staffen. 1998. *For the Sake of the Children: The Social Organization of Responsibility in the Hospital and the Home.* Chicago: University of Chicago Press.

Henwood, K. L., and N. Pidgeon. 2003. "Grounded Theory in Psychology." In *Qualitative Research in Psychology: Expanding Perspectives in Methodology and Design*, edited by P. M. Camic, J. E. Rhodes and L. Yardley, 131–155. Washington, DC: American Psychological Association Press.

Hirschauer, S. 2010. "Editorial Judgments: A Praxeology of 'Voting' in Peer Review." *Social Studies of Science* 40 (1): 71–103. doi: 10.1177/0306312709335405.

Hoang, K. K. 2015. *Dealing in Desire: Asian Ascendancy, Western Decline, and the Hidden Currencies of Global Sex Work.* Berkeley: University of California Press.

Hoang, K. K. 2018. "Risky Investments: How Local and Foreign Investors Finesse Corruption-Rife Emerging Markets." *American Sociological Review* 83 (4): 657–685. doi: 10.1177/0003122418782476.

Hooker, E. 1957. "The Adjustment of the Male Overt Homosexual." *Journal of Projective Techniques* 21 (1): 18–31. doi: 10.1080/08853126.1957.10380742.

Hughes, E. 1971 [1945]. *The Sociological Eye: Selected Papers.* Chicago: Aldine-Atherton.

Hunter, M. A., M. Pattillo, Z. F. Robinson, and K. Y. Taylor. 2016. "Black Placemaking: Celebration, Play, and Poetry." *Theory, Culture & Society* 33 (7–8): 31–56. doi: 10.1177/0263276416635259.

Hunter, M. A., and Z. F. Robinson. 2018. *Chocolate Cities: The Black Map of American Life.* Berkeley: University of California Press.

Jerolmack, C., and S. Khan. 2014. "Talk Is Cheap: Ethnography and the Attitudinal Fallacy." *Sociological Methods and Research* 43 (2): 178–209. doi: 10.1177/0049124114523396.

Jerolmack, C., and A. K. Murphy. 2017. "The Ethical Dilemmas and Social Scientific Trade-Offs of Masking in Ethnography." *Sociological Methods and Research* 48 (4): 801–827.

Jerolmack, C., and E. T. Walker. 2018. "Please in My Backyard: Quiet Mobilization in Support of Fracking in an Appalachian Community." *American Journal of Sociology* 124 (2): 479–516. doi: 10.1086/698215.

Jiménez, T. R., and A. L. Horowitz. 2013. "When White Is Just Alright: How Immigrants Redefine Achievement and Reconfigure the Ethnoracial Hierarchy." *American Sociological Review* 78 (5): 849–871. doi: 10.1177/0003122413497012.

Karell, D., and M. Freedman. 2019. "Rhetorics of Radicalism." *American Sociological Review* 84 (4): 726–753. doi: 10.1177/0003122419859519.

Katz, J. 1975. "Essences as Moral Identities: Verifiability and Responsibility in Imputations of Deviance and Charisma." *American Journal of Sociology* 80 (6): 1369–1390. doi: 10.1086/225995.

Katz, J. 1997. "Ethnography's Warrants." *Sociological Methods and Research* 25 (4): 391–423.

Katz, J. 2001. "From How to Why: On Luminous Description and Causal Inference in Ethnography (part 1)." *Ethnography* 2 (4): 443–473.

Katz, J. 2002a. "From How to Why: On Luminous Description and Causal Inference in Ethnography (part 2)." *Ethnography* 3 (1): 63–90.

Katz, J. 2002b. "Start Here: Social Ontology and Research Strategy." *Theoretical Criminology* 6 (3): 255–278.

Katz, J. 2012. "Cooks Cooking Up Recipes: The Cash Value of Nouns, Verbs and Grammar." *American Sociologist* 43:125–143.

Katz, J. 2015. "Situational Evidence: Strategies for Causal Reasoning From Observational Field Notes." *Sociological Methods and Research* 44 (1): 108–144. doi: 10.1177/0049124114554870.

Kaufman, S. R. 2005. *. . . And a Time to Die: How American Hospitals Shape the End of Life*. New York: Scribner.

Knorr-Cetina, K. 1999. *Epistemic Cultures: How the Sciences Make Knowledge*. Cambridge, MA: Harvard University Press.

Krause, M. 2021. *Model Cases: On Canonical Research Objects and Sites*. Chicago: University of Chicago Press.

Kuhn, T. 1962. *The Structure of Scientific Revolutions*. 2nd ed. Chicago: University of Chicago Press.

Lainer-Vos, D. 2013. "The Practical Organization of Moral Transactions: Gift Giving, Market Exchange, Credit, and the Making of Diaspora Bonds." *Sociological Theory* 31 (2): 145–167. doi: 10.1177/0735275113489123.

Lakatos, I. 1978. *The Methodology of Scientific Research Programmes*. Cambridge: Cambridge University Press.

Lakoff, G., and M. Johnson. 1980. *Metaphors We Live By*. Chicago: Univeristy of Chicago Press.

Lamont, M. 2009. *How Professors Think: Inside the Curious World of Academic Judgment*. Cambridge, MA: Harvard University Press.

Lamont, M., and A. Swidler. 2014. "Methodological Pluralism and the Possibilities and Limits of Interviewing." *Qualitative Sociology* 37 (2): 153–171. doi: 10.1007/s11133-014-9274-z.

Lareau, A. 2003. *Unequal Childhoods: Class, Race, and Family Life*. Berkeley: University of California Press.

Lareau, A. 2012. "Using the Terms *Hypothesis* and *Variable* for Qualitative Work: A Critical Reflection." *Journal of Marriage and Family* 74 (4): 671–677. doi: 10.1111/j.1741-3737.2012.00980.x.

Lareau, A. 2021. *Listening to People: A Practical Guide to Interviewing, Participant-Observation, Data Analysis, and Writing It All Up*. Chicago: University of Chicago Press.

Latour, B. 1987. *Science in Action: How to Follow Scientists and Engineers through Society*. Cambridge, MA: Harvard University Press.

Latour, B. 1999. *Pandora's Hope: Essays on the Reality of Science Studies*. Cambridge, MA: Harvard University Press.

Lee, J. 2016. *Blowin' Up: Rap Dreams in South Central*. Chicago: University of Chicago Press.

Lichterman, P., and I. A. Reed. 2014. "Theory and Contrastive Explanation in Ethnography." *Sociological Methods and Research* 44 (4): 585-635.

Link, B., and J. C. Phelan. 2001. "Conceptualizing Stigma." *Annual Review of Sociology* 27:63–85.

Link, B., and J. C. Phelan. 2014. "Stigma power." *Soc Sci Med* 103:24–32. doi: 10.1016/j.socscimed.2013.07.035.

Liszka, J. J., and G. Babb. 2019. "Abduction as an Explanatory Strategy in Narrative." In *Bloomsbury Companion to Contemporary Peircean Semiotics*, edited by T. Jappe, 205-234. London: Bloomsbury.

Locke, K. 2007. "Rational Control and Irrational Free-Play: Dual Thinking Modes as Necessary Tension in Grounded Theorizing." In *The SAGE Handbook of Grounded Theory*, edited by A. Bryant and K. Charmaz, 565–579. Los Angeles: SAGE publications.

Lofland, J. 1974. "Styles of Reporting Qualitative Field Research." *American Sociologist* 9 (3): 101–111.

Lopez, D., and Y. Espiritu. 1990. "Panethnicity in the United States: A Theoretical Framework." *Ethnic and Racial Studies* 13 (2): 198–224. doi: 10.1080/01419870.1990.999366.

Mancillas, J. D. 2017. "'Live Life, Get Life, or Die Trying': The Cosmology of Death and Dying amongst L.A. Gangs." *Berkeley McNair Resarch Journal* 4: 12-27.

Martin, E. 1987. *The Woman in the Body: A Cultural Analysis of Reproduction*. Boston: Beacon.

Mauss, M. 1954. *The Gift: Forms and Functions of Exchange in Archaic Societies*. Translated by I. Cunnison. Glencoe, IL: Free Press.

McMillan Cottom, T. 2019. *Thick and Other Essays*. New York: New Press.

Mears, A. 2017. "Puzzling in Sociology: On Doing and Undoing Theoretical Puzzles." *Sociological Theory* 35 (2): 138–146. doi: 10.1177/0735275117709775.

Menjívar, C. 2000. *Fragmented Ties: Salvadoran Immigrant Networks in America*. Berkeley: University of California Press.

Merton, R. K. 1968. *Social Theory and Social Structure*. New York: Free Press.

Merton, R. K., and E. Barber. 1963. "Sociological Ambivalence." In *Sociological Theory, Values, and Sociocultural Change*, edited by E. A. Tiryakian, 91–120. London: Free Press of Glencoe.

Meyers, T. 2014. "Promise and Deceit: Pharmakos, Drug Replacement Therapy, and the Perils of Experience." *Culture, Medicine and Psychiatry* 38 (2): 182–96. doi: 10.1007/s11013-014-9376-9.

Mills, C. W. 1963 (1940). "Situated Actions and Vocabularies of Motive." In *Power, Politics, and People: The Collected Essays of C. Wright Mills*, edited by I. L. Horowitz, 439–452. New York: Oxford University Press.

Mische, A. 2009. "Projects and Possibilities: Researching Futures in Action." *Sociological Forum* 24 (3): 694–704.

Mishler, E. G. 1984. *Discourse of Medicine*. Norwood, NJ: Albex.

Mohr, J. W., C. A. Bail, M. Frye, J. C. Lena, O. Lizardo, T. E. McDonnell, A. Mische, I. Tavory, and F. F. Wherry. 2020. *Measuring Culture*. New York: Columbia University Press.

Mol, A. 2002. *The Body Multiple: Ontology in Medical Practice*. Durham: Duke University Press.

Navon, D. 2011. "Genomic Designation: How Genetics Can Delineate New, Phenotypically Diffuse Medical Categories." *Social Studies of Science* 41 (2): 203–226.

Nelson, K. 2021. "The Microfoundations of Bureaucratic Outcomes: Causes and Consequences of Interpretive Disjuncture in Eviction Cases." *Social Problems* 68 (1): 152–167.

Nelson, L. K. 2017. "Computational Grounded Theory: A Methodological Framework." *Sociological Methods and Research* 49 (1): 3–42.

Nippert-Eng, C. 2015. *Watching Closely: A Guide to Ethnographic Observations*. Oxford: Oxford University Press.

O'Brien, J. 2017. *Keeping It Halal: The Everyday Lives of Muslim American Teenage Boys*. Princeton: Princeton University Press.

Okamoto, D., and G. C. Mora. 2014. "Panethnicity." *Annual Review of Sociology* 40:219–239. doi: 10.1146/annurev-soc-071913-043201.

Omi, M., and H. Winant. 2015. *Racial Formation in the United States*. 3rd ed. New York: Routledge.

Ottolenghi, Y. 2011. *Plenty: Vibrant Vegetable Recipes from London's Ottolenghi*. San Francisco: Chronicle.

Pager, D. 2003. "The Mark of a Criminal Record." *American Journal of Sociology* 108 (5): 937–975. doi: 10.1086/374403.

Pasteur, L. "Discours prononcé à Douai, le 7 décembre 1854, à l'occasion de l'installation solennelle de la Faculté des lettres de Douai et de la Faculté des sciences de Lille" (speech delivered at Douai on December 7, 1854, on the occasion of his formal inauguration into the Faculty of Letters of Douai and the Faculty of Sciences of Lille). In *Œuvres de Pasteur*, edited by Pasteur Vallery-Radot, vol. 7, 129–132. Paris: Masson, 1939.

Paterniti, D. A., T. L. Fancher, C. S. Cipri, S. Timmermans, J. Heritage, and R. L. Kravitz. 2010. "Getting to 'No': Strategies Primary Care Physicians Use to Deny

Patient Requests." *Archives of Internal Medicine* 170 (4): 381–388. doi: 10.1001/archinternmed.2009.533.

Paul, D. B. 1997. "The History of Newborn Phenylketonuria Screening in the US." In *Promoting Safe and Effective Genetic Testing in the United States: Final Report of the Taskforce on Genetic Testing*, edited by N. A. Holtzman and M. S. Watson, 137–160. Bethesda, MD: National Institutes of Health.

Peirce, C. S. 1879. "A Quincuncial Projection of the Sphere." *American Journal of Mathematics* 2 (4): 394–396.

Pena-Alves, S. 2019. "Outspoken Objects and Unspoken Myths: The Semiotics of Object-Mediated Communication." *Symbolic Interaction* 43 (3): 385–404. doi: 10.1002/symb.464.

Pescosolido, B. A., J. K. Martina, A. Lang, and S. Olafsdottir. 2008. "Rethinking Theoretical Approaches to Stigma: A Framework Integrating Normative Influences on Stigma (FINIS)." *Social Science and Medicine* 67 (3): 431–440. doi: 10.1016/j.socscimed.2008.03.018.

Portes, A., and R. G. Rumbaut. 2001. *Legacies: The Story of the Immigrant Second Generation*. Berkeley, CA: Russell Sage Foundation.

Portes, A., and M. Zhou. 1993. "The New 2nd-Generation: Segmented Assimilation and Its Variants." *Annals of the American Academy of Political and Social Science* 530:74–96. doi: 10.1177/0002716293530001006.

Pugh, A. J. 2013. "What Good are Interviews for Thinking about Culture? Demystifying Interpretive Analysis." *American Journal of Cultural Sociology* 1 (1): 42–68. doi: 10.1057/ajcs.2012.4.

Ragin, C. C., and H. S. Becker. 1992. *What Is a Case? Exploring the Foundations of Social Inquiry*. Cambridge: Cambridge University Press.

Reichertz, J. 2007. "Abduction: The Logic of Discovery in Grounded Theory." In *The SAGE Handbook of Grounded Theory*, edited by A. Bryant and K. Charmaz, 214–228. London: SAGE.

Reyes, V. 2020. "Ethnographic Toolkit: Strategic Positionality and Researchers' Visible and Invisible Tools in Field Research." *Ethnography* 21 (2): 220–240. doi: 10.1177/1466138118805121.

Ricoeur, P. 1971. "The Model of the Text: Meaningful Action Considered as a Text." *Social Research* 3 (3): 529–562.

Rinaldo, R., and J. Guhin. 2019. "How and Why Interviews Work: Ethnographic Interviews and Meso-level Public Culture." *Sociological Methods and Research*. First published online November 5, 2019, doi: 10.1177/0049124119882471.

Robertson, J. 2002. "Reflexivity Redux: A Pithy Polemic on 'Positionality.'" *Anthropological Quarterly* 75 (4): 785–792. doi: 10.1353/anq.2002.0066.

Rossman, G. 2014. "Obfuscatory Relational Work and Disreputable Exchange." *Sociological Theory* 32 (1): 43–63. doi: 10.1177/0735275114523418.

Roth, J. A. 1972. "Some Contingencies of Moral Evaluation and Control of Clientele: Case of Hospital Emergency Service." *American Journal of Sociology* 77 (5): 839–856. doi: 10.1086/225227.

Saldaña, J. 2015. *The Coding Manual for Qualitative Researchers*. Thousand Oaks, CA: SAGE.

Salganik, M. J. 2018. *Bit by Bit: Social Research in the Digital Age*. Princeton: Princeton University Press.

Schilke, O., and G. Rossman. 2018. "It's Only Wrong If It's Transactional: Moral Perceptions of Obfuscated Exchange." *American Sociological Review* 83 (6): 1079–1107. doi: 10.1177/0003122418806284.

Schoenberg, N. E. 1997. "A Convergence of Health Beliefs: An 'Ethnography of Adherence' of African-American Rural Elders with Hypertension." *Human Organization* 56 (2): 174–181.

Schutz, A., and T. Luckmann. 1973. *The Structures of the Life-World*. Evanston: Northwestern University Press.

Scott, M. B., and S. M. Lyman. 1968. "Accounts." *American Sociological Review* 33 (1): 46–62. doi: 10.2307/2092239.

Sebeok, T., and J. Umiker-Sebeok. 1983. "'You Know My Method': A Juxtaposition of Charles Peirce and Sherlock Holmes." In *The Sign of Three*, edited by U. Eco and T. Sebeok, 11–54. Bloomington: Indiana University Press.

Shi, F., and J. Evans. "Science and Technology Advance through Surprise." arXiv.org. 2019.

Shim, J. K. 2010. "Cultural Health Capital: A Theoretical Approach to Understanding Health Care Interactions and the Dynamics of Unequal Treatment." *Journal of Health and Social Behavior* 51 (1): 1–15.

Silver, D. 2011. "The Moodiness of Action." *Sociological Theory* 29 (3): 199–222. doi: 10.1111/j.1467-9558.2011.01394.x.

Simmel, G. 1994. "Bridge and Door." *Theory Culture & Society* 11 (1): 5–10. doi: 10.1177/026327694011001002.

Small, M. L. 2009. "'How Many Cases Do I Need?' On Science and the Logic of Case Selection in Field-Based Research." *Ethnography* 10 (1): 5–38. doi: 10.1177/14661 38108099586.

Star, S. L. 1991. "Power, Technologies, and the Phenomenology of Conventions: On Being Allergic to Onions." In *A Sociology of Monsters: Essays on Power, Technology and Domination*, edited by J. Law, 25–56. London: Routledge.

Star, S. L., and J. Griesemer. 1989. "Institutional Ecology, Translations, and Boundary Objects: Amateurs and Professionals in Berkeley's Museum of Vertebrate Zoology, 1907–1939." *Social Studies of Science* 17 (3): 387–420.

Stonequist, E. V. 1937. *The Marginal Man: A Study in Personality and Culture Conflict*. New York: Scribner/Simon & Schuster.

Straus, R. 1957. "The Nature and Status of Medical Sociology." *American Sociological Review* 22 (2): 200–204.

Strauss, A. L. 1969. *Mirrors and Masks: The Search for Identity*. San Francisco: Sociology Press.

Strauss, A. L. 1987. *Qualitative Analysis for Social Scientists*. Cambridge: Cambridge University Press.

Strauss, A. L. 1993. *Continual Permutations of Action*. New York: Aldine de Gruyter.

Strauss, A. L., S. Fagerhaugh, B. Suczek, and C. Wiener. 1985. *The Social Organization of Medical Work*. Chicago: University of Chicago Press.

Strubing, J. 2007. "Research as Pragmatic Problem-Solving: The Pragmatist Roots of Empirically-Grounded Research." In *The SAGE Handbook of Grounded Theory*, edited by A. Bryant and K. Charmaz, 580–602. London: SAGE.

Stuart, F. 2016. *Down, Out, and Under Arrest: Policing and Everyday Life in Skid Row*. Chicago: University of Chicago Press.

Suchman, L. 1987. *Plans and Situated Actions: The Problem of Human-Machine Communication*. Cambridge: Cambridge University Press.

Swedberg, R. 2012. "Theorizing in Sociology and Social Science: Turning to the Context of Discovery." *Theory and Society* 41 (1): 1–40.

Swedberg, R. 2014. *The Art of Social Theory*. Princeton: Princeton University Press.

Swidler, A. 1986. "Culture in Action: Symbols and Strategies." *American Sociological Review* 51:273–286.

Swidler, A., and S. C. Watkins. 2017. *A Fraught Embrace: The Romance and Reality of AIDS Altruism in Africa*. Princeton: Princeton University Press.

Tavory, I. 2016. *Summoned: Identification and Religious Life in a Jewish Neighborhood*. Chicago: University of Chicago Press.

Tavory, I. 2019. "Beyond the Calculus of Power and Position: Relationships and Theorizing in Ethnography." *Sociological Methods and Research* 48 (4): 727–738. doi: 10.1177/0049124119875960.

Tavory, I. 2020. "Interviews and Inference: Making Sense of Interview Data in Qualitative Research." *Qualitative Sociology* 43: 449–465.

Tavory, I., and G. A. Fine. 2020. "Disruption and the Theory of the Interaction Order." *Theory and Society* 49 (3): 365–385. doi: 10.1007/s11186-020-09384-3.

Tavory, I., and M. Poulin. 2012. "Sex Work and the Construction of Intimacies: Meanings and Work Pragmatics in Rural Malawi." *Theory and Society* 41 (3): 211–231. doi: 10.1007/s11186-012-9164-x.

Tavory, I., S. Prelat, and S. Ronen. 2022. *Tangled Goods: The Practical Life of Pro Bono Advertising*. Chicago: University of Chicago Press.

Tavory, I., and S. Timmermans. 2009. "Two Cases of Ethnography: Grounded Theory and the Extended Case Method." *Ethnography* 10 (3): 1–21.

Tavory, I., and S. Timmermans. 2013. "A Pragmatist Approach to Causality in Ethnography." *American Journal of Sociology* 119 (3): 682–714.

Tavory, I., and S. Timmermans. 2014. *Abductive Analysis: Theorizing Qualitative Research*. Chicago: University of Chicago Press.

Tavory, I., and S. Timmermans. 2017. "Mechanisms." In *Approaches to Ethnography: Analysis and Representation in Participant Observation*, edited by C. Jerolmack and S. Khan. Oxford: Oxford University Press.

Tavory, I., and S. Timmermans. 2019. "Abductive Analysis and Grounded Theory." In *The SAGE Handbook of Current Developments in Grounded Theory*, edited by A. Bryant and K. Charmaz, 532–546. London: SAGE.

Tavory, I., and S. Timmermans. 2020. "Sequential Comparisons and the Comparative Imagination." In *Beyond the Case: The Logics and Practices of Comparative Ethnography*, edited by C. M. Abramson and N. Gong, 185–209. Oxford: Oxford University Press.

Teplitskiy, M. 2015. "Frame Search and Re-Search: How Quantitative Sociological Articles Change during Peer Review." *American Sociologist* 47 (2): 264–288.

Thoits, P. A. 2011. "Resisting the Stigma of Mental Illness." *Social Psychology Quarterly* 74 (1): 6–28.

Timmermans, S. 1994. "Dying of Awareness: The Theory of Awareness Contexts Revisited." *Sociology of Health and Illness* 16 (4): 322–339.

Timmermans, S. 1999. "Social Death as a Self-Fulfilling Prophecy: David Sudnow's 'Passing On' Revisited." *Sociological Quarterly* 39 (3): 453–472.

Timmermans, S., and T. Stivers. 2017. "The Spillover of Genomic Testing Results in Families: Same Variant, Different Logics." *Journal of Health and Social Behavior* 58 (2): 166–180.

Timmermans, S., and T. Stivers. 2018. "Clinical Forecasting: Towards a Sociology of Prognosis." *Social Science and Medicine* 218:13–20. doi: 10.1016/j.socscimed.2018.09.031.

Timmermans, S., and I. Tavory. 2012. "Theory Construction in Qualitative Research: From Grounded Theory to Abductive Analysis." *Sociological Theory* 30 (3): 167–186.

Timmermans, S., and I. Tavory. 2020. "Racist Encounters: A Pragmatist Semiotic Analysis of Interaction." *Sociological Theory* 38 (4): 295–317.

Tobin, V. 2018. *Elements of Surprise: Our Mental Limits and the Satisfactions of Plot.* Cambridge, MA: Harvard University Press.

Trouille, D. 2021. *Fútbol in the Park: Immigrants, Soccer, and the Creation of Social Ties.* Chicago: University of Chicago Press.

Trouille, D., and I. Tavory. 2019. "Shadowing: Warrants for Intersituational Variation in Ethnography." *Sociological Methods and Research* 48 (3): 1–27.

Vaisey, S. 2014. "Is Interviewing Compatible with the Dual-Process Model of Culture?" *American Journal of Cultural Sociology* 2 (1): 150–158. doi: 10.1057/ajcs.2013.8.

Venkatesh, S. A. 2000. *American Project: The Rise and Fall of a Modern Ghetto.* Cambridge, MA: Harvard University Press.

Wacquant, L. 2002. "Scrutinizing the Street: Poverty, Morality, and the Pitfalls of Urban Ethnography." *American Journal of Sociology* 107 (6): 1468–1532.

Wagner-Pacifici, R. 2017. *What Is an Event?* Chicago: University of Chicago Press.

Whyte, W. F. 1943. *Street Corner Society: The Social Structure of an Italian Slum.* Chicago: University of Chicago Press.

Willis, P. 1977. *Learning to Labor: How Working Class Kids Get Working Class Jobs.* New York: Columbia University Press.

Winder, T. J. A. 2015. "'Shouting It Out': Religion and the Development of Black Gay Identities." *Qualitative Sociology* 38 (4): 375–394. doi: 10.1007/s11133-015-9316-1.

Zelizer, V. A. 2005. *The Purchase of Intimacy.* Princeton: Princeton University Press.

Zerubavel, E. 2018. *Taken for Granted: The Remarkable Power of the Unremarkable.* Princeton: Princeton University Press.

INDEX